THE ULTIMATE GUIDE TO
VIDEO GAME
WRITING AND DESIGN

By Flint Dille and
John Zuur Platten

Edited by Skip Press

Executive Editor: Robert Nirkind
Project Editor: Steve Atinsky
Production Manager: Katherine Happ
Series Interior Designer: Carla Green
Jacket Design by Carla Green
The principal typefaces used in the composition
of this book were Minion and Officina Sans.

First published in 2007 by Lone Eagle Publishing Company,
An imprint of Watson-Guptill Publications, the Crown Publishing Group,
A division of Random House, Inc., New York
www.crownpublishing.com
www.watsonguptill.com

Library of Congress Control Number: 2007922221

ISBN-10: 1-58065-066-X
ISBN-13: 978-1-58065-066-3

Printed in the United States

First printing 2007

3 4 5 6 7 8 9 / 14 13 12 11 10 09

TABLE OF CONTENTS

AcknowLedgments

Throughout our careers, we have met and worked with so many talented people who have helped us, influenced us, challenged us, frustrated us, occasionally paid us, and ultimately, given us the opportunity to work on a number of great projects. While we can't possibly thank them all, we're going to try anyway.

Thanks to: Rich and The Confederates at Union; Cos of numerous missions; The villain from High Noon; WGAw New Media—Suzanne, Bruce, Tim, Dean; The Strike Team—Mike, John and Rod; Sir Francis Drake and the Descendants; The Not-So-Secret Agents—Larry, Jared; The Ruby Spearmen—Joe, Steve, Marty, Meg, Buzz; Warner Bros. Interactive—Jason, David, Heidi, Gary; ZM; Christian B.; Chris Swain, who is pushing the academic discipline.

Also, thanks to Cliffy and the other Prime Justice Society; Dan Jevons; Dana and the Spectrobytes; The Neo-Cybertronians—Dan and Robb; The Legion of Superheroes—Mr. Nee and Ames; Artificial Minds: Remi, Denis, Christophe, Nathalie; Agent 13; Eric and The Big Easy, where we've smoked out ideas.

The Lions and Tigers of Tigon, especially Carthaginian Vincent Barca and Sister Tanit; The Taxi Drivers, Dean M. and Joey; The CT-RPS Team—Dr. K., Joe, Jerome, Dick, David W., David A., Steven D., Danny, Paul, Chris, Eric, the Mensa Boys of ICT, and the non-attributables from some nominative corporation; The 'Connections' Alumnus—Col. John Warden, Major Matt, Evan, Dunnigan, Perla,

Bon; Ed 209; Foo; The Kryptonauts and the sharks—Gary, David, Sergio, Marv, Sam, Chris; Drake and the Inquisitors; Ricky G.; Gary; Harris; Hildy; Howard B; Andrew and Gatewood from the class; and Eric and Vi from the Institute.

In the beginning, there was Sunbow—Megatom, Joescream, Ultra Jayus, Carole and the Commandoes, and those who know the secret of Cybertron; The Code Monkeys; Nickelodeon—Ralph and Jenna; Jon Taplin and the Enigmites; Joseph, Alyssa and the AIAS; Luigi.

The Quixotic Knights of Isix—Turmell, Welsh, Zito, Mary and Jerome Gary, Jim and Jim; King Gornishe; The T.R.A.X. Team—Peter, Matt, Renny, Chris, and Juliette, Gordon, Craig, Bob L., Larry; The P.F. Magicians—Rob, Mike; The Talisaurus; Rachel and the Cyber-warriors.

Huge thanks to Legal Eagle and Pioneer of the real game—contracts—Richard Thompson; Rick, Tarrnie; The Backwater Boys—Scott and Rick; Sagard and The Barbarians—Sultoon Jazeer, Ergyg the Wastrel, Lucian; TSORG; John W., Douglas G., Louis N. and the Mnemonics; The Flying Yugarians, Leggy Peggy and various dear departed; The Attack Ships on fire off the shoulder of Orion.

Skip Press; Seven; The Fire Studio; Starbreeze; Jack Slate and Andre; VUG (Sierra)—Pete Wanat; TSR Knights of the Pomegranate and Puce—Lorre, Warren, Ward, Grubb, Harold, Mary, Margaret, and the Battle Royale for the Future; The doomed West Coast comic folks—Justin, Lisa, Hildy, etc. and that whacky girl whose name escapes us; The Risk Treaty Breakers Society—Dave, Scott, Bill, Rod, Mike, Jeff; Fireblade Commander—Zach; The Soup Pee-er; The A-52 Debunk Team; Stan, Sandy and Mike F.; Stargate; Visual Concepts; Monolith; Stefanie H.; Gigawatt; Lin O., Jill D., Ray D., R.J. Colleary and John W., wherever you are.

For Flint, a special thanks to:
Terrie, Gwynna and Mr. Z; The Broken Coffeemaker; Paul, son of Jens, for excellent notes and encouragement.

For John, a special thanks to:
Gabriella, Jack and Kate; Mom, Dad, Sara and Justin; For Anna and Cees—your name lives on; Dr. O, The Marquis, Twenty-Cent Tony, Rico, Fred and Pocket Rockets; Big Mike, Ron and late night runs to Vegas, baby.

INTRODUCTION

EMBRACING CHAOS

This book is being written in the heat of battle. As these words hit the computer screen, we have a multitude of other game, television, and film projects in various stages of development and production. There's a meeting across town in two hours that we have to prep for, deadlines loom on the near horizon, and deliverables are in various stages of completion. In an ideal world, everyone we work with would cut us some slack and we'd have the comfort to focus entirely on one project, but life and opportunities don't work that way. So, when the chance to write this book came along, we took it, eager to see where the journey might take us. We embraced the potential chaos because that is often where real inspiration is discovered.

What you'll find within these pages is highly informed by what is happening right now in the heart of the video game business. Hopefully, what we share with you is not unduly biased by the fact that the writing has often been interrupted mid-paragraph by calls from the publishers, developers, producers, designers, and representatives (and the occasional famous actor) we work with while making games.

As with most creative activities, there are upsides and downsides. The upside is that the issues we discuss, the tips and techniques we share, and the realities of the business of game development are told from an *in the trenches* point-of-view.

We have done our best to communicate our experiences and knowledge regarding the practical aspects of writing and designing video games with you.

The downside is that the book is not a contemplative work that is meticulously structured and certain of its conclusions. There is too much flux in the video games medium for that; new platforms are arriving and new products are changing the ways we think. However, the methods and skills that we share are the way that we've successfully created and/or contributed to a multitude of hit games (and in the interest of full-disclosure, a few misses) as well as multiple-platform franchises over the years. They work for us, and we believe that they will work for you.

We are not so arrogant as to believe that ours is the only way. If there were a sure path to success in the game business, then this would be easy. It's not. We're always open to new possibilities: every situation demands its own unique mix of strategies and tactics. We don't have the magic solution or the ultimate answer. Instead, this book will provide a foundation for you to build on and help you avoid the inevitable problems you'll encounter as you bring your game to life. Sorry, but the innovation is up to you.

As working professionals in a still maturing industry, over the years we've acquired, developed, and refined a fairly extensive knowledge-base of what works, what doesn't, and why. You'll find much of it within these pages, and we hope it gives you not only insight, but also the edge you need to succeed in the game business.

There are many genres of games, and many more philosophies on the best way to approach writing and designing them. Between us, going back to pen and paper RPGs (Role-playing Games), up through every platform since the original Sega Genesis and now working on projects for Xbox 360 and PlayStation 3, we have over thirty years of combined writing and design experience. We've been extremely fortunate, and now usually work on eight to twelve titles a year (many of which overlap one another—we call it spinning plates). That being said, almost every day, we still learn something new.

OUR FOCUS

Our bread and butter is story-driven titles, which usually come in one of five flavors:

- ✳ Action/Adventure
- ✳ First-Person Shooter
- ✳ Survival/Horror
- ✳ Platformers
- ✳ Fantasy RPG

With that in mind, this book won't attempt to encompass games such as simulations, or Real-time Strategy, or MMPOGs (Massive Multiplayer Online Games), or sports, or even pure puzzle experiences. Frankly, some of these genres are simply outside our skill set. The truth is that many aspects of game creation and design have become highly specialized, and scores of successful and famous designers, programmers, and artists have made great titles (and good careers and plenty of scratch) by focusing their talents on one specific type of game.

We made a conscious decision years ago that we believe games can be both interactive entertainment and a compelling medium in which to tell stories and develop characters. Obviously, we were not alone (or first) in that assessment. The majority of the hit franchises in the gaming industry almost all include some narrative and character component. You can even make an excellent argument that one of the most profitable football titles utilizes a famous sportscaster as a "character" in the game, and that his involvement is a major reason for its continued success.

Characters and story give the player something they can invest in emotionally. Couple them with great controls, well-designed and well-implemented mechanics, creatively constructed levels, impressive graphics, and physics running within a smooth engine, and you have a potential hit. Add that certain something extra, that hook that captures players' imaginations, and you can pretty much guarantee it. At least, that's what we'd like to believe—and what we strive to achieve in every game we work on.

So, now that you know our core competencies and interests, this should give you a frame of reference: When we are discussing writing and design, we are doing so within the context of games with strong story elements. However, even if you are working on a game (or considering one) beyond our staple genres, we cover a number of universal truths about both game and franchise development that we believe you'll find useful in helping you create your own title.

WHAT WE COVER

Our intention is to help you develop the skills you need to write and design video games in a number of ways:

* ❊ By showing you where we are, where we've been, where we're going in the game business.
* ❊ By offering practical discussions, methods, and solutions of how to integrate game design and story so that they work together.
* ❊ By explaining how to work with a development team, and how that relationship evolves over the course of a project.
* ❊ By outlining the business realities of being a game writer/designer.
* ❊ By presenting exercises and projects you can accomplish (most within a single writing or design session) that will help unleash your creativity and get you thinking like a writer/designer.

If you feel confident that you can write and design your own game, and work with a developer to see that vision through to reality by the time you've finished the book and practiced the techniques you'll find herein, then we've done our job.

WHO SHOULD READ IT, AND WHY

So, for whom did we write this book?

* Aspiring writers and designers who have a desire to get into the game industry.
* Experienced writers who would like to learn about the unique challenges of constructing narratives for games.
* Working professionals in the game business who contribute to a game's content.
* Creative executives and licensors who are interested in the challenges of developing and delivering Intellectual Property through video games.
* Anyone interested in an "insider's view" of game development.
* And, if you don't fall into any of the above categories, but have still gotten this far . . . obviously you.

Throughout the text you'll see descriptions of exercises, as well as practical, tangible actions you can take to improve not only your writing and designing, but also your chances of getting into the video game business. We call these Action Items, and categorize them by terms we've bastardized from game development: Alpha (first steps), Beta (second steps), and Gold (final steps). Each Action Item has some relevance to the topic at hand, so take the time to do them, and it will reinforce what we are covering. An added benefit is that when you've finished the book, you will have already generated a decent body of work to start building on.

OUR ELEVEN VIDEO GAME SURVIVAL COMMANDMENTS

Everyone has a core set of beliefs that they rely on. These are the ones we follow in our careers. (Note: Since the market on ten commandments is already cornered, we decided to make ours go to eleven.)

1. **We're In the Entertainment Business, Not the Game Business**. We look at the content we create as entertainment. Our platform for distributing that entertainment experience is games.
2. **Build Your Design and Story to Break**. Every game design and story will be subject to multiple technical and production realities that will stress them to the breaking point. Inevitably cuts will happen, so get out in front them.

3. **Somebody Always Knows Something You Don't.** Just when you think you know it all, someone proves you wrong. Instead, learn from everybody you work with.

4. **Dialogue Is the Tip of the Dramatic Iceberg.** Throwing dialogue at a broken story never fixes the problem. Good dialogue and stories come from well-conceived characters in exciting dramatic situations.

5. **You Are Only as Good as Your Relationship with Your Team.** All the great ideas in the world are meaningless if no one wants to listen to them or implement them in the game.

6. **Be Willing to Kill Your Babies**. Don't be precious with your ideas, or fall in love with one in particular, because it will, almost without fail, be the one on the chopping block. But . . .

7. **Protect Your Vision**. This is the flip side of killing your babies. If you lose your vision for a project, or lose what was meaningful about it that inspired you in the first place, then what's the point in doing it?

8. **Make Your Deliverables.** You are only as good as what you contribute.

9. **Don't Shine a Spotlight on a Turd.** Every game will have its shortcomings. Don't go out of your way to highlight them.

10. **Choose Collaboration Over Compromise.** Collaborating gets you to the same place as compromise, but without the negativity.

11. **Making Fun Should be Fun.** We're not digging ditches or performing brain surgery here, we're making games. Lighten up, for chrissakes.

WHY WE'D RATHER BE CRAFTSMEN THAN ARTISTS

We don't look at ourselves as artists, but instead, as craftsmen. Let us put it this way: We make tables. We've been making tables for twenty years now. They are made of the finest wood, they have style, they are functional, and they add value to a home. If you need a table, you come to us. We'll build you a table, on time and on budget. We'll put our heart and soul into building you the best table we can make. We are craftsmen when it comes to tables.

Weeks later, we'll deliver the table to your house. You'll put it in your living room. It'll fit perfectly, meet your needs and be more than you were expecting. Like we said, we know how to build tables. As we're leaving, you might say to us: "This table is beautiful, it's a work of art." And to you, it may be a work of art. To us, it's a table.

This is the way we approach our craft. An artist touches his "work" when he is stricken by inspiration, when the "muse" alights upon his shoulder, when the stars are aligned. Like the artist, a craftsman has knowledge and passion and skill and experience, but he also picks up his tools every day and gets busy. Semantics, yes, but we believe that they are important to how we approach writing. Every day, we strive to be the best craftsmen we can be. And we build a lot of tables.

LET'S GET STARTED

As you read, you'll notice that within our focus lies one of the essential lessons of any kind of writing: We believe in the maxim made famous by a sneaker company, "Just do it!" Start somewhere, anywhere, and get cranking. You may not show your first work to your client, your coworkers, your friends, or even your dog, but at least you are getting it done.

And it is important to remember this: A huge part of the designer's job is communicating effectively his or her vision. This is always done on the page. In fact, some of the best writing we've ever seen has been in design documents that will never be shown to the public. Almost every designer we work with is a good writer. So even if your core interest is design, take the time to study the writing elements we present. It'll make you that much stronger as a designer.

In this book, we offer techniques that we hope will get you away from the blank page as quickly as possible. We want you to start generating content, so that you will get your subconscious motivated. Seasoned professionals know that most of the time, your creations will organize themselves later.

And what if your ideas don't come together? Well, like any discipline, writing takes practice. Sometimes, the act of creating is more important than what is created. If your expectation is that whenever you hit the keyboard only genius springs forth, then you are setting yourself up for disappointment. But know that each time you sit down to write, you'll be more comfortable and confident than the last time. So never be afraid to explore ideas. And chances are those ideas won't go to waste, but instead, will find their way into your next project, or the next one.

And so we welcome you to our world—the world of video games. Varying points of view are normal, emotions can and do run high, milestones are always looming, and crunch-time is just around the corner. It's a world full of wonderful, imaginative, difficult, brilliant, and brash individuals. It's a business of big budgets, amazing technologies, and multinational corporations. It is also a creative playground of endless opportunities to expand the horizons of what we define loosely as entertainment. And every day, we feel blessed to be a part of it.

If you think you have great ideas for games, this book should help you shape them into something you can sell. It's how we do it, and we're happy to share it with you.

—Flint Dille and John Zuur Platten, July 2006

THE INFLUENCES OF STORYTELLING IN A DIGITAL UNIVERSE

AN INTERRUPTED INTRODUCTION

Books often begin with a history lesson. Sometimes that lesson seems to be there so that the writer can (START) vamp for pages, or wax nostalgic about the past. We won't attempt to do that in discussing video games (SELECT). We're a new medium. We're not mature yet (X) and we don't know (X, X) where we're ultimately going. We barely know where we are.

The best way of figuring out (TRIANGLE) where something is going is to take a look at where it has been (SQUARE) and plot a course from there. So bear with us (CIRCLE) as we take a fast and facile tour of the history (START, SELECT, START) of entertainment media. Let's take a trip through the last five thousand years in about a page per millennium (START, START, START, START, START).

Okay, by now you're wondering what all the interruptions are about, so let's get one of the first, and most valuable, pieces of business out of the way right up front. If the above paragraphs were a *cut-scene* in a video game, for about half of your audience, this is what it would look like: frantic button presses on their controller to skip over the narrative and get to the action. In fact, chances are, you've done it yourself while playing a game. We all have. "Why are these people talking when I've got cool weapons and all this stuff to blow-up? Get on with it!"

ACTION ITEM (ALPHA)—PLAY A GAME

Within the next day, make time to sit down and play a game, preferably a console title. Give yourself at least a half-hour. When you are done, write a brief summary of the experience.

Remember that when you are creating content for an interactive medium like video games, there are expectations on the part of your audience: to be engaged. To be in control. To be playing. Of course, as in real life, control is an illusion or at best, a temporary condition, but it is one that humans like.

In his book *Why Don't Zebras Get Ulcers*, biologist Robert Sapolsky argues that the two things that create happiness are *control* and, if you can't have control, *predictability*. Since much of game design is predicated on engaging the player in potentially unpredictable ways, control becomes that much more important.

All of your writing and design is influenced and informed by the medium in which it will ultimately be delivered. For video games, one of the biggest challenges you have as a writer is creating compelling and engaging content that captivates the player and enhances the overall gaming experience, not distract from it or slow it down. Okay, we'll cover all of this in detail later, so let's pick up where we left off . . .

A BRIEF HISTORY OF HOW WE GOT HERE

For thousands of years, professional storytelling was done by someone sharing tales with an audience, probably around a fire. People would remember these stories for millennia, passing them on from one generation to the next in an oral tradition. Some tales were constantly embellished, updated, and distilled. Fables were recast, set to music and meter, and their story elements recomposed to suit the teller and his audience.

Finally, somewhere around the time of Homer, somebody started writing down the old anecdotes and legends, and the oral tradition in the West began to die. Different media flourished. The epic poem and its smaller cousin, the ballad, were popular. Theater evolved, and so did the novel. By the fourth century, dramatic convention had reached the point where Aristotle could write the seminal *Poetics*.

Then, somewhere near the dawn of the twentieth century, the process began accelerating. The movie industry was born. At first, it was simply a novelty; then, a way of recording plays for posterity. It seems that every medium reflexively defaults to what came before it (and games were no different). But early innovators such as D. W. Griffith discovered that you could edit film, move the camera, and use different lenses for varied effects. You could tell a story not only through words, but images. Where you set the camera, the lighting, the angles, the editing, the way you juxtaposed action, the music—all of it could tell a story when words could only exist as cards flashed on the screen. Then, when sound was added, an entirely new pallet of vocals and effects became available to filmmakers. A cinematic language was born.

CINEMATIC LANGUAGE

Everyone now understands that if you start by showing the exterior of a restaurant, and then cut to a couple of people sitting at a table inside a restaurant, that the exterior shot establishes the location of the characters we are seeing. Having seen thousands upon thousands of hours of filmed entertainment, we now have an inherent understanding of what is happening when we watch this sequence: the visuals and edits lead us to the conclusion that the two characters are sitting inside the restaurant we saw in the previous shot. It's simple and it's obvious. But for the early filmmakers, and audiences, this was all new. A dissolve didn't mean the passage of time until someone had the inspiration, and creative courage, to make it so. Part of what the first directors struggled with was an effective way to communicate and shorthand information with an audience.

ACTION ITEM (ALPHA)—BREAK DOWN THE LANGUAGE OF CINEMA

Watch a sequence from a film or television show and list each element of it. How did the scene begin, how did it end? What cinematic language "tricks" were used to shorthand information to you?

We have a similar struggle as we make video games: to create a language that is unique to the medium. For now, we often rely on the exact same techniques for time and location transitions as film, often in the form of cinematics or cut-scenes (noninteractive story moments within the game).

MEDIA FOR THE MASSES

The arrival of radio gave us mass media that millions of people could experience simultaneously. There was no time lag in communal entertainment. When Orson Welles dramatized H. G. Wells's *War of the Worlds* on the radio, it changed the world by showing us what could happen if the line between truth and fiction were blurred. A generation earlier, William Randolph Hearst had taught us a similar lesson with yellow journalism in which fiction, printed as reality, was able to have a profound influence on political debate within the United States.

And while we're on the subject of newspapers, we must mention the comic strip. Graphic storytelling was not a new art when strips like *The Yellow Kid* came along, but the idea of daily installments of an unending story was unique. Now, for the first time, we had characters and a universe that persisted day after day, year after year. This medium was constantly being updated, constantly kept interesting. To the kid of the 1930s, Buck Rogers was as real as anything else he saw in the newspaper. No doubt the daily comic strip helped spawn the *cliffhanger* movie serial of the day—a medium that itself is very relevant to the subject of video game writing and design. Many of the best comic superheroes have a transcendent appeal. For example, both Batman and Superman were created generations ago, and yet they remain viable franchises that we've worked on in the game business. The same can be said for popular games based on Spiderman and The Hulk.

Around the time that comics were gaining in popularity, we also saw the rise of pulp magazines and novels. Pulp fiction offered an even better format for the continuing character. Every month, The Shadow would show up with a new adventure, and every week he could be heard on the radio. Not that continuing characters were new: Hercules predated comic and radio heroes by millennia. The fresh idea was this: characters could be an industry. They weren't relegated to one medium, but could encompass multiple formats within the entertainment business. Eventually, the pulp heroes bifurcated to two different and equally important mediums—the comic-book superhero and the hard-boiled detective—and the two branches accelerated their growth.

Then radio and the movies had a bastard child called television. While the first television shows were filmed radio shows (which remain some of the best old shows from the "golden age" of television), they all presaged a whole new medium. And what was it? (START, SELECT, START, X, START) Wait for it . . .

THEME PARKS RATHER THAN AMUSEMENT PARKS

Another piece of evolution fell into place when Walt Disney came along and did an amazing thing with storytelling: he created the theme park. Think about the word *theme*. It is a classic component of writing. And here was a man applying it to roller-coasters. At Disneyland, you could physically experience the fictional worlds that previously existed only in TV and the movies. The Matterhorn ride was easier than mountain climbing and safer than tobogganing, while offering a fantasy version of these things. You could become an adventurer with little personal risk. The goal of the Jungle Cruise or Pirates of the Caribbean was to re-create the fictional experience created within Disney's entertainment properties and not the real experience of going to Africa or meeting actual pirates. It is, and was, fiction about fiction. No scurvy here, matey.

If you feel that carnival "tunnel of love" rides were precursors to the Disneyland approach, you're right. But Disney was a visionary in that all too many people told him his fantasy theme park would never work. More important, Disney rides put people inside a story in the real world.

ROLE-PLAYING GAMES

Somewhere in the mid-1970s came the role-playing game. This fusion of miniatures war gaming, statistics, theme-park immersion, and synergized fictional worlds allowed us to mentally interact with our friends and families in a player-generated reality. In many ways, when *Dungeons & Dragons* was created, Gary Gygax and his compatriots did for gaming what Einstein did for physics. Gaming was no longer about moving miniature figures around on a board; it was about moving whole worlds around in your brain, which at the time was called "the ultimate personal computer." In role playing you became somebody you weren't, a hero, or a villain, in a world that didn't exist. Other players, in the persona of their characters, were "your fellow adventurers." Everyone agreed that this was for real. Within the structure of the game, you could "play war" just like in the backyard when you were seven. You could scavenge the lair of an evil dragon, rescue a sorcerer from a dungeon, battle mythical creatures, and create adventures that spanned both time and distances too great to map. Even more important, players were able to share an alternate reality together and, thanks to an elaborate set of rules, it was "fair."

The reason it all worked, and continues to work, is because each participant, each player in the game, became a content creator (for our purposes, a writer) within the context of the game. The game exists as much in the imagination of the players as it does in any physical reality. And it was persistent: the character that you created became your "avatar" within the *D & D* universe. The brilliance and the main addictive quality of *D & D* was that it simultaneously created rules and structure for the players while also freeing their imaginations to go places and have adventures that no traditional board or military miniatures game had previously allowed. But perhaps the biggest paradigm shift it created was this: you weren't controlling a character, you were the character. The First-Person game was born. The impact on both players, and the entire gaming community, was profound. Within the video game business, the influence of *D & D* can still be felt to this day.

Before we leave role-playing games, we should mention another important element. For the first time, games had a built-in storyteller. The Dungeon Master isn't a player as such, but a storyteller (and sometimes referee) who guides the players on their adventure. In this way, the game didn't always need to be competitive. In fact, cooperation became a major element of the experience and part of the fun of playing, as gamers accepted the same reality and believed the same adventure the Dungeon Master presented.

BIRTH OF THE MEGA-FRANCHISE

Not long after *Dungeons & Dragons* became a phenomenon, the movie *Star Wars* overhauled the entertainment universe because of the way it blended comics, cliffhangers, television, and film in a way we'd never really seen before—it seemed both breathtakingly new and comfortably familiar at the same time.

George Lucas's star-child was a collage work at every level. It was a Homeric epic and it was a Western and it was a *Dawn Patrol* movie and it was a cliffhanger and it was *The Wizard of Oz* and it had comic-book influences such as Jack Kirby's *New Gods* and an Asian Zen-meets-New-Age gospel aesthetic all at the same time. In many ways, it synthesized all that came before it and served as a road map for most of what would follow. *Star Wars* also set the standard for what we would come to define as a franchise. It is an entertainment property that transcends medium. In addition to the films, it spawns a seemingly endless stream of toys, games, costumes, books, magazines and collectables. And like *Star Trek* (which had cult status with the original series, but didn't really become a franchise until *Star Wars* led the way), it has a fervent fan base that is always eager for more.

When the first *Star Wars* movie came out, people were playing a video game called *Space Wars* (you can still find emulator versions of the game on the Internet). Obviously it wasn't like playing a *Star Wars* game today, with the same characters that you see in a movie, but it did provide a sense of interaction with a similar universe to one you had experienced in the movie theater.

ACTION ITEM (ALPHA)—ICONIC ELEMENTS
Take a franchise you enjoy from games, film, television, or books. Now, write down five iconic franchise elements that come to mind when you think of it. For instance, you might think of the *Enterprise* if your franchise is *Star Trek*. Or the CTU badges from
Continued on next page

Continued from previous page
24. Or Lara Croft's guns (wherever your mind went is valid—the ones on her hips or the ones in her T-shirt—they are both icons of *Tomb Raider*). Whatever you choose, ask yourself why you remember them? If you can, write down why you think they are important elements of your chosen franchise.

EARLY STORYTELLING THROUGH GAMEPLAY

The original video games, Atari classics like *Asteroids*, *Missile Command*, and *Centipede* didn't have a storytelling component, but they still had a narrative. The gameplay itself dictated the fiction in which the experience existed. *Asteroids* is a space adventure in which a lone starship pilot (you) struggles to survive against an onslaught of asteroids and space aliens. In *Missile Command*, you are charged with defending your cities from certain destruction by intercepting incoming ICBMs. Although there are no cut-scenes, by simply describing the gameplay, you are in essence, defining a story for these games.

But these early titles focused almost exclusively on gameplay: the fusion of interaction and narrative would come later. Which leads us to interactive storytelling.

THE STORYTELLERS' TRADITION

It didn't start with computer games or pick-a-path (*Choose Your Own Adventure*) novels or *Dungeons & Dragons*. For most of us, it began when, at bedtime, somebody promised to tell you a story. You knew that they were trying to put you to sleep and you didn't want to go. You wanted to drag it out for as many minutes as you could before you were left all alone in your room. It was a success for everybody if the story provided a launch platform for sweet dreams and you were sound asleep when it was over.

The nightly story probably started with something familiar. Pick your fairy tale—one of those great old chestnuts that everybody everywhere has known for generations. *Hansel and Gretel*, *Cinderella*, etc. Any adult could tell those stories. Everybody remembered different parts and everybody had their own agenda. Some left out the scary parts and you would dutifully remember them. Some accentuated the scary parts and then got in trouble for it when you had nightmares. Or perhaps they put things in the wrong order and you would remind them of what they were missing. Some added whole parts, or even sent the story off in some wild direction.

Who told you stories? Maybe it was your grandmother with a unique sense of free association who got you laughing with a wild story that may have even contained some Freudian stuff. The point is that when you shared stories with people who cared about you, everybody won. Maybe you didn't have a vivid storytelling experience again until playing *Dungeons & Dragons* with friends. When you did have interactive experiences, even if they were separated by miles of time and intent, they seemed remarkably similar.

Regardless of the tale, the bedtime story is a continuation of the oral tradition started thousands of years ago. The stories we heard, and gravitated toward, as children continue to be influential on our creativity today, whether we realize it or not. Study any famous artist and inevitably you will find the references that they make to childhood interaction with film, television, literature, and now, with the latest generation of filmmakers and actors, games.

ACTION ITEM (BETA)—TELL A BEDTIME STORY

Tell a bedtime story, preferably to a small child. Don't read it . . . do it from memory, or make up your own. Embellish it wildly. This is the only time we will encourage you to put your audience to sleep. Write down your thoughts about the experience. What worked and what didn't. Did inspiration hit? If so, think about how. Do you think you could do it again?

That's the thing about games—they are exciting experiences we share and talk about. They can, and do, have an impact and leave an impression, often in ways that traditional entertainment can't, because when we play a game, we are active participants in the process.

The video game business is now in its second generation of talent, so today's designers, producers, writers, artists, and programmers can all look back on the video games that they played as children. Many of the core mechanics and play-patterns of those games find their way into the titles that they create. And the experiences—the stories—we create through video games today will be just as influential on the next generation of artists.

THE TELEVISION EVOLUTION

When we play console games, we are almost always looking at a television. It is the ultimate visual delivery medium through which we interact with program content. The same chair or sofa we sit on when watching TV is the one we sit on when we are playing a game. It is a different experience than playing a PC game. There is an immediacy—and an intimacy—to playing a game on your computer. You sit next to the monitor; you control the game with mouse and keyboard. Your mind is keyed-in to the space that you've created for your computer. For many of us, the computer is also where we work, so we create an environment for ourselves that is conducive to using the computer.

The same holds true for our televisions and where we are most comfortable watching them. Usually, when we are sitting in front of our televisions, we anticipate that we will be entertained or informed. We don't look at "the idiot box" as a place where we work, and the environment we create for our televisions reflects this. Therefore, our mind-set for console video games has already subtly been influenced by the fact that we are watching it on a television. The relationship between the two mediums is often overlooked when we write and design games, but the overall connection between what we are watching, and where we are when we are playing a video game, can have a profound effect on our gaming experience.

People who grew up in the latter years of the twentieth century gleaned linear stories from movies, books, magazines, and other media. But, the closest thing to nonlinear storytelling (if we view it in the context of a metastory) was the weekly television show. It was as if the same deck was laid out and shuffled in a new way every week. For example, let's take a look at an early classic television series, *The Andy Griffith Show*. Every week, Andy and Barney would be sitting at the station/jail/courthouse when somebody would open the door and lure them off on a story. It didn't much matter whether it was Opie trying to win a spelling bee, or the governor arriving in town, or Aunt Bee trying to set Andy up on a date. At the end of the episode, it would be a complete reset and next week everybody would be back in place at the Mayberry Police Station, waiting for the next story to start. Of course, there was some continuity. Thelma Lou and Barney seemed to be kind of an on-and-off thing, and Andy's relationship with his girlfriend grew until they were finally married. Some incidental characters came and went: Gomer left to do his own show (*Gomer Pyle, U.S.M.C.*), a spin-off (*The Andy Griffith Show* was itself a spin-off of *The Danny Thomas Show*) and Goober arrived. Somewhere along the line Ernest T. Bass appeared and people liked him so much that he kept coming back. There were probably other characters that were intended to continue in the series, but never took hold and so they were packed off to Mount Pilot, never to be seen again. Eventually even Andy was gone, and so we got a continuation television series called *Mayberry R.F.D.*

TV shows of that time lead to a new kind of interactivity—one in which fans played a huge role in the development of a show. In fact, *Star Trek* was the first show that ever lived and died simply by its fans, which saved it for an entire season. Now, thanks to the Internet and instant feedback, producers and show runners (the writer/producers who keep the shows running) learn very quickly how to tune their shows to suit the fans—and in an increasingly splintered market, more and more television shows are dependent on Fans with a capital "F."

Television also established a format for its shows, a pattern that would become second nature to the viewer. Like film before, television had its own language. A viewer knew what to expect if he was watching a sitcom, or a drama, or a doctor or cop show. Regardless of the content, the way that each was presented was predictable, formulaic and, some might even say, comfortable.

That all changed in 1981 when *Hill Street Blues* came along and broke all the rules. Part crime drama, part black comedy, part ensemble character drama, *Hill Street Blues* followed multiple storylines simultaneously, had chaotic scenes (and camera work) with characters talking and yelling over each other to the point where some of the dialogue was almost indecipherable. Action was framed in ways that multiple events were happening within a single shot and without the camera racking focus to tell you which one you were supposed to pay attention to. It had continuing storylines that didn't resolve themselves each week, and had convoluted plots involving the idiosyncrasies of a large cast of flawed heroes. Although it had Capt. Frank Furillo at its center, the show was just as likely to follow any of the characters, making them "the star" of an episode. Things were never tied up with nice little bows.

At first, the audience didn't know how to respond, so they stayed away. But as people caught on to the unique language of *Hill Street Blues*, they began to find themselves captivated, and the series went on to become a success with both the public and critics. Its influence can be seen in any number of past and current television shows. It also helped audiences become comfortable with alternate forms of storytelling and entertainment, which is, of course, a big part of what we are doing today in video games.

In any case, the seeds of interactivity were planted in popular television shows. And, because we are humans and live in a time continuum, shows had to move forward whether they wanted to or not. Actors playing roles got older every year, died, or left shows to pursue movie careers. Animation, the next paving stone on the road to video games, didn't have this problem.

TRADITIONAL ANIMATION LEADS THE WAY

Cartoon characters don't age. They don't put on weight. They don't have scheduling problems. They don't want to change their careers. Animated characters do whatever the writers and animators want them to do, just like video game characters. They don't intrinsically change; they grow as the medium grows. Think of the longest running show on television, *The Simpsons*. There have been minor changes to the art over the years, writers and producers have come and gone, and there has been the occasional contract dispute with the voice actors, but for the most part, the series has remained essentially the same since it began in the late 1980s. In addition to the considerable talent involved in creating the show, a big reason for its success is its familiarity and continuity: Bart and Lisa are still the same kids we met almost two decades ago.

In fact, with digital media, we can go the additional step of not just stopping aging, but reversing it. As this book was written, actor Sean Connery returned to his most famous character, James Bond, for the game *From Russia with Love*, looking the same age as he did when he made the film in 1963. So what if the real Sean Connery is a grandfather? In the game, as on the DVD, he is Bond, James Bond, and can remain thirty-three forever.

VIDEO GAMES AS ALTERNATIVE ANIMATION

In many ways, today's video games bear more of a similarity to animation than to live-action, despite the race to "photo-realism" on the part of console makers. Games rarely rely on filmed assets. Instead, characters and worlds are built in 3D, using software packages that are essentially the same as those used to create computer-generated movies and visual effects, and by animation artists that may work in both the game and traditional entertainment fields. Voice talent is utilized in much the same way as animation. The same goes for music and sound. Of course, the big difference comes in design, engineering (programming), and content creation. But if you were step into a top CGI house, and then visit a top game developer (also known as an "A-Level" developer), you'd see a large majority of people doing essentially the same thing.

THE THREE MAIN ERAS OF VIDEO GAME DEVELOPMENT

Let's take a quick look at the three main eras of video game development, and how they inform our role in the game business.

PRIMITIVE

The first era of video games (we don't mean primitive as a pejorative term). Hardware was so limited that story either took center stage (text-based games) or was relegated to the back seat (arcade games). Games of this era were defined in large part by the imaginative investment that the player was willing to make with the gameplay experience. The graphics may have been basic, but if the gameplay was addictive, then the player filled in the blanks that the technology couldn't deliver.

Twitch games (titles that rely on fast interaction and input from the player) dominated the early console market that was trail-blazed first by Atari, and then later by Intellivision.

MULTIMEDIA

Then, we moved into the *Multimedia Era—or (Sillywood)*. This was the period when the first CD-ROMs came out and everybody jumped on board. *Myst* is one of the most memorable and influential games from this era. It was a sweet, naïve time when "repurposing assets" became the key buzzwords. Everything could be made interactive; everything could be made into a game. Timothy Leary declared multimedia as the new psychedelic drug. Hundreds of released titles had no reason for being other than they were interactive.

While console-based games flourished under both Nintendo and Sega, they also dabbled in the multimedia explosion, most notably with interactive FMV (Full-Motion Video) games on the Sega CD (of which we were a part).

Interactive stories with branching narratives were in vogue and everyone arrogantly believed that they were on the verge of some great breakthrough in entertainment (in many ways, game storytelling is still dealing with the backlash that was created during this era). Alas, it was not to be. The *Multimedia Era* died hard somewhere around Christmas of 1996, but it did serve as a great foreshadowing of the dot.com boom/bust that would follow.

SOPHISTICATED

Then came the era of the *Sophisticated Platform*, heralded in by the arrival of PlayStation. Now, games were achieving a level of graphic realism that was captivating eyeballs as well as thumbs (in the game business, a visually-stunning game is referred to as "eye candy," while a fast-paced twitch game is referred to as "thumb candy"). PC games began utilizing 3D Video Cards. Realism became the new standard. First-person shooters came into their own, on both consoles and PCs. Arcade-quality platformers such as *Crash Bandicoot* became huge franchises. And we saw the first hints of multiplayer and Internet connectivity.

We now find ourselves in a midphase of the *Sophisticated Platform* era. We'll see if the Xbox 360 and the PlayStation III, or perhaps the Nintendo Wii, move us into a new period. At the moment, games have increased in their visual wow factor, and in their depth, but we haven't seen a great leap forward in design.

ACTION ITEM (ALPHA)—RETRO IMAGINATION

Take your favorite game of today, and imagine it designed to run on technology from the early days of video games—say the Atari 2600. What elements of the game could be implemented? If you could play the core mechanic, would it bother you that the graphics would be primitive? If you don't believe that your favorite game could translate back in time, ask yourself why? Write down your thoughts. Would it be fun? Would the game still be any good?

As with the midperiod of any phase, there is very little innovation other than increased aesthetics and polish. We see a lot of licenses, sequels, and knockoffs. Advancement is incremental. Don't expect much that is blindingly different (although it may be blindingly more beautiful). We can all think of the exceptions, but they only serve to prove the rule. However, don't look at this as stagnation, but instead as stabilization. Often, the most innovative ideas come not from constantly pushing the envelope, but from looking at the envelope in a new way, or using it to do something completely unexpected. Creativity need not, and in fact should not, rely on constantly advancing technology.

The exciting prospect of this time, the time we are working in right now, is that more than ever before, the game business is able to compete with other forms of entertainment at their level. Television is losing its audience to people who would rather play a new game that watch a re-run. Hit titles have sales figures that outperform movie box-office receipts. It is said that you cannot demand respect, only earn it. Well, the game business has earned that respect, and now it is demanding to be taken seriously. And the entire entertainment community has taken notice, and in many cases, wants to come along for the ride.

NOW IT'S YOUR TURN

And so now we start our journey through the video game universe together, where all storytelling methods that have come before are integrated, where worlds and characters can be manipulated in ways previously unimaginable, and where you are allowed to participate. There has never been anything quite like it in the history of entertainment. Video games enthrall us, addict us, shock us, fulfill us, anger us, frustrate us, thrill us, appall us, delight us, and on that rare occasion, become a part of us.

Okay, enough theory and history. Let's get our fingernails dirty.

Press START.

LEVEL 2

VIDEO GAME
STORY STRUCTURE
AND WORK APPROACH

THE DIFFERENCE BETWEEN LEAD GAME DESIGNERS
AND GAME WRITERS

Throughout this book, we will often talk about tasks and responsibilities of lead game designers and game writers. While many times their jobs overlap, there are distinctive differences we should discuss for clarity.

LEAD GAME DESIGNER

A designer is responsible for all of the creative content in the game. This includes characters, worlds, core gameplay, level layout and design, core mechanics, weapons, player character (PC) abilities, story, usable objects, inventory systems, game-shells, controls . . . you get the idea. Think of the lead designer as the director of a film. If the player can see it, use it, shoot it, modify it, explore it or master it, then it is the responsibility of the lead game designer.

The lead game designer works with all of the other members of the development to execute the vision of the game.

GAME WRITER

The game writer is primarily concerned with the narrative content of the title and how it integrates into gameplay. This includes the story, characters, worlds, mythologies, creatures, enemies, mystical powers, grounded or enhanced realities, technologies, and so on. The game writer will oftentimes be involved in High-level Design, as the story and gameplay should blend together seamlessly into a compelling experience: story-related set-piece often make for good gameplay.

The game writer will write the game script for all of the narratives, whether pre-rendered or in-game cut scenes, as well as the dialogue for the characters. The game writer may also create the mythology of elements that are uncovered in the game (sacred scroll text, for example).

The game writer usually works directly with the lead game designer and the game producer.

THE UNIQUE CHALLENGES OF CONTENT CREATION IN VIDEO GAMES

There are a number of ways of structuring your story. They range from a linear path at one extreme, to a free-flowing narrative at the other. In this section, we're going to roughly break down the different kinds of stories that games attempt to tell. The disclaimer we insert before you read this is that the categories are not hard and fast and there are a million hybrids in between the options we offer. A discussion has to start somewhere, so we're laying out the different kinds of stories as to how they affect the writer.

If you come from a screenwriting background, you should realize that there are unique aspects of game writing versus film. An iterative process means that things are constantly in motion and revision. While that might sometimes be true when a movie is nearing or even in production, it is continually true in game writing. Changes are part of the process. The writer needs to embrace them, because it means that you are moving forward. If movies were made like games, shooting an establishing shot of a street would go something like this:

> Shoot the street;
> Look at it, add rain;
> Shoot the street;
> Look at it, paint the storefront red;
> Shoot the street;
> Look at it, move the cars;
> Shoot the street;
> Look at it . . . liked it better without rain;
> Shoot the street;

> Look at it . . . maybe at night, with rain;
> Shoot the street.

And so on. The main issue is that in traditional production, it is too expensive to show up on the set without everything fairly thought out in advance. In game production, ideas build on ideas, levels, and even core gameplay. The project can be in a constant state of flux for months on end until the game reaches *Beta Stage* (just prior to release).

Often, when we start writing, we trust (hopefully) that the issues at the core of the story will resolve themselves. Unfortunately, this rarely happens, and at some point in the process, we are forced to go back to deconstructing the narrative to find the elements that sit at its center. When your story has a reached a roadblock that seems unsolvable, chances are good that the problem, and the solution, can be found back at the basic structural elements that should be in place before, or fairly soon after, you begin writing. That's why we pay a lot of attention to prep work when we get started. So now let's take a look at how we begin structuring a video game.

PLAY IT, DISPLAY IT, SAY IT

It is important to remember that your story is working in unison with gameplay. The more your story can be told through gameplay, the better. Much like the film axiom "Don't say it, show it," you should be thinking in a similar fashion for the game: "Don't show it, play it."

If it is possible to do so, let the player have control of key narrative moments, either by triggering them through their actions, or in fact, having the game reveal key story moments (a sidekick character is killed because the player didn't defend him, for example). In other words, when dealing with your narrative, create a priority for telling your story as follows: *play it, display it, say it.*

ACTION ITEM (BETA)—STORYTELLING PRIORITY

Write out three versions of the same gameplay sequence using the Play It, Display It, Say It model. Create each possible solution. For example, if your hero must blow up a door, write a version in which this can be accomplished in gameplay, a version in which the hero detonates the door in a narrative, and a version in which the hero recounts blowing up the door to someone else. Think about the implications of each. Which is more satisfying for the player? Which is the most cost effective for the production? Is there a way to split the difference?

DON'T DIMINISH THE HERO

One of the big problems with game narratives is the fact that oftentimes the needs of the game conflict with the needs of the story. The hero is the player, and the game needs to give the player information, so the way some games go about this is to make the hero the dumbest character in the game. Everyone is telling him what to do. He doesn't have the same knowledge as everyone else. He asks too many questions. The hero has a "controller," such as a guy in a parked van. He is lost. And then there's that classic gambit: he has amnesia. We find that this often happens with larger properties and established characters. The end result of this too-common condition is the hero is the weakest character in the story.

It is understandable why this happens when one considers what the designers are trying to get across to the player. In practice, however, it diminishes not only the hero, but it leaves the player feeling less than powerful. No one likes to be bossed around, especially in a game. Games are about empowerment, and creating a situation in which the narrative conceit of the game puts the player in a subservient role is not a winning formula. This is especially true of licensed property where doing so violates the character. When you have Nagging Nancy storytelling, where every other character in the world is saying: "Go here . . . go there . . . see this guy . . . get this thing," the game has become a series of chores, and the hero is now a messenger boy.

This is one of the main problems with story-driven games. For their future titles, developers and publishers are going to be looking for writers and designers who have innovative solutions to this dilemma. Here's a perfect example where your creativity can open doors.

For us, we address this problem by first keeping the hero *in character*. Then, we make the hero proactive rather than reactive. Instead of asking for information, he demands it. Simple changes of focus keep the hero out front. If the hero is running out of time, we have him call his handler, rather than the other way around. We need to know the hero's agenda and how he is striving to achieve it. When the narrative doesn't diminish our hero (and by extension, us) we get a more satisfying gameplay experience and feel better about our advancement.

Our character grows if he moves from taking orders to making them, but this is not a hard and fast rule. Nevertheless, you should always be aware of how many times the hero is being nagged, or ordered, or bossed around in the game. This particularly makes sense in a military simulation. If the hero is a gangster running the south side of Chicago, however, taking orders from a bartender doesn't make sense. What you could do instead is have the gangster have his goons beat the information out of the bartender. And whatever you do, remember to keep your character in character.

ACTION ITEM (BETA)—DON'T DIMINISH THE HERO

Here's the setup: Three characters have information that your hero needs to advance. One knows who he must see. One knows where he must go. And one knows when he must be there. Write a sequence in which the hero remains proactive and gets the information. Perhaps he threatens the characters, or fools them, or overhears conversations, or offers something of his own that gets him what he needs. The one thing that your hero can't do is ask for the information. Be creative and keep your hero in character.

CONSTRUCTING THE STORY

Where do you start in putting together your story? The following are some idea of places to start. There are probably a thousand books out there that will tell you how to pace your story. We don't intend to be number 1001. The best advice for story progression in a game is to design it like a roller coaster.

Consider the following elements:

* Exhilaration
* Slowing
* Building suspense
* Bigger exhilaration
* Surprise "bump"
* Huge suspense
* Final wild ride
* Victory lap
* Get off the ride

A game constructed like that gives you a gamestory *beat chart*.

If you've had experience with writing fiction, you'll notice that we haven't yet touched on the classic three-act structure. Usually, we save this for last, as trying to force game stories into traditional structure can inhibit the creative process. Eventually, our game story will have a beginning, middle, and an end. But unlike screenwriting, we aren't thinking of what is happening over the course of Act One. Instead, we focus on our characters, the world, and the gameplay challenges that the player will face as he accomplishes the objectives of the levels. When these are firmly in place, we turn back to more traditional storytelling techniques to create the narrative arc of the game.

WRITER-FRIENDLY FORMATS

The more linear a game is, the more writer-friendly. Linear path games are controllable. You don't have to think of the five thousand different things a player will do and cover every contingency. You know where he is, what he's doing and why he's doing it at all times. The art here is to make the story compelling enough that the player keeps playing through it to see how it all comes out.

In a linear path you are given no choice as to what you do in the story. Success or failure is dependent on whether you are able to accomplish preset goals. In this kind of game, often as not the player is judged by how well he plays the character that is laid out for him. How good a Spankman are you? Maybe there are variations on how you play *Spankman,* but basically, the range of what the character does is determined solely by the game designer.

The difference between linear and nonlinear stories is that a linear story drives the player through the game, and in a nonlinear story, set pieces are created that may live on their own or, when added to other set pieces, build toward a larger unfolding narrative.

In a *mission-based* game we have a kind of open-world design in which you are able to wander around all you want, but here and there you are given either mandatory or optional missions that pin you to a sense of story progression.

WRITER-DIFFICULT FORMATS

These formats are by their very nature much less controllable. They tend to lead to a lot of situations in which the writer will have to write endless alts (alternatives) and fairly generic exchanges with NPCs (Nonplayer Characters). In practice, however, these games tend to have linear, mission-based components so that the player can experience varied gameplay.

In a *free-flow* game there are no cinematics or obvious breaks in the story. This effectively refers to an open world design in which your adventure is whatever you happen to do in the world. There is no clear sequence of events.

A *consequential story* offers a way of balancing free-flow and structure. The idea here is that the world is alive and remembers things and there are consequences for your actions. For instance, if you kill a guy who is a member of a certain gang, that gang will hunt you for the rest of the game or until you perform a mission for them.

In a *role-playing game* (RPG) you are not so much progressing through a story as trying to build up your character to better deal with the world of the game. So, the journey of the character becomes the story. The problem is that you have to anticipate thousands of different kinds of alts depending on who your character is and how an NPC will relate to them. For instance, a character will react very differently to a sexy woman thief who poses a limited physical threat to him than a battle-scarred barbarian who is frothing at the mouth. The ensuing dialogue tends to come out really "canned." Such games tend to be best realized in online, massive multiplayer games where the players create their own dialogue.

TYPES OF BRANCHING NARRATIVES

As the name implies, think of *branching narratives* like the branches of a tree. The trunk forms the spine of the story, and events within the narrative reach outward in a number of different directions at specific decision points, or branches, along the journey.

LIMITED BRANCHING

Limited branching stories tend to revolve around a series of "yes/no" or "black/white" objectives. Depending on the outcome, or the choice of action that the player takes, the game will branch to the appropriate story thread. Many early adventures games relied on this structure. Today, it has fallen out of fashion. Limited branching usually will only go one or two branches deep before it returns to the main story arc. This often means a story contrivance that puts the player back on the "correct path." This type of branching can lead to more than one ending.

OPEN-ENDED

Open-ended branching stories are the complex and ambitious version of this type of storytelling. The player may be faced with a multitude of storylines to follow in the game, and each of these may have multiple permeations. This type of game story can very quickly get out of hand. It's pretty simple to do the math, and see how quickly the various branches and variations can get out of hand. Another major problem with this type of story is that often you are devoting creative energy, time and money to elements of the game and the story that will not be seen by the player (he takes another branch and entirely misses it).

FUNNELING NARRATIVE (CHOKEPOINTS)

Using a funneling or *chokepoint* structure for game stories is fairly common, and the reasons are obvious. First, you have a controllable and definable way to set the player back on the narrative arc of the game. Second, you give the player more freedom to explore, but ultimately, you can elegantly determine where and when you will allow story and game progression to take place. For example, you can allow the player to move throughout an environment, and explore multiple story-threads, but he will not be able to progress deeper into the game until he visits the bartender at the edge of town. The bartender becomes a gameplay and story chokepoint, and ultimately, all the gameplay will begin to funnel the player toward his conversation with the bartender. Chokepoints in this type of structure tend to be the story set pieces for the game.

CRITICAL PATHS

Similar to limited branching, a *critical path* game has one success path, and allows the player to deviate from it in very small ways. However, nothing of consequence in the game or story happens outside of a predetermined path that winds its way through the experience.

NODAL STORYTELLING

Many open-environment games utilize this type of story. *Nodal* stories are either location and/or objective dependent. Each node of the game story is a self-contained piece, with a setup, midpoint, and payoff. In totality, each of these story nodes may lead to a larger reveal, or they may be just cool things that you play and see on your journey through the game. Usually, this story structure doesn't function as a traditional branch (and it is valid to debate whether or not it belongs here), but since moving from node to node of the story is often dependent on a previous element of the story, we believe that nodal structure does function as a pseudo-branch.

STORY STYLES

There are several story styles currently in use. All of them, interestingly enough, can be compared to other mediums that preceded video games.

EPISODIC

Think of episodes of an old-time TV series like *The Cosby Show*, which basically hits a reset at the beginning of every show. This phrase "episodic" has taken on a pejorative meaning in the movie business that basically means: "This is a series of episodes that doesn't add up to a story." Well, have you ever played a game that was truly episodic, in which each level starts out exactly the same way as the previous level? Though there is a lot of talk about episodic content what they really mean is that you sell a game a level at a time online as opposed to selling a giant game product.

FILM STYLE

This is a common game structure. Basically, you take the structure of an action film and use the game parts to play the action sequences. You use cinematics to mimic the dialogue scenes in the movie (and maybe a few big payoffs).

SERIAL

Serial exists somewhere between episodic and film style. Many games are structured this way. You are following a distinct story that ends in one level and then teases you at the end of the level with a cliffhanger that leads you to the next level.

The truth is that there is no right or wrong kind of story. Many players are perfectly happy just working their way through a story—sort of like watching a movie while playing the action scenes. There should always be games out there for these players. Likewise, other players are sold on an RPG style (which has a multitude of mutations and variants) in which the player builds their character in order to face ever more challenging objectives.

The more role playing a game goes, the more your player determines who their character is, the less applicable this is to licensed or franchise characters. For example, it is unlikely that DC Comics will allow any version of a Superman game in which the Man of Steel is allowed to wantonly kill civilians.

CUT-SCENES AS GAME AND STORY DRIVERS

Unlike passive entertainment, in games the script is doing more than simply existing as a story. While helping to create a fully realized experience for the player, the story also serves very specific functions within the game. To bolster it, narrative cut-scenes are used. Therefore, putting those pieces in place can give you compass points on which to build your game.

Below are some of the most common types.

SETUPS

Narratives are often used to set up the challenges that the hero will face in a particular level, or sometimes, even a set piece within the level. Elaborate setups will usually involve a cut-scene at or near the beginning of the level, while a shorter one can be created *in-game*. Sometimes, setups may be nothing more than voice-over dialogue.

PAYOFFS

We also call these *attaboys*. They are the narrative equivalent of a slap on the back. Often, they are the most visual sequences (like when the bridge blows up as our hero jumps to safety). In addition to resolving issues with the story, payoffs are also a way in which we reaffirm to the player that he is accomplishing the challenges of the game.

AUTOPSY

Narratives can also be used to show the player where he made a mistake. When the Hero is killed because he stepped into a minefield or was ambushed, a cut-scene can be used to replay the event, and show where the hero (and by extension, the player) went wrong.

ADVANCEMENT

Similar to payoffs, but usually on a larger scale, advancement cut-scenes establish new worlds, or technology, or characters, or weapons, or skills, etc., that the hero has earned by progressing forward through the game.

CHARACTER JOURNEYS

In games, the player is creating the journey for his character as he plays. The story can support this with a specific scene that shows how the character is evolving, getting more powerful, or wiser, or even more damaged. The characters can also be on emotional journeys, or journeys of discovery that will manifest themselves both in story and gameplay.

IMPART INFORMATION (MISSION BRIEFING)

You might need to creatively tell the player what he needs to accomplish. For instance, if we create a cut-scene that has a commander telling our hero that he must reach a bunker at the top of the hill, then in essence, we are telling the player what his objectives are that must be accomplished. This information need not be something that the player needs to know immediately. In fact, things can get very interesting when we give the player some information that he will find useful later, and then let him experience the joy of discovery when he puts it to use.

Cut-scenes can also be used to let the player know that something important has changed within the game that he will be forced to deal with. For example, when you are exploring an underground cavern and a cave-in blocks your passage.

ESTABLISH RULES AND EXPECTATIONS

One of the most important things that game narratives can do is help the player understand the rules of the game. Narratives also serve as a way to help establish player expectations. A few in-your-face narratives at the beginning of the game will set the tone for what is to follow.

ACTION ITEM (GOLD)—WRITE A SETUP AND A PAYOFF NARRATIVE SEQUENCE

Okay, you can do this. Using your idea for a game, or if you prefer, creating your own version of a property you like, write both a setup and a payoff narrative. Think about what the sequences must convey to the player. Think about the pacing of the scene, remembering always that the player expects to be in control of the game. We've included samples for you to review later in the book.

USING DIALOGUE TO CONVEY INFORMATION

Dialogue in games serves two main purposes: advancing story and conveying information. When it comes to advancing the story (which can have any number of interpretations from learning more about a character, to creating some interesting reveal, to setting up a gag that is paid off later) you have a lot of flexibility in how your characters will talk and interact with one another. Other than the creative limits imposed on any project, and of course, the player's patience (which is a function of how interested they are in the story you're telling), you have a virtually unlimited palate that you can use for your dialogue. However, always remember that finger hovering over the action-button.

Conveying information through dialogue is another matter entirely. Here, you are relaying specific details that the player needs to move through the game. Let's take a look at some examples:

> "I need to go to the store. I'm out of batteries, and I need to check my account balance at the ATM."

Okay, what exactly is important to know from the above? That I need to go to the store? That I'm out of batteries? That I need to check my account balance? All three? Is the ATM at the store? Do I need to see if I have enough money to buy them, and that is why I need to check my balance at the ATM?

The point is, as far as dialogue goes (as un-compelling as it is), it does convey some needs and objectives that need to be accomplished. However, it gives no real direction or context in how to do so. And it doesn't prioritize the goals that need to be achieved. Instead, let's break this up into something more useful:

> "I gotta stop by the ATM first. I think I'm tapped, and I need to buy some batteries. Better to hit the ATM at the store and know for sure than to be embarrassed at checkout."

Now we are doing much better. We have a plan of attack clearly laid out. First, we are going to the ATM, then buying the batteries, and then we are going to the store's checkout. We have made one action contingent on the previous one. We have identified where the ATM can be found, and the objective we are trying to accomplish (buy batteries).

As you are writing your dialogue, remember that lines are there to add depth to the story, and note which lines are giving instructions to the player. Is it necessary to always hit people over the head with direction? Of course not. Subtlety is key to not shining a beacon on instructional dialogue. However, always keep in mind the context of your dialogue. Unlike other forms of entertainment, the words your characters speak are often the clues your player needs to advance through the experience. You can inadvertently fool him and frustrate him with a careless piece of dialogue that he believes is direction and sends him off on a wild goose chase, but one you believed was just a clever turn of a phrase. Remember that words matter.

ACTION ITEM (BETA)—YOUR DAY IN VOICE-OVER

Think about what you did yesterday: where you went, who you met, what you had for lunch, etc. Were there any specific tasks you had to accomplish, such as going to the mall, or school, or a meeting? Was any part of your daytime critical? Now, write the events of that day in dialogue, as if you were talking to yourself, but also providing information to someone else in the process. In essence, turn yourself into a video game character, and let the player in on your thoughts. Make sure that you are including all of the information needed so that someone else would be able to make the same logical choices you did as your day played out. But leave out the specific details of what resulted from your actions, and write only in the present tense. For instance: "There's a shirt I gotta pick up. I told them to go light on the starch." From this, we can infer that the shirt is at the cleaners, rather than something you need to buy. The second line is a "hint" that points the player in a direction. When you are finished, share your document with a friend. See if they can deduce what you did that day from your dialogue.

ELEMENTS OF PLOT

Okay, we're going to start with the basics. If you're an experienced writer, you've probably heard (or studied) some variation of this before. However, for those that may be new to the craft, we've included some universal truths about constructing narrative.

When someone says to us: "Tell me a story," our first instinct is to reveal the plot, filling in the details along the way. The plot of the story is an account of the dramatic tension we experienced as a result of the jeopardy our hero faced. The dramatic tension is created by conflict and the stakes that are being contested within our narrative over a set period of time. If we were to put the creation of a story into an equation, it would look something like this:

Plot = Dramatic Tension (Conflict x Stakes/Time = Hero Jeopardy)

Let's dissect those elements to make them more understandable. When we are constructing our plot, we look at the following:

Conflict	What is the nature of the fight?
Stakes	What are the stakes that this fight is about?
Hero Jeopardy	How do the conflict and stakes put our hero at risk?
Dramatic Tension	What are the results of the conflict and the stakes, and how do they impact our characters?
Time	Over what time period does this conflict take place?

What is interesting about this equation is how we can use the same basic structure to describe the core elements of almost any game. Replace plot with the word gameplay. The equation works just as well.

Without conflict, there can be no game and no story. Blanket statements like this can be dangerous, but in this case, we believe it is totally defensible. Conflict is the core of any game, and the core of any traditional narrative. Watching people we care about and are emotionally invested in as they overcome adversity forms the basis of almost all traditional storytelling. In games, we have the added benefit of not only watching the characters, but of controlling them, and, if we get the suspension of disbelief right, actually becoming those characters as they face these conflicts and struggle against them.

TYPES OF CONFLICT

Conflict can take many forms, and have many expressions, but by their very nature, games rely on conflict. You are presented with a series of objectives. You must overcome obstacles if you are to reach these objectives. This is also the underlying structure of narrative, and this is what makes writing for games both challenging and rewarding. Listed below are the main types of conflict used in gameplay. (Note that most stories depend on more than one type of conflict.)

MAN VS. MAN

This is the big one: protagonist versus antagonist, our hero against a villain. This can be personal, or "just business." Note that our hero can sometimes be a bad guy, in which case the roles reverse. Almost all stories rely on this type of conflict. First-person shooters, third-person action-adventure, and sports games are usually centered on this type of conflict.

MAN VS. NATURE

Our hero is trapped in the wilderness, or fighting to survive in a storm, or out to kill the great white whale. In gameplay it might encompass a sport like snow-boarding, or hunting. We can also broadly define nature to include aliens and monsters (of biological origins).

MAN VS. SELF

Although not often used in games, this conflict is our hero at war with his own demons, such as addictions and phobias. In gameplay terms this might be a survival horror scenario.

MAN VS. DESTINY (LUCK)

Often used in Role-playing Adventures, this is our protagonist battling with his destiny. Often, our hero doesn't want to fulfill it.

MAN VS. MACHINE

This is man in conflict with technology. Fighting unstoppable machines, usually after they've become self-aware, is a staple of science-fiction stories and games.

MAN VS. SYSTEM

This is our hero versus the world. Usually our protagonist is misunderstood, or a loner who "knows the truth" but can't get anyone to believe him. This is a common theme of action-adventure games.

MAN VS. PAST

Our hero is trying to escape his past, but it keeps coming back to haunt him. Sometimes, no matter how hard he tries to break from his past, our hero finds it impossible to do. This type of conflict is often overused in the amnesia stories and is common in mysteries.

While all the aforementioned are classic story conflicts, they also represent some of the main types of gameplay challenges that designers create. Note that as our story progresses the level of conflict will often escalate. We are headed toward a showdown confrontation at some point in our narrative, and the ever-increasing intensity of our conflict is an indicator that we are reaching the climax.

ACTION ITEM (ALPHA)—IDENTIFY THE CORE CONFLICT OF A STORY

Using the main types of conflict, write a page that describes the core conflict of your favorite game, film, television show or book. Consider it carefully; often the obvious conflict is masking something deeper. For instance, a man at war with the world may actually be lashing out at society because he is really at war with himself. Now think about the game you want to create. What is the core conflict of the experience? Is it the same for the hero as it is for the player? How does this conflict manifest itself in gameplay? Write as much of this as you can. This will become the foundation of both your game and story content.

THE STAKES

This is what we are playing for, both in the game and the story. Let's look at the various types we see in gameplay.

LIFE OR DEATH

The highest of stakes. When you are playing for your life, things are about as serious as they get. Most first-person games use these stakes. If there is too much damage, you're dead.

WEALTH OR POVERTY

Greed is a powerful motivator and is something that is understandable by everyone.

LOVE OR LOSS

This is more esoteric and isn't used in games as much as it should be. It is the most emotional of stakes, and when done properly, love is probably the most compelling emotion.

HAPPINESS OR SADNESS

Who doesn't strive to be happy? If our character starts at the bottom emotionally, his or her journey to happiness can be rewarding for us as well. To make these stakes work, we really need to be invested in our hero.

TRIUMPH OR DEFEAT

Win the battle, win the war. Save your people, save your family . . . and yourself. Fairly straightforward.

SECURITY VS. INSTABILITY

Bringing chaos under control, or succumbing to outside forces. As with conflict, the stakes of our story will very often change. When the stakes increase, the level of dramatic tension intensifies as the jeopardy our hero faces becomes larger. As we build on one, we are building on the other, pushing us ever closer to a resolution.

All of the above examples fall into the win/lose category. As you can see, the stakes that we use to make a good story are the same ones that we can use to make interesting gameplay. The goal is to have the stakes of the story and the stakes of the game in harmony. When both of these elements are working together, it creates an even more immersive experience for the player. Since the stakes are either a win or a loss for our hero, it is easy to start plotting out an arc for our story when we can see how our hero will either win or lose, not only the game, but also in the narrative.

Your conflict and stakes must be in sync with the core gameplay or your story will seem out of place. When the gameplay and story are in sync, the experience is seamless.

ACTION ITEM (ALPHA)—UP THE STAKES

Write a sequence of events in which the stakes keep escalating. For instance, you are trying to drink coffee in the car and hit a bump, spilling it on your clean white shirt. As you react to the mess, your distraction causes you to bump into the car in front of you, crumbling the front end of your car and shattering the taillights of the car you've just hit. As you come around, you see the other driver exiting his vehicle and you realize that he is carrying a baseball bat. And so on. Think about the affect stakes have on your story, from a stained shirt, to an insurance claim, to potentially fighting for your life against a man with a hand-weapon.

JEOPARDY: HOW STORY ELEMENTS AFFECT TENSION

The level of conflict and level of stakes determine the intensity of the jeopardy our hero faces, and therefore the dramatic tension that exists within the story. All stories rely on some type of conflict to create tension. Sitting between the conflict inherent in the story and the stakes that are being played for is where the core dramatic tension of the gameplay narrative takes place. Here's an example: If you are playing cards around the dining room table for nickels and dimes, then the jeopardy you are facing is at one level, and the tension you experience matches accordingly. If you are playing professionals in Las Vegas for your entire life savings, then the tension is obviously different. You now have a great deal at risk. The conflict is the same but the stakes have been elevated, and in the process, the amount of dramatic tension that can be introduced into the second scenario is dramatically increased.

Remember this as you go about tuning your narrative to match the game—heavy conflict and high stakes tend to be more serious stories than minor conflict and low stakes. It is possible to mix and match to create interesting situations. For instance, some comedy relies on heavy conflict but light stakes. Black comedy often relies on minor conflict but high stakes. The idea is to tune these to match the gameplay. You need to figure out how your story uses conflict and stakes to create the tension of the narrative. Having an understanding of these elements at the core of your story will help you with all aspects of the narrative.

TIME

The ticking clock drives action. Time establishes the "rules" under which the characters in the story function. Conflict and stakes can escalate over time. Our story can take place in the blink of an eye, or over many centuries. Stakes tend to go up when there is less time to accomplish our goals. Time can heal wounds or aggravate them, causing them to grow even deeper. Unique to games, time can be nonlinear, allowing the player to see action from multiple perspectives, or even out of sequential order. Also, we can speed up or slow down time to create tension.

PLOT

This is a function of conflict and stakes, the intensity of both and the time in which it occurs, which generates the risk, or jeopardy our hero faces, and dramatic tension we experience that forms the basis of the plot of our story.

When all of these elements have been well thought out, the ultimate story that is created is much more compelling, and the chances of running into a creative impasse during the development of the game are significantly reduced.

What is interesting is that what makes good storytelling also makes good design. It might help to think of the carrot and the stick, rewards versus punishment (the stakes again). How we push and pull the player through a gameplay experience is also the same type of action we want to take when we are driving the narrative forward. This all ties back into character, world, tone, and theme.

CHARACTER(S)
Your hero(es) need not be the protagonist of the story. They can also have their own inner-tension and turmoil, not just that which is generated within the game.

WORLD
Again, this is not only the location, but also the reality in which the story takes place, e.g., Hong Kong Physics, Comedic World, Sci-Fi Oppressive, etc. The world itself will contribute heavily to the conflict.

TONE
What is the tone of the piece? Is it light, heavy, serious, playful, black, or irreverent? This is the area where stories often go "off the rails" because a tone is set within the narrative that the player becomes comfortable with, and then something comes out of right field that throws the tone out of whack. When this happens, it is usually instantly noticeable. This can be used for powerful effect, but it must be well thought out because at that point you are removing the safety net. Examples of this technique are: killing off a main character unexpectedly in a comedy, or suddenly switching to heavy horror overtones in an otherwise light action adventure. When done right, it has quite an impact. When done incorrectly or unintentionally, it can cause you to lose your audience.

THEME
Underneath the game story is the theme: redemption, salvation, falling from grace, power corrupts, money can't buy happiness, revenge. All of the clichés tend to be the big themes that fuel the story. The importance of understanding the theme of your story cannot be overstated. Whenever you run into a brick wall in the narrative, go back and review your theme. What scenes do you need in order to advance the hero forward in a way that will deliver the theme?

PLAYER EXPECTATIONS
Think of character, world, tone, and theme as the cornerstones of your story. To build your narrative, you are going to add a plot that is driven by conflict and stakes, and in the process you put your hero at risk. This risk generates the dramatic tension of the story. If people care about your characters, they will forgive a lot. In most storytelling, characters are the main figures we follow through the

narrative. What makes games unique is that the player is the character. What is happening to the character onscreen is happening to us. Therefore, we can create even stronger connections, and get our players more emotionally invested in their hero with effective storytelling. Breaking down the barrier that exists between the player and the character is a big part of creating the kind of compelling experience we are striving to achieve. So what are players looking for?

Your "audience" is playing a game. They expect to interact, not watch. They will watch, but it must be compelling, and tied into setting up or paying off gameplay. Thus, long scenes of exposition should be avoided, and information should be imparted to the player creatively.

Always think about the player holding the controller, with his finger hovering over the "start" button (ready to jump past the sequence). If something is essential to advancing the gameplay, front-load it rather than have it at the end of the sequence. Think of timing. What is the pace of the game? Fast-paced action games require a different pacing than more leisurely role-playing games. The pacing of the narrative should match the pacing of the game.

Keep dialogue as tight possible. Avoid long expository speech like a wise old wizard who tells us lots of interesting things that we never get to see. Don't tell what you can show. Don't show what you can play. Backstory is only important if it has direct relevance to the narrative.

Eventually, you'll need to arc out the story, planning setups and payoffs along the way. Ask yourself what are the essential narrative set pieces that must be included to advance the story to its conclusion. Then think about the information that must be imparted to the player during the game and creative ways these can be incorporated into the story. Remember, your narrative is not there for narrative's sake; it is there to serve the larger gameplay experience.

DECIDING WHAT GOES IN

Ockham's Razor is a philosophical principle attributed to a fourteenth-century Franciscan friar, William of Ockham. His basic idea was that simple explanations should be preferred to more complicated ones, and that the explanation of a new phenomenon should be based on what is already known. This is also known as the law of economy.

We use a rule of philosophical simplicity in all issues revolving around games. Our basic question is: "Does this (feature, product, winky) belong in the game that we're selling to the player?" If it does, great. Now it is just an issue of prioritizing this proposed element in a range from (1) it would be kind of cool, to (10) we can probably be indicted for fraud if we don't include this in the game. However, when in doubt, we always keep it simple.

Problem areas to consider include:

* **Animations**. Do you have your hero sliding across the hood of a car? If so, is that an animation that is possible to do while playing the game? If not, then it is going to have to be created for the sequence.

* **Character Emotions** (getting better with next generation consoles). We are fast reaching the point where our characters can convey subtle emotions and reactions. However, if you are not writing for a next-generation title, and aren't sure what is possible with "a look," it is probably better to find another way to communicate this stage direction. Is there a broader action, or a line a dialogue that can accomplish the same thing?

* **Creatures and Animals**. Be very careful about adding any type of creature or animal without thoroughly thinking how it will impact production. Animals and creatures require unique models, and even more significantly, unique animations, to be convincing. One final note: Real is more difficult than fantasy, because we all know how a cat moves.

* **Crowds**. Crowds are usually a problem for the obvious reason—they are a lot of assets to build and get into the game. If the core design doesn't include crowds (and this would of course include masses of armies, hordes of aliens, etc.), then consider setting the action somewhere other than near a big mass of characters.

* **Settings**. Avoid creating special locations just for narratives. Wherever possible, you should use the game worlds for the cinematics.

* **Special Lighting or Effects**. If you have some big dramatic effects (such as lightning, for instance) in your sequences, consider how this will be accomplished. Does the game support these types of effects, or are you calling out for something that will have to be a custom creation?

* **Vehicles**. As with creatures and animals, any vehicle will have to be modeled, textured, animated, and have associated Sound Efx, so stay away from introducing vehicles that only exist with cut-scenes unless this is part of the core design of the game (choppering in and out of missions, for example). Also, remember that if the vehicle is cool enough, player expectations mean that they will want to control/play it.

ACTION ITEM (BETA)—REALITY CHECK

Take a sequence from your favorite game and break down all of the elements that went into creating it. Think about the characters, the worlds, the animations, the textures, any special effects, the creatures, the weather conditions, the sounds, the music, etc. Detail as

Continued on next page

Continued from previous page
much as you can. It will give you an appreciation for the amount of work (and money) that was needed to put the sequence together. Can you envision how the sequence could have been done another way? For your game, think about how your big set-pieces would stand-up to similar scrutiny.

THE CREATIVE PROCESS

Somewhere sitting in some producer's office is a schedule. It is usually an elaborately laid-out chart with milestones, dependencies, tasks, and resource allocations. This chart often serves as the nerve center of the project. It is often treated like a sacred text inside the Holy of Holies. It is perceived as reality. It is, of course, as much of a fantasy as the story the game is hoping to tell.

You will notice that people refer to the creative process. Nobody who has ever been through it refers to it as the creative act (a singular thing). The more that you and everybody on the project realizes that you are part of a process; the more likely it is that you will succeed. Conversely, the more people on both sides of the chart fight the reality of the creative process, the more likely you are to fail.

3

GAME STORY THEORY AND DIALOGUE

In screenwriting, amateur screenwriters often indulge in elaborate explanations for scenes and situations that stop the motion cold. How workable is that in a game? Similarly, professional screenwriters have written innumerable "now the villain explains" scenes that might not have much place even in the climactic battle of a game. Stories, which are all around us, are what interest us most. In a game that's the story we can see, not the ones we are told about. That isn't the case in real life, where every day we hear stories and tell them—great and small. We instinctually know which ones are worth telling and which ones aren't. We've honed that skill since we were children.

FROM THE MOUTHS OF BABES

If you want to see somebody learning story skills, get a seven-year-old to tell you a tale. There's an incredible feedback mechanism. Usually, the story isn't very compelling and your mind starts to wander as the child meanders away. Then, the kid telling the story will sense that you're glazing over. He says: "So guess what?" And you're supposed to say, "I don't know, tell me."

With the "Guess what?" he is forcing you to pay attention, putting you on the spot. He's leveraging you, buying your attention for another beat. Think of that

"Guess what?" as a creative beacon, his attempt to draw you in. If you answer "What?" then he's got you. No, he can iterate, refining the story to hold your attention. He's revising and creating on the fly.

That young storyteller is probably learning fifty different narrative skills at the same time. He's learning what holds interest and what doesn't. As often as not he's telling an elaborate story about people or giant robots you don't know anything about. Or maybe he hasn't told you where or when the story took place (likely as not, you have no sense of context). He hasn't given you the cues that tell you where you are in the story and you're afraid that it may never end. If he tells the story more than once, he begins to learn what parts work and what parts don't. He learns what characters are important and what characters aren't. He learns to sell you on the villains, the mean teacher, and the bully. As he gets older and more sophisticated, he learns to set up the victims and the protagonist. At some point, he hits a crossroads where he either gets better at telling the stories or he finds fifty different ways of saying "Guess what?" The former is a good conversationalist; the latter is a bore.

Which type do you want to be as a game writer?

"Guess what?" is so naked, so clear. It is about someone trying to get you excited about whatever is exciting him or her. It's a way of saying "Something interesting is about to happen." Usually nothing interesting happens. Sometimes children just haven't learned how to communicate. If they saw a food fight break out in a diner, then they might just get to the part where the guy has a banana stuck on his nose, without giving you the setup or the right characters to root for. If someone asks a child: "So what did the man who threw his food look like?" the child who anticipates the question and develops a strategy for answering it, has become a storyteller. This child will most likely develop an ear for dialogue as well.

ACTION ITEM (ALPHA)—CHILDLIKE STORYTELLING

Try writing a quick story as if told by a child. What are the elements of the story that you focus on? How much detail do you provide? Do you obsess over a small point, or quickly jump from one to another? Do you lay out an overview of the coming narrative, or just let it unfold during the course of the story? If possible, read your story to a child and see what questions they ask. Do they think the same things are important now as you did when you wrote it?

DIALOGUE IN VIDEO GAMES

Like it or not, you will live or die by your dialogue. Ninety percent of the people you work with think that writing is dialogue. You as a game writer know that dialogue is the tip of the iceberg that starts at the bottom with

* an interesting world.
* a great plot with twist and turns, setups, and payoffs.
* compelling characters that are affected by and create the conflict and stakes.
* an immersive style that depends as much on the entire game experience as it does on the story.
* great challenges (manifested in gameplay) that you encounter and overcome.

In short, to have great dialogue you have to have great characters talk about fascinating things, often in conflict with each other. You might want them always in conflict with each other at some level. Put another way, the greatest characters in the world will be flat if they don't have something interesting to talk about and the greatest plot in the world is a pancake if there aren't interesting characters driving it. On yet another tack, a great script is the omelet that comes out of a chicken or the egg situation. And if you don't like that analogy, rewrite the dialogue.

ALTS, ALTS, AND MORE ALTS

Great screenwriters and great novelists have suffered horrible fates in the game space because game writing has a unique set of challenges. First of all, a great deal of gameplay dialogue is too expositional. Everyone hates exposition, and game writers have more reason to hate it more than most. A novelist isn't expected to write compelling dialogue to tell somebody how to use the controller to open a door, or why he is wandering around a barren world. Screenwriters only need to write, "I'll be back" once. They don't have to write twenty alts (iterations) of it. (Let's face it, things get kind of flat around phrases like "I shall return" and "I shall pass this way again.") In fact, the whole concept of alts and verbose dialogue is a battle with the concept of characters, because one of the ways you define a character is by the way he says things. "I'll be back" was perfect for Schwarzenegger characters of the 1980s, but it wouldn't have worked for General Douglas MacArthur in the Philippines in a serious circumstance required gravitas.

Nevertheless, games need alts. Games need a hundred ways of saying, "I'd better check this area again." At the end of the day, game writers have to play the hand they're dealt. We're in a medium that by its very nature demands a lot of repetition, and our job, as dramatists are to conceal this fact.

THE STORY LOOKS BACKWARD WHILE THE GAME LOOKS FORWARD

Another problem endemic to game story is reliance on backstory. More often than not, when you read character bios in a game, you are reading about the player's past, or what happened before the game, rather than what happens during the game. Just as an experiment, imagine a character with virtually no backstory. If you think about great action franchise characters it's amazing how few of them have much of a backstory.

For example, if James Bond had parents, and we assume that he did, have you ever heard about them? If he has inner doubts, are there any more than one or two awkward moments onscreen when he expressed them? This is the most successful character-based movie franchise in history, and he was seemingly born anew in every movie. There is no need to tie up old stuff unless it is fun and interesting. James Bond ended up with Pussy Galore at the end of *Goldfinger*, but he wasn't with her in *Thunderball* or any of the movies that followed. While it might be interesting for some novelist to write a novel following Pussy's life, it isn't of interest to the viewers. All they need to know about James Bond is that he has a license to kill and he's good at it . . . and he has an eye for cool cars and hot babes.

SHORTHAND BACKSTORY WHEREVER POSSIBLE

Sometimes, huge amounts of backstory are covered by a visual. *In You Only Live Twice*, Bond shows up as a naval officer and we have reason to believe that he actually is or was one. And that's it. Done, backstory covered. We don't know what happened to him in the navy and it doesn't matter.

Sherlock Holmes is similar. We don't know who his parents are. We do know from (*A Study in Scarlet*) how he came to live at 221B with Watson, but there seems to be very little need to belabor the subject. In fact, Conan Doyle in creating the character of Watson cared so little about his backstory that he couldn't remember the location of his wound from Crimea or Afghanistan or wherever Watson served in the army. Even Moriarty only shows up in a few stories and it was left to late twentieth-century writers to speculate on their childhood.

So there are very successful franchises without much character history. If you are going to have a backstory, it should only exist to propel your story and your characters. We know that Odysseus has a wife and a child on Ithaca, and he wants to get back to them. This doesn't stop him from dawdling with Calypso or Circe, and we don't worry much about his infidelities given his insistence that he wants to get back home. It has been suggested, however, that *The Odyssey* is two stories: the one he told his buddies when he got home and the one he told to his wife. We can pretty much figure out which is which. The point is, we have a guy who has fought a brutal ten-year war and wants to get home, but the gods, most specifically Poseidon, are against him, as are the odds.

If you're old enough, think back to when *Star Wars* (now designated *A New Hope*) came out. Even though we now know that there is a workday's worth of backstory (not counting the numerous books), Mr. Lucas only told us what we needed to know to propel the story.

Games fell into a backstory obsession by necessity of the technology. *Myst* was a "discover the backstory" type of tale, but that was necessary due to the limits of the medium at the time. An artifice that was brilliantly designed to conceal a technical limitation, has, all too often become *de rigueur* without the writers stopping to think about why or what their creations serve. We call these things *vestigials*—conventions that are hanging around from previous incarnations that we don't need anymore.

ENGAGING THE PLAYER TO FILL IN THE BLANKS

In the classic game *Asteroids*, the Player was free to impose meaning on a straightforward, addictive game mechanic. You were an intergalactic space pilot and you had to get to 100,000 points. You couldn't lurk (sit in the corner when there was only one asteroid left and shoot the ships). The game pilot had a distinct personality—he was noble. He was a knight. He played by the rules. You were pitted against an evil enemy who was too accurate and didn't play by the rules.

There was the story, and it even had a structure. There was a phase at the beginning where it was just asteroids, then asteroids with big ships that hit you just often enough, and then a scary little world with lots of asteroids when the little ships came out. Then there was that moment of dueling, and there was hyperspace, which almost had a mystical element. Asteroids offered a hostile world because the creators wanted to knock you out of the game for another quarter, but they had to make it seem fair. When playing, you created your own story to give context to what you were doing.

At the moment when you are fully engaged you are thinking like a game writer. It's the moment when you say: "This time, I'm going to dodge the boss until he makes a mistake." Then: "Oops . . . that didn't work." Then you declare: "This time, I'm going to attack him and see what happens." Only you get killed, but you knocked his health down half way. Then you get it, and realize you have to wait until he's taken his big shot, dodge it, and attack him while he recovers. When you finally get your strategy to work, you get the cinematic where this guy who was taunting you dies. And all the hassle was worth it, just to feel victorious.

THE CESSATION OF FRUSTRATION

There are other thrills to gaming besides feeling victorious. There's the thrill of being *in the zone*, which is that moment when you are so smooth with the controls, so engaged that you are unstoppable. If this goes on too long, however, you get bored. You need one that you can't beat right away—the frustration that balances the competency factor. It is like life: growth, learning, mastery, moving to a higher level, defeat, more growth, more mastery, and so on. Remember, though, that game success should never feel like the cessation of frustration. That is not the emotion that you want your players to experience if you want to have a hit. Overcoming the frustrations is what will make the player feel victorious. "Yes!" not "Thank God, it's about time I finally got through this," is what we are after.

As game writers and designers we are faced with a fundamental problem: We live in a world of finite resources, finite characters, finite levels, branches, finite enemies, and finite worlds. We have to make the finite seem infinite. We need to make the seemingly unbeatable, beatable. In short, we have to play a lot of tricks on the player, because, we are in the entertainment business, not the frustration business. How we do that is the art of game design.

GUESS WHAT?

Back to game writing and being judicious with dialogue, we're still saying, "Guess what?" a lot. Often, the player doesn't feel so much like he is living a story, as he is *unlocking* a story. He or she beats an opponent and unlocks a cinematic that moves the story along. As of right now, a lot of our storytelling is borrowed from previous mediums, mostly film and television. We aren't exploiting what our medium does the way movies do. You walk into a movie, you know that the whole story is already laid out, and all you have to do is pay your ten bucks, sit for two hours, and it will open for you.

When games are a fully developed medium, the stories will probably mimic life even more so than films. That is to say that the story will happen to you in present tense. You'll really feel like you're experiencing the story for the first time, not receiving somebody else's set-down adventure. Think about it this way. When you watch *NFL Week in Review* on TV, you are watching a narrative laid down over a game that has already been played. It is a totally different experience than watching the actual game in progress. Both are interesting experiences, but watching the two-minute recap of a game is almost never as interesting as watching the actual contest. The bonus is that you don't have that nervous feeling of "anything can happen." You know it has already taken place.

LIVE IN THE MOMENT

The difference between a film or a TV show and a video game is immediacy. You want the player to live in the moment. Games can deliver that over and over. A film can usually only deliver it once. A great game is re-playable and the each replay can give the player a different experience. He may be going for more points. He may be trying to get all the way through it without dying even once. He may want to explore areas he didn't explore the first time through. He may want to play it a completely different way; if he shot his way all the way through a commando game, he might want to try stealthing his way through the game the next time.

Great gameplay is about solving problems the first time. Solving problems means making choices and the more choices you give a player, the more addictive the gameplay becomes. When writing the story you must first view the game from your player's point of view. When your player buys your game, they have an expectation of what the game will be. Your job is to deliver on that expectation—even over-deliver. You want your game to get under people's skin, and live inside their head. You want to give people that sense of missing this virtual world they've been living in.

RELATIONSHIPS AND DIALOGUE

Good game relationships and the dialogue that builds them fully engage the players. Like anything else, the best relationships are give and take. Here's Danny Bilson's (our friend who is an accomplished screen and game writer himself) classic analogy: "If you meet a guy in Level 2 and he double-crosses you, then you're going to have very strong feelings about him in Level 3. Now what happens, if this time, he helps you? What's changed? What's his agenda? What are you going to think when you run into him on Level 4?" These are the things you need to consider to make your story more interesting.

What if, in the above example, you decided to kill the guy in Level 3 by shooting him in the back? Would you have a problem with (a) him turning around and saying, "That would be a really stupid move, you are going to need me," or your own character saying, (b) "No, bad idea." In this case, dialogue is determined by a choice of actions that come from the internal motivation of the various characters. Twists and turns and the dialogue that reflects them keep the game fresh.

AVOIDING STOCK TEXT

One of the least pleasant things to write is numerous variations on stock text. For instance, you show up at the shopkeeper's establishment and have some repetitive dialogue with him, often nuanced with slightly different dialogue either in text or voice-over. The animations are usually re-used. The problem with this is that it tends to show the limitations of the game. Avoid them when possible.

Repetitive situations are almost always better handled automatically and abstractly, without dialogue. The fifth time you hear the same wisecrack from the same character, the game feels stale. The question to ask at any moment in gameplay is: "What choice am I making?"

STYLE

The more abstract the style, the more abstract the dialogue can be. Then again, the art might dictate extremely user-friendly, earthy dialogue to contrast the stylized characters. Ultimately, it is what you're personally trying to say. Sometimes games aren't trying to say much except express the pure joy of being silly games. In that case, the real dialogue is sound effects that merge with music or dialogue that becomes a sound-effectish kind of laugh track. That's okay, too. The point is that you want to know what you're doing and why you're doing it.

THE PRESENT TENSE

Game dialogue is written in present tense. Like this. Very present time. Very tense. It's happening right now, right here, right in front of me. See it as the viewer sees it. No sense in thinking that it happened in the past. It's the difference between opening on a *smash-cut* in your face visual, and opening on an *establishing shot* that tells us where we are.

This is true of all writing for games, film, and television. Always use the present voice. Describe action as if you are witnessing it in real-time. Never use past-tense descriptions. For example:

> *Present Tense (Correct): Karl enters the room, flipping the safety off his .45.*

> *Past Tense (Wrong): Karl entered the room. He'd already flipped the safety on his .45*

In one example, you are describing events that have already taken place. In the other, you are talking about events that are happening now, right in front of you, and you are relating them to the reader as fast as you can call them out. If you are writing a book, you can use the past tense. However, for a game-script, you are always in the here and now.

METASTORY

Metastory is closely related to world. It is stuff that happens on the edges of your stories, things implied, but never explicitly stated. Perhaps the most famous example of this from a film is *Chinatown*. There is a clear implication all the way through the movie that something bad happened to Jake Gittes in *Chinatown* long before the story started. Our guess is that his wife was killed there, years ago, but that's only a guess. It is never stated.

At the end of the film, when another character says to Jake, "Forget it Jake, it's Chinatown," we get the implication. We know there's code being spoken. Chinatown is a metaphor for a dark place where bad things happen. It's about a dark secret in the past. It is something that can't be fixed. It is a place where the normal rules don't apply.

Another example of metastory is when the driver, in any version of *Dracula*, doesn't want to take Jonathan Harker to Castle Dracula. He might write it off to local suspicion but we, the viewers, clearly know what this means: bad things happen to people when they go to Castle Dracula. This also tells us something interesting about our character: He probably knows that it is an unsavory place, but he believes that somehow he is exempt from whatever happens at Castle Dracula. Think about that for your game characters and the dialogue you write.

Another interesting example that is pure brilliance in execution is in the opening scene of *Raiders of the Lost Ark* (arguably one of the best opening sequences in film history). Not far into the tomb, Indiana Jones comes upon a corpse. It's a ghastly sight, but it doesn't particularly disgust Indy, telling us that he's hardened. Instead, he recognizes the guy and mentions his name. This tells us an incredible amount about Indy, about his world and about what is coming.

One incident, one line, and you know a lot more than you knew before that fifteen or so seconds of film. We know that we're in an ancient tomb that kills people, we know that Indy is part of a subculture of archeologist and grave robbers who all know each other and compete (which sets us up for the scene where Belloq steals the idol from him) and we know that Indy thinks he's better than good—he's got an ego. Of course, throughout the rest of the sequence he'll prove this, but he'll also make mistakes. He'll botch the idol transfer and he'll discover, the hard way, that he's trusted the wrong people when his lackey betrays him. In short, it's incredibly economical storytelling. In the next scene, he's a guy who is easily embarrassed by a schoolgirl. This is a good example of a lot being learned about a character in a short time.

DON'T WEAR OUT THE F KEY

Rough language does not instantly translate to tough narrative. Edgy is a four-letter word, too. Effective profanity can heighten action and tension, and is also useful for establishing character, but don't overdo it. Overuse of profanity is amateurish and ultimately distracts from the story. Exceptions are when the characters, world, or tone can use it. Remember your audience and tune accordingly. Create alternates. After all, it is possible that your voice talent may not want to do a rough line as written. Give them a chance to record more than one and then leave it to others to decide.

For some reason, a lot of rookies feel that their writing is going to get a lot better when they say "fuck" a lot in their scripts. They would probably point to Paul Schrader or another great screenwriter, but our advice is that unless you are Paul Schrader you should avoid doing this, because in game scripts it tends to just look like you're a rookie imitating Paul Schrader or perhaps the writers of HBO's *Deadwood*. Without mentioning names, we literally did a "doctor" job on a script in which the first phase involved globally searching and replacing the obscenities and making a couple of minor tweaks. We called this process "defuckification." We shared the script to discuss some other points and people couldn't believe how much work we'd done and how much better it was. Sure, if you're making a game rated "M" it allows you to use rougher language, but having the opportunity doesn't mean that you are required to use it.

Our friend Frank Miller told us that during the filming of *Sin City*, actor Clive Owen was trying to figure out his character and came to Frank and said, "You don't like using the word fuck, do you?" Frank, whose work has never been described as prudish, said, "No."

One fun exercise is to try and dodge the usual masculine clichés. For instance, we always have the tough sergeant telling the player to, "Get your ass in gear." Try to find a way to say it without mentioning a guy's gluteus maximus. It's tough. The most insidious clichés are ones that you do almost automatically. Sometimes you can create interesting characters by simply avoiding clichés.

STORY PHYSICS

The physics of game story break down to: action/reaction/action/reaction; escalating tensions; foreshadowing and reveals. It takes in spectacle—the use of big, glossy effects. It includes reversals—nothing should go the way you expect it to. And don't forget writing as magic: deception and sleight of hand. Scene templates include elements of classic scenes. When approaching an idea consider the strategy. Is it story to scene, or tactical (from scene to story)?

Building games is like making movies in 3D. You have all of the plot, character, style, and other concerns of a movie, but you also have a technological component. As you can see, there are many elements to consider and constant evaluation and re-evaluation of elements. So now that we've discussed various strategies in the creation of games, let's get more specific, and talk about structure.

CLICHÉS AND STEREOTYPES

There's a reason we fall into clichés—it's easy and, at a certain level, they work. The problem is that they are never fresh; they always feel derivative. Writers use clichés sometimes because of laziness, sometimes because they don't want to waste valuable real estate on seemingly unimportant things.

Try and surprise the audience when you can without confusing them. By confusing them, we mean we've all seen instances when writers have gone so far out of the way to avoid a cliché that it is difficult to figure out what the character is about. Sometimes a small twist will do it. For instance, if your character is a cop, it might be amusing to give him a boss who is simply lazy. He doesn't care whether you do your job dirty or clean; he just doesn't want a lot of paperwork and gets ticked off if you make him do any. In other words, give your work some extra beat of thought to figure out why the boss is always coming down on your guy.

Sometimes you just give the character a quirk. Who would have expected Kilgore in *Apocalypse Now* to be a surfing fanatic? That quirk would relate directly to his dialogue. It's easy to get the impression that he invaded an entire town because he wanted to see if the surf was any good. In that case, it tied into the underlying theme of the movie, which was sanity. Everybody in the film was a little bit whacked. The film was a little bit whacked. You create a world like that and you get lines like, "I love the smell of napalm in the morning . . . that gasoline smell. It smells like . . . victory." It doesn't get any better than that.

Sometimes it's good to give your character a code. It's one thing to write in your story bible: "Harold doesn't kill criminals without giving them a chance to save themselves." What kind of dialogue would that generate? What about something like, "I know what you're thinking: 'Did he fire six shots or only five?' Well, to tell you the truth, in all this excitement I kind of lost track myself. But being as this is a .44 Magnum, the most powerful handgun in the world, and would blow your head clean off, you've got to ask yourself a question: Do I feel lucky? Well, do ya, punk?"

DIALECTS: LET THE ACTORS BRING SOMETHING TO THE PARTY

Some people have a gift for dialect, some don't. In general, our feeling is that your first goal is to have clarity in the dialogue. Your average reader should be able to make it through your script without having to say the lines out loud to understand what they mean. The other inadvertent issue comes in the touchy area of racism. There is a mighty fine line between writing certain kinds of dialect and appearing to be prejudiced. When in doubt, get the sense of the line without taking the additional risk of offending people. Often as not, we try to write a line in such a way that an actor can embellish it in the read, but isn't pinned to a specific accent or dialect (unless it is important to the story).

Allow your actor to bring something to the party. Your work, unlike in a novel, is written to be spoken by (hopefully) a professional actor who brings his own skills to the table. Whenever possible, allow your actors to get comfortable in the recording session and bring their own unique twist to the lines. One caution here: If you deviate too much from the written, approved line, make sure you have a usable "take" of the line as written. This gives everyone something to work with in post.

While doing the script for *Rise of Sin Tzu*, a Batman game, we created a new villain, Sin Tzu. While prepping the character, we wrote a character bio for the DC executive on the project, Ames Kirshen. Unbeknownst to us, Ames forwarded the bio to Cary-Hiroyuki Tagawa, the actor playing Sin Tzu. At the recording session, Cary read the bio in order to warm up for the part. His reading was so great—so much better than the words on the page—that DC decided to commission a novel of the game script, which was later novelized by Devon Grayson with a little help from Flint. The point is, no matter what dialogue you write, sometimes the actor brings much more to the party than you expect.

PLAYER'S RELATIONSHIP TO THE CHARACTER

One question, more or less unique to games, is the player's relationship to the character he's playing. The most obvious characters are surrogates for the player. When you play James Bond in a game, you're presumably playing someone you would want to be. What heterosexual male wouldn't want to be James Bond? In some cases, however, the player plays a character that is wildly different than he or she, like a guy playing Lara Croft. In that case, there's a different relationship with the character. Lara is a girl; the player is a guy. Okay, so there's something great about being able to control a woman (no man can hope to do that in real life!). In the case of Lara Croft, her gender doesn't matter for gameplay (the game doesn't require a female protagonist), but she's certainly more fun to watch.

Perhaps there is a deeper relationship lurking in there somewhere. Is Lara a surrogate date for a guy who doesn't have one that night? (Hey, it's a common occurrence for hard-core gamers.) What is the player's relationship to the character? In the case of Lara Croft, most of the players aren't fantasizing that they are Lara, so something else is in play. Discovering the relationship between the player and his or her surrogate(s) in the game (the player's character) will go a long way to helping you establish exactly what story elements should motivate action.

ACTION ITEM (ALPHA)—THE PLAYER/CHARACTER RELATIONSHIP

Play a game with a hero, studying how you feel about your relationship with the character. Do you feel like you have become the character? Or are you more like a sidekick? Or a god? Is the action of the game happening to you, or to the character you are controlling? Do you "care" about the character, or only their predicament? Write down your thoughts and then see how this would apply to a character you want to create.

Let's move these questions to gameplay. What if there is a tension between you and your character? When you play a criminal in *Grand Theft Auto* is that because you want to be a criminal or is it because you think it would be kind of fun to be something wildly different than what you are? It's a vicarious thrill: I'm not this guy, I don't want to be this guy, but it is kind of fun to be one of the ponytailed guys from *Miami Vice* for a few hours. It's fun to be bad in a virtual world, and find out what types of conversations they have and language they use.

There's a slightly different thrill to a realistic combat game. No sane person wants to get any closer to the real D-Day landing than as a viewer of a film or a player in a virtual world. Nevertheless, if sales figures are an indicator, there's a vicarious thrill to being a virtual GI in World War II. So what about the dialogue? Naturally, it needs to be accurate.

CONSEQUENCES

Some games experiment with a world that has consequences. The world watches what you do and you have to suffer the consequences of it. If you go around killing people, the cops are after you, and so are the friends of the people you've been killing. All of a sudden, the world you live in is a very hostile place. This is really cool, but bear in mind that, as a game writer, you're going to need alts for every possible relationship another character can have with you. The bits of dialogue that result range from utter indifference to blind hatred or, in other cases, blind love. The production realities of such games can be staggering. That's a lot of alt lines of dialogue. It is a lot of coding as well as a massive play balancing challenge (because it is very poor form, not to mention design, to give players choices that ensure that they will lose the game).

At one level or another, there is a balance to be struck between playing one story really well or fifty stories less well. In game writing, you often don't get to pick your challenges, so you play the hand you're dealt the best way you can play it. Breakthroughs come from people working their way through impossible situations. If you want to do something that's easy all of the time, don't go into this line of work.

LEVEL **4**

VIDEO GAME CONSTRUCTION TECHNIQUES AND STRATEGIES

SETTING UP THE WORLD OF YOUR GAME

Video game storytelling primarily exists to give meaning to game play. This should be obvious, but how many times have we held our controllers expectantly in our hands, waiting to start playing, only to have to watch endless cinematics throwing a bunch of backstory at us about characters and situations we don't yet care about?

As you approach your story, remember we're not making a movie, we're creating context for a game. Maybe someday Hollywood will want to make a movie out of your game, but not today. So keep it lean. Get the player up and running as quickly as possible. Unlike a movie where you're pinned to somewhere between ninety minutes and three hours, you have somewhere between eight and twenty hours to tell your story. If that doesn't seem like much think of it another way— the average gamer often spends more time playing one game than viewers spend watching the entire *Star Wars* saga. Maybe they spend less continuous time, because a lot of game playtime is try/fail, but you get the idea.

If you come from screenwriting and are not that familiar with games, here's an overview of the differences between films and games in terms of story. Console games are usually episodic in nature (levels) so we need multiple opponents, locations, and environments. Levels then have sub-levels and missions (objectives) throughout these areas. The reality of story-driven games is that you usually have an optimal path: the spine of the game where the main action and events take place. The art of design and fiction is to create the illusion of freedom of movement or nonlinear gameplay. Figure that (and we are using very broad-stroke averages here and throughout this discussion to illustrate our points) you are going to need eight different environments for a full-length game, with different locations within that environment.

You're likely to need a *Level Boss* for each of those environments and he (or she, or it, depending on your content) will have three types of semi-unique *palookas*. You'll need something that represents money. You will need to have some kind of new activity every level or so. It might take the form of a mini-game (a term we use generically to mean anything that isn't the main gameplay in the game). Story and dialogue needs to be restricted to short bursts. Rarely do we have—nor do we want—long cinematics. As a general rule, a cinematic shouldn't be over a minute long unless there is a compelling reason for it. Think of cinematics as the "landmarks" in your story. They provide information, reward the player, and move the game along.

However, there are all sorts of different ways to get exposition across.

Scenarios that involve shooting need to be stretched out to give the player an objective. That is, shootouts need to be against several opponents to become a challenge. Enemies range from canon fodder through midbosses, to bosses and an ambient villain that is usually killed at the end of the game. And it all has to make sense.

Game logic is often more far-fetched than film logic because of the structure of the medium. The player always needs an objective or challenge, so in many cases reasoning behind areas of story are flimsy. For example, in films people do not normally leave keys for sensitive areas lying around. Since we are aiming for hyperrealism in games, it pays to endeavor to circumvent such situations whenever possible. It is necessary for gameplay to have a punishment/reward system to drive the objectives. The ultimate punishment is game-over death and the ultimate reward is winning the game.

THE PALLET

We have two media in which to tell our story: audio and video. Audio divides into voice, sound effects and music. Video divides into game graphics, text, and interface graphics. Let's break that down further:

AUDIO—VOICE

There are three ways to use voice: onscreen, off-screen, and voice-over.

* Onscreen is when you actually see your player speaking.

* Off-screen is when you hear the voice of a character, but don't see him speak because he is out of the shot. This includes your main character speaking if you can't see his mouth.

* Voice-over (and often this is mistakenly used interchangeably with off-screen in scripts) is when the character could not be present in the scene. This can either be an omniscient narrator or a known character speaking outside the context of the game—like a private eye in a film noir.

AUDIO—EFX

Sound effects come in two forms:

* There are sound effects that are organic to the world of the game such as a sword striking or a waterfall crashing.

* Inorganic sound effects are game conceits: effects that tell us that we have opened up the secret doorway or have picked up a treasure star or other important item.

AUDIO—MUSIC

Like sound effects, music comes in two forms:

* Source music comes organically from the game, like when a character is playing a guitar, or a radio is playing in the background.

* Sound track music comes from outside of the game; it is the musical score that plays underneath the action, setting the mood. Context sensitive music is part of the sound track that is triggered by something in the game, usually used to tell the player that he has hit a specific moment of importance.

VIDEO—CINEMATICS

For our purposes, story cinematics (or cut-scenes) divide into pre-rendered and in-game (game engine controlled real-time animation).

* When you are writing an in-game narrative, you are restricted to what is possible within the limits of the game engine. This means that while you can have custom animation and effects, you can't suddenly cut away to

some new location (as this would mean loading those assets into the game's memory).

* Pre-rendered cinematics allow you infinite possibilities, but at a price—the gamer loses control, they tend to be more expensive and elaborate to produce, and they may not match the in-game graphics.

Both types of sequences have their value, but in-game cinematics are currently in favor with most designers and developers. If a title has pre-rendered sequences, they now tend to be the bookends at the beginning and end of the game.

VIDEO—TEXT

Text has two forms:

* Printed text, which is meant to be read.
* Iconic text, which is designed to be understood with a simple icon (for example, a question mark over the player's head).

VIDEO—GRAPHICS

Pop-up interfaces are things like health meters, radar screens, etc. They are usually abstract game conceits that are superimposed on the game in order to aid the player.

EXPLOITING THE PALLET TO TELL YOUR STORY

These are the media elements you have with which to tell the story. Think of them as story elements. Don't forget—story in video game terms is anything that helps you immerse yourself into the game-playing experience.

Story isn't just characters and dialogue. An interface element can be a story-telling device. Think of it like something you might read within a novel. For example, the moment in which your ammo counter tells you that you only have two shots left would appear in a novel as: "He only had two bullets left . . . two bullets. He had to use them well or die. He knew that just up ahead there was more ammo, but he had to figure out how to get there. Could he sneak past the gunmen waiting for him around the next corner? Not likely, they knew he was here. He'd have to make his last two bullets count."

Sorry about the pulpy writing. The point is that low ammo isn't just a game-play issue; it is a story issue. The player has an emotional, intellectual, and character decision to make. Any time you have a decision to make, it is a character opportunity. How your character deals with it depends on the relationship between the main character and the player. A spy might take the stealthy route, while a brute will face the enemy head-on. The design and the story can encourage the player to do one or the other, and sometimes both.

ACTION ITEM (ALPHA)—PLAYER CHARACTER'S POV OF METER

Here's your chance to write pulpy dialogue, too. Take a meter from a game (ammo, health, armor, etc.) and write a description of how it affects the player character from their point of view.

TYPES OF EXPOSITION

Exposition is the hardest and most awkward part of game writing. It is necessary when you have to convey intellectual information. Dramatic exposition is used to get across story elements. It divides broadly into plot, character, and world exposition. Also, unique to the game writer, there is gameplay exposition.

Plot exposition at its worst it is the endless briefing from a character like Sergeant Gloff, who says something like: "As you know, our enemy, Colonel Vorlosh, is bent on destroying the United Global Federation of Affiliated Nation States in a diabolical attempt to subvert our motherland." (We're using intentionally bad examples here to make the point that "B" movies might not be the best place to draw your influences from.)

Character exposition attempts to tell the player something about characters. Sergeant Gloff now stands before Operative Susan Brabuster stating: "I don't much like sending you on this mission, Susan, but you're the best stealth operative we have, so I'm forced to do it. I know I sent your father to his death, but I promise I'll do everything I can to bring you back alive."

Once again, we use the clunky example of bringing up her father. Is this relevant? It had better be. We need to make sure the player knows the characters, but we need to keep the exposition trimmed to only what is relevant to the game. If it turns out that the evil Colonel Vorlosh is really Susan's father, horribly mangled, that is relevant to the game. If it is just a lame attempt to provide character depth, you might want to rethink using it, or at least do it in-game so that the player doesn't have to sit idly, controller in hand, watching clunky dialogue.

Gameplay exposition is a kind of writing that exists uniquely in games and instructional manuals. It ranges from: "In order to jump, press the Y button" to "I'd better check out this door" to "Sergeant, your mission is to take Hill 17." It is pure exposition that needs to be overt enough that the player knows what to do, but it should also provide some character benefit.

GAME SCENE DRAMATIC LEVEL TEMPLATE

We use the following template for constructing the overall dramatic structure of each level. Most everything here is something that every writer knows. It is divided into two parts, the *Dramatic Template* and the *Game Template*. The idea is to integrate the game and the story as much as possible and turn the game into story. It is presented to make sure we fully exploit the possibilities and think through what we're doing. Note that the second template is more concerned with how we execute the scenes as levels. Obviously, not every level contains every element, but, like all templates, these are things to consider for every level. Also, in some circumstances, categories overlap. Not every category should be filled out for every level.

Universal Dramatic Level Template

Category	Description
Level Title (Name):	Just what it says it is. A lot of times it helps to have an exciting title for a level like a chapter of a book.
Brief Outline of Scene: Grabber, Bump, Climax, Resolution:	The Grabber is the thing that gets the player's interest. It can be the revelation of a shocking piece of information or it can be a sudden betrayal. The Bump is a plot development that sends the story in a whole new direction. Climax is the final conflict of the scene—we should feel the scene is winding down. In Resolution, the scene is over. We should set up a next objective.
Problem/Solution:	What the major conflict of the level is. The problem of the level should be clear and obvious, and the player should know, at the end of the level that he has either (a) solved it, or (b) will have to solve the problem later on. (Dramatic problem).
Game Objective and How It Is Learned:	This walks a line with the game template, but it is to remind us what the player thinks he is trying to accomplish in the level (often the objective changes, but nevertheless, you should go into the level with a clear idea of what is to be done). Also, the player should get his mission in an interesting way (probably at the end of the last level, but it must be restated). Journalism rules apply here: Tell the player what he is going to do; what he is doing, and what he did.
Location (Unique things about this location):	Every location should be interesting. What's unique about it? At the same time, you have to be cautious to make sure that it clearly exists in the same "world" as every other location in the story.

Universal Dramatic Level Template (Continued)

Category	Description
Mood/Tone:	Every level should have a mood that somehow compares or contrasts to the overall dramatic structure of the story. The idea here is to avoid every level feeling the same way. Examples of moods are: Creepy, Explosive, Tense, Frenetic, etc. The mood can evolve in the course of a level, but we should give a feeling of mood to key art, music, and sound effects. Mood also reflects the activity (i.e., a stealth episode has a very different mood than a run and gun).
Time of Day/Weather:	Should fit the mood and give us a sense of story progression. It should be noted that the same environment could feel totally distinct depending on the time of day and the weather.
Initial Intention:	This is what the player thinks he is going to try and do in the scene. You can get a lot of mileage by having the player think he is going in to do one thing, and having it suddenly shift (with the opening conflict or the Bump). For instance, the player might think he's going to sneak into a place and suddenly get into a gunfight and it is a furious combat level or vice versa. He goes in there loaded for bear and finds the location deserted—except, maybe for some assassins waiting for him. Implied in this is that there is another way things could go. What is that way?
Opening Conflict:	In games, the conflict almost always means fighting. What triggers the fighting? Make it interesting and surprising.
Major Characters and How They Develop in the Level:	Who are the major characters in the scene? What are we trying to say about them? Characters should have a "gut level" motivation.
Level Boss, Minibosses, Thugs (Gun-Fodder), and Other Enemies or Potential Enemies:	Who is the enemy you are fighting in this level? You may or may not kill that character or actually contact them at all, but every level should have a sense of an identifiable enemy rather than faceless minions. Once again, it might not be who you expect it to be.
Plot (Game info to get out): Raw Exposition.	What does the character learn from the level?
Threatening or Actual Crisis:	This gets into the area of ticking clocks. What are the stakes of failure if a bomb about to go off? Is a friend being held hostage? Do you hear sirens and have to get out of the level before the cops arrive?

Universal Dramatic Level Template (Continued)

Category	Description
Bump/Reversal:	This is a revelation in the middle of a level that changes the nature of the level (i.e., Hero sneaks into the funeral home and plants a time bomb to blow up the mobsters attending a funeral. Then he goes outside to watch the fun. Then, the Bump is that an innocent heads into the building. Now the hero has to race in there before the bomb goes off). The other term for a Bump is a Reversal by Fate. Something happens that changes the dynamic in the middle of a scene. Watch any great scene in any great movie and there is a reversal in it.
Final Action Taken:	The story should advance at the end of every level. The world is different. The player has gone in deeper. There is no going back.
Keep Other Story Threads Alive:	Subtle point. Stories are composed of numerous threads that are wound together. There are numerous ways of keeping other threads alive: dialogue, voice-over, physical reminders, ephemera (pictures), symbols, etc. The crass way of doing this is simply to have the character state his intention or throw in a "recap." It is a little like in sports—always display the score and the current situation.
Value System:	What is valuable in this world and how do you show it? What is life worth? Money? What is important?
Presence of Other Realities Existing Simultaneously:	Anything you can do to make the world and story seem real. See the city out the window, hear a radio, show signage—anything that makes us feel we are existing in a living, breathing world, not just trapped in a video game.
Payoff from a Previous Level:	Levels don't exist in a vacuum. Scenes don't exist in isolation. If we've set up a conflict in a previous level, we should pay it off here. We should remind players of the previous conflict.
Setup for Future Level (Revelation of future possibilities):	Each level should create anticipation for the player. If we hear about a particularly nasty hit man in a game, we know that sooner or later our hero is going to be in a duel with him. Nintendo games often show you an interesting area in a level, but don't let you reach it until later. In this way, they both tease you and foreshadow future gameplay.
Matching Elements (Repeating symbols, etc.):	Something games miss out on. Returning to the same location you have already been at reminds the player of how far the story has progressed. It can save on art and build story. The second part of this (repeating symbols) is where we set something up (like birds as a metaphor in John Woo films) and then keep returning to them.
Bridging Out:	Mirrors bridging in. Get out of the scene in an interesting way. Leave the player with a sense of expectation of what the following scene is going to be, then surprise him. Tell the player what he accomplished in this scene either verbally or visually.

ACTION ITEM (GOLD)—DRAMATIC TEMPLATE

Fill in the Dramatic Level Template for your game. This may take a few sessions to complete, as it will start to force issues you may not have considered into focus. Take your time and explore what you can create.

Level Design Template

Category	Description
Name of the Level:	What is the name of the level? Rather than simply a description of a location, you can also tie this to action and story. For instance, rather than "Space Station Alpha," you might name the level "Gunner Finds the Girl."
Mission Objective/Stakes:	Player has a clear idea of what he is going to try and accomplish in this level. He may or may not do it (he may be trying to kill an enemy or two and only succeed in vanquishing them for a while, or may end up fleeing them, having obtained valuable information), but at every minute, the player should know what he is trying to do.
Sub-Objectives Both Known and Surprising:	Let's try and think of something more interesting than getting the three passkeys. What surprising challenges can you add into the game?
Experiments (Out-of-the-Box Ideas):	Approach every level as if it is going to be a unique and most wonderful level in history and that there's going to be something in it that nobody has ever seen before. You may not get it, but there should be some lofty ambition in every level.
Primal Impulse (Activities and feeling the level should give):	What is driving the character? Is it a frantic chase to stop a weapon of mass destruction? Is it the exhilarating thrill of a run and gun? The methodical challenge of slipping through an environment undetected? This ties a little bit to mood, but at a reflex level.
References:	If there is another game or film that is inspirational to this level, tell everybody what it is and what elements of that scene you want.
Music and Sound Effects:	Where should key stings go? What are the ambient sounds? If you pass an open window, remember to describe the sound outside (street traffic, etc.). This is not only a manifestation of mood, but it is also a way of creating a living, breathing world outside of the game, even if we have no visuals or characters to support it. (Jim Cameron calls the sound track the "invisible actor.")
Interesting Starting Point:	How does the character get into the scene? Do it in the most interesting possible way. Remember the old axiom, "If your guy comes through the door, you don't have a situation. If your guy comes through the window, you have a situation."

Level Design Template (Continued)

Category	Description
Carrot/Stick:	What keeps the player moving? What is he chasing, what is chasing him?
Exciting Gameplay Opening:	How and why is the first shot fired? If all you're doing is scooping a faceless guard with a high-powered rifle, it's been done.
Jolts:	The dogs crashing through the window in *Resident Evil*. Players are very vulnerable to scares in a game. If it makes sense within the context of the game and story to scare them, do it.
Expositional and Visceral Knowledge (How does the player know the mission?):	The player should know, at every moment, what he's trying to accomplish. The days of endlessly wandering corridors are over. The lazy way is to have a "Bitching Betty" (see Glossary) or Nagging Nigel tell him what he is supposed to be doing. Instead, try to set up levels so that they are intuitive. The entire level should be laid out to reinforce the mission objectives. For instance, if the player is trying to find the secret vault, he can pretty well figure the tougher the guards are, the more he's on the right track.
Resources:	What Power-Ups, Reloads, First Aids, etc. are scattered along the way? Surprise players with these things.
Ticking Clock:	Use visuals, audio, and music to remind players of tension.
Hidden Objectives and Easter Eggs:	What fun surprises can we put in the level? These are things people will talk about.
Ahas!/Puzzles	The best feeling there is. It's the moment of pure inspiration when you figure out how to beat a level. "Aha!"
Enemies—Ambient: Boss: Confrontational:	Emperor in Star Wars (you feel him more than confront him). Darth Vader Storm troopers. The cannon fodder thugs you have to fight. Who are they? Motivation? Will they run away or do they fight to the death?
Systems and How to Defeat Them:	This is the logic of each scene. If you're going into an enemy's lair, spend a little while thinking about how the enemy would logically defend his place. What it the Achilles' heel? For instance, if he has video cameras all over the place, rather than knocking off every camera, you go first to the control room and off the guys. Likewise, if cops are hunting the hero on the streets, he might find the rooftop route across town is very effective.
Save Points:	Don't make people redo something really hard over and over again. Don't make players watch the same cinematic over and over again, no matter how much you spent on it.

Level Design Template (Continued)

Category	Description
Save Scores:	Is score or virtual score in this game? If so, how will it be expressed? Scores come in many different forms.
Traps:	Traps are great. They can take all sorts of forms, from falling out floors, to ambushes, to surprise alarms and electric eyes, and so on. They're really great if you stumble into one and think, "I should have known better" (i.e., the cheese was just a little too easy to get to).
Weapons/Tools:	What does your character have and how does he get it? How does he move it around the world? What's special about each weapon? What surprise use is there for tools? Think about the relationship between weapons and tools. For instance, if you can get into an area by shooting a door, your gun has suddenly become a key.
Gadgets and Breakable Items:	Players love to break things and they love cool tech or magic.
Interface Issues:	How does the player know what to do when we provide him with a unique situation?
Navigation/Geography Issues:	If we're going to avoid having maps all over the place, how do we allow players to find their way around an environment? For instance, if you have a cityscape out the window, the player can pretty well figure out north, south, etc. If you are heading through the nightclub, you can follow the sound. The louder the music, the closer you are to the dance floor.
NPC Scenes (Nonplayer characters):	What surprise encounters can the hero have with these characters?
Cinematics/NIS (Noninteractive scenes):	What are the major cinematics? Are there set pieces in the level that need to be addressed with narratives? Are we using in-game or pre-rendered cinematics?
Plot Props:	What objects are particularly important to this level?
Different Deaths and Mission-Overs (Surprise mission ccontinues):	Every now and again, a character might get shot up, but instead of killing him, we can introduce a submission where he stumbles to the sleazy doctor who patches him up . . . that kind of thing. As far as death in general goes, it's really cool to have the player learn something every time he dies so it doesn't happen again.
Clichés to Avoid in This Scene:	What is there that we see in every game and want to avoid. Removing clichés forces creativity.
Theme of Gameplay:	What is the main theme that you are trying to communicate with the player through the gameplay and the story?

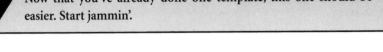

ACTION ITEM (GOLD)—LEVEL DESIGN TEMPLATE
Now that you've already done one template, this one should be easier. Start jammin'.

THE *WORLD* IN VIDEO GAMES

Usually, when you use the word *world* in the context of games, people think of the art department and what kinds of trees and cliffs and buildings they're going to put into the game. That's a natural thing to assume, but such things are only part of what we mean when we talk about the world of the game. World has profound impact on gameplay. Tom Clancy games live in a *one-hit death* world.

If you think about it, the decision to have "one-hit death" has significant implications beyond a thematic decision. It implies a real world. In fact, we'd bet a lot of money that that edict came out of some early development meeting where a project overseer (maybe Mr. Clancy himself) said: "I don't want any med-kit crap. I want it real. In a real firefight, when a guy gets shot in the chest or stomach, he's down. If he's wounded, superficially, yeah, he could stay in there for a while, but only for a while before he's got to get some serious medical attention." One-hit death was an extremely important result of making the decision to set the game in the real world, and it had a profound impact on the gameplay experience.

Game people throw around the phrase "real world" a lot to describe things that aren't real world at all, for example: "The great thing about *The Matrix* was that it was set in a real world." Sure it was, if your real world includes people running on walls and mysterious phone messages and strange seductresses at secret clubs and high-tech hit men in limousines. What they mean is that it is not in a *Lord of the Rings*-type fantasy world or in some highly stylized cyberworld.

Just as world dictates gameplay (e.g., one-hit death), gameplay dictates world. One-hit-death-commando world implies a photo-realistic treatment, characters that are governed by the constraints of real physics (Sam Fisher can't lift five hundred pounds or jump across a thirty-foot chasm with a running start). It also tells you that the environments in those games should look realistic in comparison to a *James Bond* villain fortress.

IMPLYING STAKES AND VALUE SYSTEMS THROUGH WORLD

World also encompasses what matters, what is of value, and what the stakes are in the game you are playing. In a one-hit-death game life implicitly has value. In such a game, the velocity and density of kills drop off. The ferocity of firefights changes dramatically. One-hit death demands patient, deliberate gameplay, no macho frag-fests. Your story should reflect the world. One-hit death implies threats in the world that we believe are potentially real.

If, however, your story is about liberating the Sunshine Princess from the Black Void jail at the Core of the Lava Kingdom, you are working with a very different value system that calls for a very different world. These types of games by their very nature have colorful, unreal worlds. The trick is to make that world and its values understandable and meaningful, because the dirty secret of world building is that player stakes and gameplay intensity are in no way related to reality.

While there is no law against it, you would not expect to see M-16s and garrote attacks in the Lava Kingdom. In certain genre-bending cases things like that appear, but then we are looking at the deliberate violation of a convention as a sales tool, or at least an attention-getting device. *Conker's Bad Fur Day* is an example.

HOW CONTENT IS PERCEIVED RELATIVE TO THE GAME WORLD

World tends to reflect the intended market of the game. Kids' games tend to take place in highly stylized cartoony worlds. Mature games tend to take place in photorealistic worlds. World creates context. Sly Cooper and Sam Fisher both sneak up behind characters and do away with them, but the execution and rating are very different. The funny thing is that this actually appears to fool people. Somehow, *Ratchet and Clank* make it past Mommy's violence radar, while *Metal Gear* isn't a consideration. In the 1980s, when people in Congress were decrying violence in entertainment, somebody figured out that it would look stupid to be waving a picture of a cartoon turtle around on the Senate floor, so *Teenage Mutant Ninja Turtles* got a hall pass while the somewhat more traditional *GI Joe* did not. Critics ignore the fact that real violence levels are different.

Such things speak to cultural differences. Americans are squeamish about sex in games. Japanese don't like to die too often. In Germany, there are huge issues about blood. It has to either not be there or be some funky color. Real world culture affects the worlds inside your games.

THE SAME BUT DIFFERENT—IT'S IN THE PRESENTATION

Whatever *moustache* you put on the game, there are certain characteristics. Sam Fisher and Sly Cooper have more in common than would immediately meet the eye. Both of them need ammo, information, health, etc. The differences are in presentation. The more realistic the world, the more likely that people may find things offensive. The less realistic, the less offensive people find it.

61

World is also about the kinds of spaces depicted. Is it a free-roaming city or is it a point-to-point hoppy-jumpy world? When you collect money (whether it comes in the form of cash or goody globules), what can you buy that is tactically valuable in the world? What are your objectives? Whatever you get at the end of the quest is what is really prized in this world. It might be treasure or it might be information.

FINDING YOUR WORLD BY KNOWING YOUR CHARACTERS

The world determines its inhabitants, though you might come at it in an opposite way. Suppose you know that your world contains sentient mice. Pretty quickly, you can decide that cheese is valuable, along with breadcrumbs. Cats are dangerous (though you might befriend one). Dogs are friends because they hate cats, so if you get in trouble and can raise Muttsy from his slumbers, you can stay alive. Secret passages are valuable. Small holes in the wall are, too. You might be afraid of the human doctor with the syringe, because he wants to use you for experiments, and he might at some point in the story capture you and put you in his diabolical lab. Mice often find themselves in labyrinths or mazes, and what maze is complete without the Mousataur (a mouse Minotaur) for a boss level.

Worldview is another thing to think about; it's subtler. What is the worldview of your mouse game? Are your mice innocent characters attacked by evil outsiders, or are your mice adventurers, thieves, or neutral? Are your mice pleasant little things or foul-mouthed rats? You could go either way, and the mice's attitudes toward their missions might be markedly different. The kind of dialogue they have with the nasty cat could be wildly different.

World is also setting. Is your story set in the past, present, future? Is it set in America, Russia, China? Is it set across a vast city or in a petri dish? All of this has huge implications in the world you create.

WORLD QUESTIONS

One of the core strengths of video games is that they provide an immersion into other realities—into other worlds—in a way that can be more engaging, compellingm and addictive than other mediums.

Here are some questions you can ask to help you in creating the environment of the world of your game:

* What is the most valuable thing in this world? In a commando world, it might be a weapon of mass destruction. In a fantasy world, it might be a magical orb. In a racing world, it might be a SuperNitroTurbo.
* What does the hero (and by extension, the player) need to do to win?

- Who and what are trying to stop him?
- What will happen in the world if the hero or heroine fails?
- What will happen if he or she succeeds?
- Who is trying to stop the hero and why?
- What does a bar look like in this world? (It often seems like bars are the most common buildings in games.) Is it a swank James Bond thing on the Riviera or is it a low-life dive populated by bug-eyed-monsters?
- What stops you from going places you aren't supposed to go? Does the world channel you or do you have freedom of movement? How do you know if you've left the world? How do you know if you are on the wrong track? What stops you from endlessly wandering through an open world and getting bored? Likewise, what gives the illusion of choice in a largely linear world?
- Does time matter in this world? Is gameplay often determined by time? Does the time of day change in this game?
- Is there an artist whose work is relevant to this world?

OTHER CONSTRUCTION TECHNIQUES

Another way to think of story is as a chain reaction of events, like the old wacky Rube Goldberg devices depicted in popular cartoons of the mid-twentieth century. By comparing a game to a Rube Goldberg cartoon construction, we basically mean that an action is taken, a certain thing happens, the bad guys respond, etc. It is an exercise in physics. As you know, physics exercises only work if we understand the world and its rules. This either means that you have to spend a lot of time establishing the physics of the world you create or you have to piggyback on an existing reality.

You might also try writing from the *key scene* or *mythic moment.* You have one scene you love. You write that and then write everything that leads up to it and leads away from it. What has to have happened beforehand and what has to happen afterward?

Scene within a scene works well. Every scene has another scene sitting inside of it. Think about the other way the scene could have gone. In games you have flexibility, and can have the other way.

When you build from the world you can construct story. You have a world that is intriguing you. Build from it. What is valuable in that world? Who has it? Who wants it?

Similarly, try building from your hero or villain. Let's say you know who your hero is. Now design a world that needs the unique abilities of your hero.

ACTION ITEM (BETA)—CREATE A HERO AND HIS WORLD

Create a hero for your game, and then detail the world in which he inhabits. Think about the ways that the hero and his world connect. Could your hero exist in some other world? If so, how do you modify the character and world so that they depend on each other for survival?

Interactive writing deals with unknown outcomes. It presents the other way that scenes can go: every story contains the story that didn't happen. Every scene must have a twist. In branching stories you can have it both (or multiple) ways.

5

BUILDING CHARACTERS

CHARACTER TYPES

There are five major types of characters that can exist within any game. They are:

PLAYER CHARACTER (PC/HERO)

This is the character that you, the player, control as you play the game. This will either be the role that you'll play during the experience, or the character that you'll control (depending on the point of view that the game utilizes). There can be more than one Player Character that you are allowed to control. Sometimes this character switching will come about by *force* (the character that you control switches based on a triggered event within the game and you have no choice but to play the new character). Many linear games that utilize multiple characters employ forced *swaps*. Usually, each of the Player Characters in these games has different skills sets to help you get through the experience. Ideally, you allow the player to choose which hero he wants to play, and make the character switches an element of gameplay. In multiple character games, we are usually splitting attributes among the heroes; so in essence, they all function as a meta-character. Some games will also allow you to either choose or generate your own character.

Most of the major franchises in the game business are built around well-defined Player Characters. The best have become icons of the industry: Mario,

Lara Croft, Master Chief, Crash Bandicoot, Solid Snake, Sam Fisher, Sly Cooper, and Jill Valentine to name but a few. Note that your character is often something other than human.

Player Characters are the heart of your franchise. How they live, fight, behave, rebel, quest, change, grow, interact, and even die within the worlds you create will have the greatest influence on the success of your game. Player Characters are our surrogates while we play; within the game, they are the vehicles by which we overcome obstacles, conquer fears and reach our eventual goal. Do not discount the power of the bond that can be created between you and your Player Character.

NONPLAYER CHARACTERS (NPCS)

These are the other characters (and creatures) that populate the worlds of the game. Each of these characters will have some relationship to you: ally, enemy or neutral. As their name implies, you cannot directly control these characters. However, you may be able to influence their actions by choices you make during gameplay. The majority of the characters that exists in any game are NPCs. Let's take a look at the various types of Nonplayer Characters you'll encounter:

Ally

An ally is a character who either helps you or has to be helped by you. This can be a member of your commando squad or the princess you have to save.

Neutral

A neutral character in the world is neither friendly nor hostile to you. This can be a member of a milling crowd or it can be the trader that sells weapons. Neutrals give your worlds life . . . and establish the reality in which your game takes place. Think about the *Star Wars* cantina, a place populated mostly by neutrals (some of whom didn't like droids). The neutrals in that scene provided the color and told us a lot about the world that existed on the edges of the empire. In fact, they told us a lot about the empire and the rebellion itself. The world had dimension. It wasn't all black and white. One of the issues with fiction in games is that everything tends to be all black and white. Neutrals can provide interesting shades of gray.

Enemy

An enemy is a foe that will actively attempt to thwart whatever you are trying to accomplish. Enemies come in a variety of shapes and sizes, and with differing levels of power. In a First-Person Shooter, enemies can range from generic cannon fodder to specific soldier types like snipers and grenadiers.

Remember that the category that the NPC falls into can be dynamic, and change on the fly, based on the player's actions. Rescue a neutral and he may become an ally. Attack a neutral, and she may become an enemy.

Another thing to keep in mind about NPCs is that they can be self-motivated characters. They can have their own agendas, which may conflict with the hero's. If the Player Character is a Treasure Hunter, for example, then an NPC might be another treasure hunter, who, in the grand scheme of things, is competing with you. For a time they may find it in their interests to cooperate with you in order to obtain some short-term objective. At other times, you'll be in competition with them to find the loot.

Or they might be characters that are on their own mission that is unrelated to yours, but ones you develop an interdependency with during the course of the game. One example is a female spy who is on a vengeance mission against the main villain. She's willing to help your hero as long as it leads to her eventually getting her chance at revenge.

Obviously, characters this complex require both additional coding and story development if they are to be fully integrated into gameplay, so you'll often find these characters functioning as part of the *primary cast* for the game.

Level Bosses

Unique NPCs, Level Bosses are the *uber-enemies* that the player will encounter throughout the game. They usually have distinctive gameplay associated with their actions. They are more powerful than other enemies and may also have dedicated story elements attached to them. To get through a level, or finish a mission, you'll often have to defeat the Level Boss. The main villain of the game is often called the End Boss. Usually there will be gameplay associated with this character that makes him the most difficult to defeat. There is often a narrative conceit that ties the End Boss and the Player Character together.

PLAYER-DIRECTED CHARACTERS

Becoming extremely popular in Squad Combat style games and *questing* adventures, the Player-Directed Character(s) can be given orders by the player. For example, in a combat game, you may control a small group of fellow soldiers. You can issues orders, telling them to attack enemies, move to certain locations, or even defend you.

Player-Directed Characters function as a subset set of your Player Character. Issuing the right commands to them as you move through the game (and keeping them alive) is often as essential to success as controlling your Player Character. Once you have given a Player-Directed Character an order, his A.I. takes over to best execute your command. However, you never take direct control of these characters. Interactions and story elements that relate to these characters can often be quite deep, as you'll spend a great deal of the game fighting and adventuring alongside them. Throughout the game, you may control a variety of Player-Directed Characters.

PLAYER CHARACTER RELATIONSHIPS AND INTERDEPENDENCIES WITH NONPLAYER CHARACTERS

A writer/designer has a relationship with every character that he creates. Some (like your heroes) you spend days, weeks, even months, fine-tuning and developing, while others (cannon-fodder) are almost boilerplate. But regardless of the time you've spent getting that character in the game and on the screen, when you have done your job properly, the player will have an emotional investment in the hero he's controlling, and varying levels of involvement with all of the other characters in the game.

While we discussed them above, we want to spend a little more time on NPCs, because their actions are dictated by design, and therefore can have the greatest overall effect on the gameplay experience.

Every NPC is at any given moment an ally, neutral, or an enemy. The possible relationships the Player Character can have with other characters fall into a kind of tic-tac-toe board pattern, like the one on the facing page. We've filled in typical examples of each type of character, but they by no means exhaust the list of possibilities.

For our example, let's assume you are designing a game set in World War II in which you take on the role of an American Doughboy in the trenches that face no-man's land.

ACTION ITEM (BETA)—CHARACTER RELATIONSHIP CHART
Fill in the Character Relationship Chart for your game.

CHARACTER REVERSALS AND THEIR RAMIFICATIONS

Static situations are not the stuff of drama. Drama happens when motivations change (or are revealed). Drama happens when an enemy changes into a friend or a friend turns into an enemy. It happens when a neutral changes and becomes committed to one side or the other, or when a friend is revealed to be an enemy or vice versa.

Character Relationship Chart

	Ally	Neutral	Enemy
Player-Centric	A character that will fight alongside you, give you valuable information, and help you on your journey through the adventure. This NPC is usually a "featured" character in the game. Example: Sgt. Dunphy, your squad leader	A character that may be willing to help you, depending on the conditions. They are neither a friend nor foe, yet. They're conditional. This type of character can sometimes play a large role in the game's narrative. Example: Sofie the French Barmaid	An antagonist whose only mission is to stop you or kill you. These tend to be bosses or recurring antagonists, and are therefore often at the center of the game's narrative. Example: Lt. Lukas, German Infantry Commander
Location-Centric	This is the soldier who is protecting the outpost. You fight by his side while you're there and then leave him behind when you move on. These characters also tend to be the "red shirts." Example: Private Walsh (soon to be KIA)	Any character that is specific to a level or location of the game. Unlike a Player Centered Neutral, these tend not to be recurring characters and are more easily motivated to become a friend or foe. Example: Peasant Refuge escaping his shelled out village	The vast majority of the enemies that you'll face in the game are this character type. They are usually guardians; that is they patrol and protect a specific location (they may also attack one). It's not personal with these characters—they are just doing their job. Example: German Machine Gun Crew
Self-Motivated	This is a character aligned with you that is fulfilling an agenda other than yours. They sometimes indirectly cause trouble for you. Example: French Freedom Fighter	Characters attempting to achieve their own goals while operating without allegiance to either side. Example: Louis the Profiteer, trading in collected battlefield gear.	An enemy wandering around the world who is your competitor on a mission. He is not necessarily in league with your enemy, but he is your enemy. Example: Private Foxall, your rival to make Corporal.

During the course of gameplay, character alliances can and do change. We can all recall the game where our sidekick, or our commander, or our fellow traveler, turned out to be the villain. Because narratives for games need to be fairly compact, there is often only a small cadre of characters to work with, and this leads to structures where betrayal is often at the center of the story. For example, suddenly it is revealed that Lord Gornishe, who you believed to be helping you, is, in fact, your enemy. Now, you have to fight Lord Gornishe.

While we know this betrayal is going to happen (we've designed it), the player hopefully doesn't see it coming, and is surprised and delighted by this revelation. If we get it right, it's a satisfying twist (and if we've foreshadowed it properly, the player will realize that we left clues for him and played "fair"). Drama, and a world that seems alive, happen when relationships evolve and change over the course of the game. But if we get it wrong, it can and does hurt everything that has come before. Nothing is worse than playing a title and beating the gameplay only to feel cheated by the story.

Unlike other forms of entertainment, you can be the reason that motivated change in other characters: your actions during gameplay can affect how other characters react to you. Since character motivations and alliance can be dynamically subject to alteration, this leads to some great opportunities to explore relationships and interactions in ways that are unique to games.

Reversals, especially when caused by player action, are more powerful than simple revelations.

The Lord Gornishe betrayal turns from a hackneyed cliché to a more compelling piece of plot development the minute you motivate it through gameplay. Perhaps Lord Gornishe says: "I will join your fight to defeat Vorlosh the Incontinent if you will help me recapture my castle." Indeed, he helps you defeat Vorlosh, but you decide to blow off the castle mission; after all, it isn't on your mission list. Now, Lord Gornishe turns on you. Your betrayal (through gameplay), has led to his betrayal (within the game and narrative).

Now you have to pay for it with an unexpected fight. If you're killed, or if you saved before you made your decision that led to the betrayal, you can go back and do the castle mission and maybe get an unexpected boon. In either case, your future adventure, and the story, has been altered by the decision you made: if you help Lord Gornishe, his subjects will help you later on; if you don't help him, they will oppose you.

Choices with these types of ramifications have to be carefully considered during design. While they add depth, they also add assets and complexity. It almost goes without saying, but we'll say it anyway, that no consequence should doom the player for the rest of the game. It may make his life harder, but it shouldn't doom him.

Alternate possibilities and consequences are something that can only be done in an interactive medium. Multiple character and story arcs need not be done with *branching* but instead by creating a set of conditional triggers that directly affect how any character in the game that will interact with you. The above example is just a slightly more complicated version of a neutral NPC that becomes an enemy because you shoot at him. The underlying concept is essentially the same. Of course, if you are going to allow such dynamic changes with characters that are fundamental to your game, you'll need to generate the various alternate missions and storylines to support it.

CHARACTER REWARDS AND PUNISHMENTS

Rewards and punishments are truly the core compulsion of game play. They are the carrot and the stick that either lure or drive you through the experience. Since we are playing a game, by its very definition, we expect rewards (advancement, winning) and punishments (obstacles, losing).

Rewards come in numerous forms ranging from power-ups to victory cinematics. Punishments arrive in numerous forms ranging from loss of life (which adds up to loss of player progress up to a point and loss of player's time) to missed opportunities.

Normally the rewards and punishments in a game are the province of the designer. However, there is little that tells you more about a world and your character's place in it than how they are rewarded or punished for their actions. This is the *value system* of the game and it needs to align with the narrative. In any world, especially a game world, everything depends on what is valued.

Characters are defined by the choices they make; this has always been true. A hero reveals himself by what he decides when faced with adversity. A villain shows his true colors when temptation presents itself. The beauty of games is their unique ability to put you in the position of making those choices for the characters.

Let's suppose for a moment that you're playing a game, and your character is in the following position: he has low armor and he's working against a timer to rescue a hostage. If you attack with low armor you'll probably die rescuing the hostage. If you go for armor, the hostage will die. It is a conundrum that is revealing on a number of levels. What will you do? Your choices are things that need to be anticipated, and manipulated, by both the game design and the narrative. How the game rewards or punishes you for the choice you ultimately make is one of the keys to your overall gameplay experience. Will these little dilemmas encourage you to move forward, try again, or hurl the controller across the room?

If you are playing a well defined (licensed character), then the gameplay and fiction will be derived from the persona of that character. For instance, many major franchises have injunctions against their hero character knowingly hurting an innocent human being. Therefore, collateral damage is heavily punished. Conversely, if you are playing a sociopath you might be rewarded for the number of people your character kills. That's a huge decision. In gameplay you must decide what your character will and won't do. Do you allow the player to do things that are out of character or do you punish those actions?

Not all rewards need have direct consequences to be satisfying. For instance, what if, given the richness of a franchise property, we feel that we should embed *info nuggets* in the game. Think of them as trivia pieces about bosses or locations that may serve as clues to the player, but are basically there for collectibility based on franchise history. Players collect them and can then view them in an archive, like little movies or slideshows. In this way, you are offering a reward that is outside the fiction of the game, but is inside the fiction of the franchise.

Here are the most common ways to reward and punish a player. Consider how you can integrate them into your design and story.

REWARDS

* **Resource** (Lives, Health, Fuel, Ammo, Weapons). In many games these are sprinkled throughout the environments, and by exploring, you can find them. In this way, the designers are able to "breadcrumb" you in the direction they want you to take. Resource can also be spawned from dead enemies, forcing you to put yourself at risk to reap the reward.

* **Power Ups**. Power Ups will give your character increased power and abilities to specific tasks they can perform. They are usually temporary.

* **Information**. This can take many forms: letting you know where you can find a character you need to talk to, or giving you a clue to where you can find the treasure, or which door is a portal to the next world, or how to defeat a dragon, or where enemies may be waiting in ambush. Information is a great reward because it encourages you to keep advancing further into the game.

* **Keys** (to unlock new areas of the game). We are using *keys* in the generic sense to mean any object, which allows you to solve a problem (although games still show up with find the "red keycard" to get through the "red door lock" gameplay, mainly because it still works and players understand it).

* **Skills** (Fighting, Climbing, Stealth, etc.). This is a way of *leveling up* your character, gaining new abilities. For example, the further you get into the game, the more acrobatic you become, opening new areas of levels that were previously off limits because your character couldn't reach them.

* **Points** (if the game is keeping score). There is still something very satisfying about seeing a number that let's you have some objective standard (no matter how arbitrary the scoring system) you can measure your progress against.

* **Upgrades and Add-ons**. These enhance the weapons and gear you already have. For instance, silencers for weapons, or enchanted chain mail that improves your armor.

* **Collectibles**. Added value elements that may or may not have a direct effect on your advancement in the game.

* **Difficulty Level Unlockables**. This reward allows you to play the game at higher difficulty levels (usually by successfully beating the game at a lower one first).

* **Reveal Hidden Areas or Characters**. These are very satisfying because they come with an added benefit: the joy of discovery.

* **New Alliances and Allies**. Often, success will bring new fighters and friends to your cause, and to your side.

* **Game Saves**. Many games are tuned to create maximum tension by placing *save points* in strategic locations that makes reaching them before you are killed a major reward.

* **Easter Eggs**. Easter Eggs are added value items, hidden gameplay, special codes, etc., (and often in-jokes) that you can discover.

PUNISHMENTS

* **Progress**. This is the most obvious one, usually in the form of character death (which can mean restarting from the last save or at the beginning of the level).

* **Capability**. This diminishes your capability to advance through the game. Health and armor damage are the most common ways this manifests itself in gameplay. Reduced health can affect your speed, how you fight, how you aim weapons, etc.

* **Time**. Time is and will remain one of the best ways to manipulate any situation. Everyone understands what it feels like to be at the mercy of a "ticking clock." Taking time away from you ups the ante.

* **Resources**. This usually comes in the form of a resource that you've already collected being taken away from you. For instance, you are attacked, and your wallet is stolen. Now, you're going to have to go and earn that resource (money) again before you can advance.

* **New Enemies**. Sometimes, you'll find that if you attack the wrong character, or group, or even neutral NPCs, you suddenly have a new enemy, or a whole new set of enemies, to deal with.

Rewarding and punishing the player helps to direct him through the gameplay experience. It gives him tasks to accomplish, and provides him with a metrics (standard) by which he can measure his progress (or lack thereof). We've broken out some of the main ways this expresses itself with the game utilizing the following templates.

The first category is the "base" resource. The second category is the "effect" of the resource and in the third column are some of the *moustaches* (alternatives) that games of different genres use.

ACTION ITEM (BETA)—CREATE A CUSTOM LIST OF REWARDS AND PUNISHMENTS

Imagine your life was a video game. What system of rewards and punishments would motivate and influence your actions the most? Make a list, and detail out why you think they would affect you, and how you would react to them.

Developing Characters—A Template

In narrative-driven experiences (the kind we work on most often), gameplay and story are intertwined. We are always looking for ways to not only connect the two, but to have them build on one another to create a seamless interactive experience. Much of this comes about by creating a forceful character around which the rest of the game can be developed.

The following is our template that we use for creating a *Character Bio*. It contains a lot of information that probably won't make it directly into the game. However, it will be very useful for helping you to have a clear vision of the character you are creating. Think of this as building the iceberg, even if the player only sees the tip of it. The character that you see and interact with in the game will be better because you've taking the time to explore these details.

The template includes a list of questions that won't be relevant for every character you create. Different games have different issues, so tune the list to match your project.

There are different ways of filling out this template. You can answer the questions as they come, taking a biographers approach and just getting down the facts. Often, we find it effective (and an interesting exercise) to have the character we are developing answer the questions him or herself, so we'll write them in First-Person Narrative.

If you get stuck as you work through the template, just go down the list to the next question, or jump around. Think nonlinearly . . . you can go back later and fill in the blanks based on what you have. After a while, a picture of the character

Resource Template

Resource	Effect	Alternatives
Food	You need it to keep functioning. In some ways it buys you time.	Fuel, air (in a space or underwater game). It usually either serves to buy health (food equals restored health) or time; fuel functions as a timer for vehicles.
Ammo	Your weapon's expendables. You need them to fight. Some games always give you a base weapon with unlimited ammo. Others meticulously manage ammo to encourage alternative gameplay (such as stealth).	Spells that need to be recharged.
Health	You need it to repair yourself after a fight.	Karma, awareness
Armor	Makes you harder to kill. (Use often blurs with health.)	Force fields, magic enchantments
Power-Ups	Either gives you a new power, amplifies an old one, or negates the need to scavenge for powers you currently have.	Gems, berries, auras
Keys	Allow you to access inaccessible areas of the game.	Pass cards, lock-picking devices, maps, clues, hints, information
Detectors	Allow you to see characters or objects in the environment that you otherwise couldn't see.	Infra-red, night-vision, magic
Points	There are two kinds of points: points that actually allow you to "buy" things, and points that exist for nothing other than giving players a rating, a sense of accomplishment.	Player "ratings" often come off of points earned. A player might be able to get all the way through the game, but they are encouraged to replay the game in order to get a higher rating or attain an Easter egg or some other reward.
Easter Eggs	Secret areas, off the optimal path, which give players a new kind of mastery.	These range from relevant data to Hot Coffee—style secret unlocks to hidden videos to pictures of the designers, etc.
Stealth Rating	Not exactly a resource, but a location-dependent circumstance that greatly affects the player's game state.	Shadows, alarm signals, meters, etc.

Reward Template

Reward	Effect	Alternatives
Attaboys (Cut-Scene)	Plays to let the player know that he has accomplished the objective and rewards him with visual/story/gameplay feedback.	End of level screens (statistics of play).
Enhancements	Extra kill power and health to improve player's chances of beating ever tougher enemies.	Weapon mods, new spells, ammo packs, character enhancements
Insight (Knowledge)	Information that advances the player through the game.	Opening up new levels, hidden environments, foreshadowing of actions and events to come
Wealth	"Money" that can be used to buy things within the game.	Points
Status (Character/Equipment)	Re-set health, armor, inventory.	May also replenish ammo, spells, powers

Punishments

Punishment	Effect	Alternatives
Death	Your character suffers a death animation.	This is a failure notice to the player. In and of itself it is not that much of a punishment—especially if the player regenerates at or near the same spot without other punishments.
Loss of Progress	Restart at the beginning of a level or at the last checkpoint save.	*Prince of Persia* built an entire franchise on dealing with this problem. Time rewind takes an annoying game convention (loss of progress and turns it into a game feature by allowing the player to rewind time and play again.)
Loss of Powers	Taking away capabilities that the player character had.	An alternative to loss of power is the loss of capabilities. For instance, when your character has sustained health damage, he may not be able to target his weapon as efficiently, or run as fast, or climb over objects, and so on. The difference here is that these effects may be temporary, and that when his health returns, so will these capabilities.
Loss of Time	Ticking clocks used to force and manipulate action.	Taking time away from a player in a timed level. This is a huge play balancing issue. It has to be fair. If you can lose time, there ought to be a way to get it back.

starts to develop, and you'll find that you answer the remaining questions almost instinctively.

SAMPLE SETUP

Okay, so you've created an idea for a game called *Hades Hit Man*. In the game, you play Jack Slag. He is trying to work his way out of the lowest corners of Hell, so he's doing nasty jobs for the Dark One. The rule is that he has to kill a good person every ten minutes or he will be banished into eternal torment. However, he is forbidden to kill a human who's been infested by a demon (of which there are many). That means, he must use his "power of discernment" (a variation on heat vision) to make sure he is killing an innocent.

In laying out the premise for the game, we can fairly easily extrapolate some of the core gameplay. Often, story leads to logical game mechanics and vice versa. We can see the tone (dark, controversial even). We can imagine the levels, both in hell and in the real world. We know that we'll be up against both humans and demons . . . maybe even angels. We know that we have "powers" from hell. We know that there is a ticking clock, with severe consequences for failure.

Now, let's take a look at the template. From the above setup for *Hades Hit Man*, we'll fill in the template for Jack, and see where it takes us.

Character Template

Name	Jack Slag
Story Purpose	We are going to follow Jack on his road to his own version of redemption, no matter how twisted or perverse it may ultimately be.
Gameplay Purpose	Player character
Alignment	Neutral evil. He won't kill randomly, but he will kill just about anyone that gets in his way.
Persona	Bad-ass
General Disposition	Indifferent and vacant. He may be too far-gone, although, occasionally, there is still a hint of life in his eyes.
Special Abilities	He can see an innocent soul, which he must then reap to the Dark Lord. Note that it is possible that he finally reaches a soul so pure that even he can't pull the trigger, and this leads to more chaos than he could have ever imagined.
Education/Intelligence	College educated, maybe even a doctorate degree. He has come a long way since he walked among the living.
Family	None that he can remember. He'd like to, though.

Character Template (Continued)

Name	Jack Slag
Aspirations	Jack realizes that he is eternally damned. He's just hoping to make his eventual suffering a little less worse. It's not much as far as hopes go, but at the moment, it's all he's got.
Addictions	Gambling. The only time Jack felt alive when he was at the craps table.
Occupation and attitude toward it (good or bad)	Hit man for Beelzebub. At first, he wasn't too happy about his occupation, but lately he's been warming to the task.
Objective(s)	Kill innocent souls and deliver them back to hell. Avoid eternal damnation (beyond what he is already facing).
What does this character want?	Ultimately, to be left alone. However, that doesn't look like it is ever going to happen.
Who or what does he love?	Jack has vague recollections about a family pet. He can't remember if it was a dog or a cat. Maybe a parrot. He thinks he loved it . . . he'd like to think he did, anyway. It bothers him that he can't remember.
What is he afraid of?	Nothing. That is what makes him so dangerous. If the Devil had known this, he might not have decided to use him.
Why does he involve himself in this situation?	He has no choice.
Other roles and identities?	Jack can pass among the living, able to fit in by looking very much like any other person you'd ignore if you'd passed them by on the street.
Single adjective to describe this character	Weary
Skills	Expert marksman. Lightning fast. (You would expect a hit man to know how to use a gun. We'd have a unique angle if he doesn't—maybe he has to learn how to become a hit man, this is part of his adventure.)
Reports/Answers to?	The equivalent of hell's field operative. This could be someone still living, someone dead, or the wild idea, something not human, but not necessarily a demon. Perhaps he can communicate and receive orders psychically.
Who reports to this character?	No one.
Trademark Object	Jack has a cursed gun with a sentient desire to kill. He must placate it or it will turn on him.

Character Template (Continued)

Name	Jack Slag
Common emotions (pick three): Exhausted, confused, ecstatic, guilty, suspicious, angry, hysterical, frustrated, sad, confident, embarrassed, happy, mischievous, disgusted, frightened, enraged, ashamed, cautious, smug, depressed, overwhelmed, hopeful, lonely, love-struck, jealous, bored, surprised, anxious, shocked, shy	Exhausted, sad, mischievous
Signature Move or Tic	Jack bunches up his shoulders when he talks, as if he was trying to get out of his own skin.
Nationality	Open. This character can be from about anywhere.
Ethnicity	Also open.
Religion	Fallen (and fallen hard) Catholic
Favorite Food	Sautéed Mushrooms
How does this character dress? (Note: Characters might wear a variety of clothes, but there is a "standard" way you see them. Bond wears a tuxedo. Indiana Jones wears a leather jacket and a fedora.)	Getting tired of every anti-hero wearing a duster, so let's see what we can come up with. Perhaps a dark suit or even the clothes he was buried (or died) in. We want something iconic, but also original.
Accent	Interesting. A vague, hard to place accent could hint at backstory we may want to explore.
Dialogue Tics and Slang?	Perhaps Jack speaks with idioms from another era, and that hints at the fact that he has been trapped in hell for a lot longer than we originally thought.
Locations where this character is mostly likely to "blend in"	Hell and various locations around large metropolitan cities.

Character Template (Continued)

Name	Jack Slag
Where was the character born?	Springfield, Illinois, though Jack can't remember this. Yet.
Where has the character been?	Jack traveled the world. As he visits various parts of the globe looking for innocents, he makes deja vu of locations he visited while he was alive. There may be a connection here that becomes clearer as the game progresses. There is a larger plan in motion, and the locations he's being forced to "hunt" in are not as random as we believe.
Where does the character live?	Jack has no home.
Where will (did) he or she die? And how?	Jack died in a car accident as he was trying to evade the cops. He can't remember why, but he does remember that other people died.
Objects the character wears on his or her body (jewelry, tattoos, etc):	Jack has a set of dice tattooed onto the palms of each of his hands. The weird thing is, depending on the situation and his mood, the dice changes their face-up positions. Possible this could be a foreshadowing device . . . if Jack looks at his palms and see "snake eyes," his odds are not good. If he sees a seven, it's a different story.
Dichotomy of Character (inner conflict in the character)	Jack finds a "true innocent," and can't pull the trigger. This could be the crisis that becomes both a major story and gameplay reversal. We could also have a tone issue to contend with here.
Character reaction to different events in the game (walk through a few beats)	Early on, Jack will start as indifferent to pain and suffering (in fact, he is the cause of most of it). At some point, something will affect him in an unexpected way. Perhaps he feels joy, or dare we say, love.
Relation to other significant characters	The Devil—starts as an errand boy, and then slowly becomes a threat.
The Innocent (character to be determined)—This is the character that will help Jack stop his fall.	The Angel of Death—elbowing in on his territory while working for the "wrong side."
What we'd think if we saw this character on the street	We'd be nervous, not because of his physical appearance, but because of his intensity and vacant eyes.

Character Template (Continued)

Name	Jack Slag
Three days before the party started: Often as not your game will be about one of the peak moments in this character's life. What was he or she doing before it started?	Suffering endlessly in the lower corners of hell.
How did this character lose his or her virginity? (This is always a fun one.)	Crazy idea, maybe Jack is a virgin.
Morality: Moral choices the character makes in the game. Does this affect how the player should play him?	We are into some morally ambiguous territory with this character. We may want to consider doing a wild reversal, where we start in a world without consequences, and let Jack (and the player) go wild. Then, we turn everything on its head, by making Jack deal with all the chaos that he caused.
Emotional Stability	Jack is slowly losing his mind. He's in the first stages, but it may manifest itself through dialogue, or his interaction with other characters.
What do they do to comfort themselves?	Dreams about gambling.
Phobias: heights, snakes, darkness, etc.	Jack can't stand to be alone, although that is all he desires.
Vanity	Jack has a casual cool. Even in his present situation, he looks like a movie star without trying.
Tagline	"Time to meet your real maker."
Epitaph: What will go on the character's tombstone?	He died too soon, but he deserved it.
Actor Suggestions	Let's think about this one.
Impressionistic Age and Health	Midthirties. Failing health.

Character Template (Continued)

Name	Jack Slag
Impressionistic Height	Taller than most, but he hunches over a little when he walks.
Impressionistic Weight	In shape
Body Type	Lean and muscular
Hairline/Color	Thinning fast. Dark brown with gray sideburns.
Eye Color	Deep green
Facial Hair	None

CHARACTER TEMPLATE SUMMARY

Okay, so what did we learn about our character by filling out the template? We've definitely started to think about all the ways that we can play Jack Slag (lost soul, tormented, or even liberated, and enjoying his task now that he has already seen the worst hell has to offer). And we have an obvious question to ask: What did Slag do in life to get him into hell in the first place? This is probably one of the core plot points for the game, and one we now need to answer, but we've already given ourselves some material to work with.

In our example, you'll notice that in addition to the straightforward answers, we occasionally went off on tangents inspired by the question being asked. This is the value of developing characters with this structure. So in this simple premise, and by working through the template, we're already off the races. We can see gameplay, and story, and our antihero.

You'll notice that the driver's-license-type questions (height, weight, eye color, etc.) are at the end of the template, because you'll often discover your character morphing on you as you explore his or her motivations and desires. A character's physical appearance is often a manifestation of his wants, needs, status, current situation, and life experiences. We like these questions toward the end so we don't limit our creativity or ourselves as we think through the character.

Very little of this is straight backstory, biomaterial. It might be interesting to know where the main character was born, but the real question is: "How does it affect gameplay?" If a character is working in his hometown, it will be a different experience than if he's operating in a place he's never been before.

We want to stick to what is relevant. For instance, it matters to us to know about Harry Potter's parents, but not James Bond's. Sometimes, the design of the game, which often precedes the story, dictates certain things about the character—

if you are doing an underwater exploration game you'll obviously need to create a character that is pertinent to underwater exploration. The interesting thing about in-depth character bios is that they are often a powerful tool for helping to not only flesh out the characters, but core gameplay, levels, set pieces, etc.

Teams love the fertile ground of character templates because they stimulate ideas, discussion, and debate.

Obviously, this template is designed for major characters. When you're filling out a template for minor characters, you can delete the questions that are too deep, or you can use another template that we find useful; one that deals with organizations and their hierarchies.

ACTION ITEM (GOLD)—CHARACTER TEMPLATE
You knew this one was coming. Create a character by utilizing the template. This can be your hero or your main villain. If you don't have an original character to build, try filling it in with your personal details. Maybe you'll discover something interesting about yourself in the process (like you should be a character in a video game).

CREATING CHARACTER ORGANIZATIONS: GAME AND STORY NECESSITIES

Almost every game relies on a large number of enemies that are aligned, whether informally (zombies, street thugs, orcs) or formally (knights, crime families, military). We treat these characters as members of an *organization*, and develop a detailed story for this group. While much of this may never find its way into the game narrative, creating a consistent vision for your enemies, allies, and their organizations can have a profound effect on the design of the game. This is fertile ground to find opportunities to make your primary *targets* more than just an endless stream of cannon fodder.

To that end, we've developed what we call our Organization Template. The goal of this template is to integrate aligned character groups and their leadership into a cohesive whole in order to help level designers, artists, programmers, and other team members better understand the *agents of conflict* that the player will have to confront in the game.

We also use the same template to develop the hero's organization (if he belongs to one). For instance, if your player character is a samurai in feudal Japan, then you'd definitely want to know as much as you can about the warlord and army he fights, as this has obvious implications on the hero's motivation and backstory.

Note: in this template, we have largely appropriated John Warden's Five Rings theory of systems in combat (Warden was the architect of the air campaign during the first Gulf War). Warden identifies five unique elements of any organization, which he refers to as the Five Rings. They are: Leadership (who's in charge), Essential Systems (what the organization cannot or will not live without), Infrastructure (often the physical manifestation of Essential Systems, such as buildings, fortresses, communication, equipment, food, etc.), Population (who populates this organization), and finally Fielded Forces (who, and what, protects this organization).

Using Warden's theory as a starting point, we've developed an organization template that we use to help flesh out both game and story elements related to the larger factions that you might face (or align with) during a game.

Organization Template

Name	This is the name of the organization we are profiling (include an acronym if appropriate).
Goal or Objective of Group	Our enemies and locations should feel real; they should exist as more than a mechanism that gets in the main character's way. In fact, we should understand what they do day-to-day and how the hero is a disruption to their plans.
Leadership	Who controls this organization? More often than not, this is the level boss.
Ambient Doctrine	What is the nature of this group? Is it a hard-bitten, violent organization or are they sophisticated white-collar criminals who don't usually deal in excessive violence?
Public Awareness	Is this organization overt or covert? Or does it straddle the line somewhere in-between (a secret division running inside the CIA, for example).
M.O.	What is their method of operation? How does this group get what it wants or achieve its desired goals?
Powers	How much clout does this group have? Is this a local group or an international threat? What must the hero take into consideration before attacking this organization? If he aligns with this group, what are the benefits and risks of doing so?
Essential Systems	What do they need in order to survive? Those things they cannot or will not do without.
Infrastructure	Buildings, important places. Where do they live? Where do they hide? What kind of support do they need to stay operational?

Organization Template (Continued)

Fielded Forces	The command structure and type of troops this group has available. This includes not only manpower, but equipment as well. For example, the Fielded Forces of an armored division includes not only the men, but their tanks, and their air-support as well.
Posture	Is it on an offensive or defensive posture? How does the enemy system defend itself? What does it need to instigate an attack?
Population	What is the nature of the population of this organization? A prison, for example, contains a mixed ecology of prisoners, guards, service workers, visitors, etc.
Who does business with them?	Often, organizations are only as good as their associates.
Zealotry	Do paid mercenaries or true believers staff this organization?
Vulnerabilities and Fears	What is this group's biggest fear? Where is their Achilles' heel?
Real World Parallels	Who in the real world is like them?
Appearance	Do they wear uniforms? Street clothes? If so, what kind?
Symbols	Logos, flags, corporate insignia, etc.
Paraphernalia	Typical weapons, tools, etc.

ORGANIZATION TEMPLATE SUMMARY

As you can see, this template can help you in creating a unified structure for almost any organization, from straight-forward military units, to street gangs, to covert ops, to fantasy clans. Having a consistent vision for the organizations that your hero will be facing will make your game that much stronger. Ideas for elements such as action set pieces, locations, vehicles, weapons, and enemies often spring from this template, so as with the character template, share it with the team and encourage feedback.

ACTION ITEM (GOLD)—ORGANIZATION TEMPLATE

Using the template, detail the organizational structure of the main enemies or allies in your game.

ENEMY STATES AND STRUCTURE

Usually, your enemies are controlled by the code that is running the game (in a single player game). That means that some basic AI issues should be considered when developing your foes. Listed below is a study that we did for one of our games. It was created to help us understand how the enemy characters would function. This list includes the states that an enemy character can be in, and how they advance through the states depending on your actions.

Note that this is not intended to be a comprehensive list of AI issues (entire books have been devoted to the subject). Instead, we present them here to help you understand what you should consider when you are developing your enemies. This should also help you think about their strengths and their weaknesses, and how those reveal themselves in the game.

UNAWARE

Unaware enemies have two modes: guard or patrol. At its simplest, patrolling enemies move, while guarding enemies are stationary. Patrolling enemies will follow a preset path or activity (either direct line, nodal or regional—depending on the engine). This allows you the chance to observe the enemy (and often determine their patterns of action), and then determine the best time to take action (stealth past, attack, etc.).

Guarding enemies are fixed in place while they are unaware. This could include any number of types, such as a guard at a door, a lab-technician working at a computer, a prisoner in his cell, etc.

Unaware enemies are the easiest to stealth past, or to approach for an attack, and have the smallest detection radius.

ALERT

Alert enemies are aware of your presence, but haven't yet discovered your location.

The alert state can be reached four ways:

* Visual detection   * Alarm
* Sound detection   * Discovery of body

Once an enemy has been alerted, his state advances and he may take on a different set of actions than when he was unaware.

In addition to the actions available above, an alert enemy may also go into search mode. In this mode, the enemy is looking for you in the direction in which you were detected. A searching enemy will not move beyond his original region, or beyond his patrol area as determined by tuning.

If an alert enemy does not advance to an active state after a preset period of time, he will return to an unaware state.

ACTIVE

An *active enemy* has discovered you. The active state can be reached four ways:

* ❋ Visual detection
* ❋ Sound detection
* ❋ Alarm
* ❋ Discovery of body

An active enemy will take one or more of the following action modes:

Hunt

A *hunting enemy* has found your location and is actively moving toward it. This is different than searching, in that the enemy has found your character as is now closing in on him.

Attack

The enemy attacks you, either with ranged weapons or in hand-to-hand combat. With ranged weapons against multiple enemies, all enemies that can attack may do so. In hand-to-hand combat against multiple enemies, enemies will stagger attacks so that no more than two are actively attacking at any one time.

Protect

The enemy will defend a region or object, but not pursue you. *Protecting enemies* may flee when their health has been reduced, or they may go berserk.

Flee

The enemy will run. *Weakened enemies* may attempt to run when their health reaches a certain preset level.

NPCs will usually react by fleeing.

Warn

The enemy will move toward an *alarm button,* or if equipped, reach for his radio to warn others of your presence.

NPCs may also react in this fashion.

A warning will immediately put all enemies in the region into an active state.

Berserk

An enemy that is *berserk* will fight to the end. The only way to stop this enemy is to kill him. Berserk enemies will not warn others, as they are too busy engaging you in combat.

ASLEEP

An enemy that has been knocked out in hand-to-hand combat is considered *asleep*. The *asleep enemy* may not perform any actions. Asleep enemies lose all awareness. An asleep enemy may be awakened by another guard after thirty seconds of inaction. *Asleep guards* may also wake up on their own after a preset amount of time.

An *awakened guard* will reactivate at the alert level, and immediately attempt to return to their patrol region, unless they can detect your presence, in which case they will move to their active state.

DEAD

An enemy that has been killed through gunplay or knocked unconscious through the use of a special weapon is considered dead. Dead enemies cannot perform any action for the remainder of the level.

A *dead enemy* that is discovered will initiate an alert response in other enemies. Dead enemy models can be dropped from the buffer, but their spawned items (weapons, health) should remain.

CHARACTERS WITHIN THE LARGER GAMING EXPERIENCE

By their very nature, games force a set of basic rules on otherwise complex events and situations. Creating the rules, and then playing by them, establishes the context, the structure and the goals of the experience. Rules allow us to set expectations and define winning and losing.

In games, unlike in real life, we need to create a set of rules for our characters so that we can categorize them, and then utilize them to support the various elements of the overall design. That doesn't mean we can't create a compelling set of characters with multifaceted and convoluted relationships and interactions. However, we have to recognize that all the characters that are in the game are there to serve the overall experience. If we are developing a character that doesn't neatly fall into a category, we have to anticipate how this will not only affect the story, but the gameplay as well.

The templates that we use to create characters and the organizations that they belong to are not static; we are constantly adding to them and tuning them for specific projects. You should experiment with them in much the same way. Treat them as springboards to help you in developing your characters, and you'll be surprised by the depth of understanding you'll gain in your own creations. And if your characters become so rich, so complex that they confuse you, confound you, start talking back to you, or even take on a life of their own, well, so much the better.

STEPS TO THE GAME CONCEPT AND SCRIPT

DEVELOPING THE CONCEPT

Video game writing is a process consisting of many "deliverables" for many purposes. Unlike any other kind of writing, your deliverable does not, in the end boil down to a single focused document. It consists of a number of documents delivered at different points in the production. Oftentimes you will have to deliver unrelated items at the same time. For instance, you may write a "sample scene" for the game demo while you are writing the outline for the story.

You can think of this as a parallel process. While it is the tendency of writers to want to work from macro items to micro items (for example, from the outline to individual lines of dialogue), you'll find that you might have to do these simultaneously. The good news is that game writing is a very iterative process and you'll probably have multiple opportunities to nail down dialogue and other items.

WHAT IS THE HOOK?

Hook is one of those words designed to annoy writers. Producers who've had a dangerous amount of exposure to the film business might ask you, "What's the hook?" Of course there is no working definition to the word *hook*, but it vaguely means, "What's the thing that's going to grab people right away?" (It originated in the music business, where it is the "catchy" thing either lyrically or musically in a song that causes you to focus your attention on the tune.)

For our purposes you can think of it as the back-of-the-box copy, or even just the headline for the back-of-the-box Copy: "Joey Rose must sacrifice his soul to enter the Gates of Hell and fight Lucifer himself."

ACTION ITEM (BETA)—WRITE A HOOK
Write a single line hook for a game you'd love to create or play.

WHAT IS THE STORY?

This usually boils down to a story premise (some people call it a treatment, though technically that phrase isn't right). This is a short document (think two to four pages) that sums up your story. You want to keep the premise short because there is a natural human tendency to get sidetracked and oftentimes an entire treatment can become derailed by largely irrelevant details.

WHO ARE THE CHARACTERS?

These include your main characters, the player character (or characters), his friends and allies, the main (ambient) boss (typically who you defeat in the last level), level bosses (those guys you defeat at the end of every level) and, minions for all of the bosses. These are extremely important in games, because the player will spend the majority of his time taking on seemingly endless numbers of these guys. Also, you want to give some thought to the population of your game. Are there people in the game who are neither friends nor enemies? Who are they?

WHERE ARE THE LOCATIONS (AND WORLDS)?

Games are about *worlds*. You live or die by the world of your game. *Grand Theft Auto* exists in a world of criminals and hookers and cops and innocent citizens. The art and locations of this world obviously reflect its inhabitants. We've covered a bit about the world of a game already. The point here is that you must consider spending a lot of pixel space on the world.

WHAT IS THE FRANCHISE?

Franchise is another word that you will bump into. It means a lot of different things in different contexts to different people. The basic meaning is: What is the thing that will make people buy *Spanklords from Neptune II, III, IV* and *V*? What makes it into a movie or a TV show? What can we spin off to make another game? What makes it extensible to multiplayer and online?

Franchises are the Holy Grail of the mediasphere nowadays. You'll have to do some thinking about this: Is it understanding what your client wants to accomplish or trying to create your own franchise? This may amount to a flashy couple of paragraphs in your document, or it may be a huge issue. In the case of licensed properties, you may be called on to do a franchise document. For instance, if you are doing James Bond, you might be called on to name every mark you have to hit (e.g., he has to say, "Bond, James Bond" at some point in the script).

SCOPE AND SCALE

Ideally, you will know the scope and scale of the project by the time you make your deal, but rarely does it work out that way. Often this is unknowable, though the game will almost always get smaller over time (though sometimes your part grows exponentially—usually to compensate for the game shrinking). In any case, you want the best idea you can get at the outset of how much you'll be delivering and what your working method will be. Sometimes you'll be asked to come up with this from scratch; sometimes level designers will rough the particulars out for you for "clean up." There are questions you can ask to rein it in:

* How many levels is the game intended to be?
* How many minutes of cinematics are you budgeted for? (Don't be surprised if nobody has the answer to that question.)
* How much voice-over (V.O.) do you expect? A sneaky way to get to this is to try and figure out if they are using professional actors or not. Oftentimes the realities of V.O. budget dictate the length of the script. If they're using "in-house people" in their own recording booth, the sky is the limit.
* What is the storytelling strategy (i.e., voice-over, cinematics, text, still frames, etc.)? In this case, you want to avoid lip synch and tedious cinematics.
* What is your budget in terms of time, money, resource, and art?
* What is the game objective exposition strategy: ditto maps, IGCs (in-game cinematics—those that run inside the game's engine), pre-renders, etc.? How do we plan on telling the player what to do? If it is text, who writes the text? (This is usually working directly with the various designers.)
* What are the extrinsic deliverables? Although this is not in our direct game path, it is important if we want to go platinum: think tie-ins, website, books, graphic novels, film, TV—other stuff we want to be onboard to write.

HOW THIS TRANSLATES INTO DELIVERABLES

Hard deliverables are subject to approval, deadline, and payment. You want approval because you want to eliminate any vagaries. Things left vague have an uncanny habit of returning to bite you in the butt down the road. It is almost impossible for an executive legally and professionally to go back on an approval without a mea culpa. This buys you a lot. If he wants to make changes and send you back to premise, he is obligated, one way or another to compensate you for the trouble. In a subjective world, it is great to have things defined in black and white. It should be noted that we are not advocating distrust as a policy—quite the opposite. However, projects need benchmarks, recommitments and milestones and you should be sure that they have them.

Regarding the mission statement: It is very important that the entire team focus on a simple, memorable, one sentence or paragraph version of what the game is about. In those dark moments later on in the project (and they always come), you need clarity, something you can all focus on. You need the sign-off of everyone, both legally and creatively. You need not only dedication, but also commitment in every sense off the word. You need to have everyone on the team take the solemn oath that they agree on the project that they are making—no vagaries, no misunderstandings, and no passive-aggressive behavior.

A STORYTELLING STRATEGY DOCUMENT WITH PARAMETERS

This is a creative document that outlines what the storytelling strategy is going to be in terms of how it will apply cinematics, In game-cut scenes, voice-over, interface searching, etc. The idea here is come to agreement on these issues early on.

THE PREMISE

This is your short version (a paragraph to a page) of the story. It is your stake in the ground. It says, "This is the idea we're following in the most general terms." It gives you something to build from and it officially chases away all of the other story ideas that were flying around.

A STORY SYNOPSIS

Longer than the premise, perhaps four pages. It takes the reader from story setup to complications to resolution. Major characters and groups are described in brief; minor characters might be mentioned by name (in passing or thumbnailed). The object is to buy off on major story issues (or at least identify those issues that haven't been fully worked out).

SPRINGBOARDS FOR LEVELS

These are the basic *beats* (important moments) of the levels. The springboards are comprised of a sentence or a couple of sentences on the levels covering things like setup, characters involved, beginning, middle, end, and payoff.

CHARACTER BIOS

Offer longer bios of major characters, shorter bios of minor characters. You may also consider doing a short bio of the world if it is fantastical or mythical in nature.

LEVEL TEMPLATES

These are done for each level. There's a certain amount of debate as to whether level templates or outline goes first. Level templates are designed to be a "net to catch ideas." They contain an idea in its category and give it a context. When another person reads it, they are more likely to see where it fits into the overall concept. Whether you complete the template and then build a detailed outline or whether you build an outline and then make templates off of it is dealer's choice. (You're the dealer.)

THE OUTLINE

This is the story, laid out linearly (if it is to be linear) or nonlinear if it's a non-linear story.

BREAKDOWNS

These are scenes and voice-overs broken down.

SCRIPTMENT

We'll also sometimes write what we call a *scriptment*. This is a document that lives somewhere between a script and a treatment (hence the name). A script-ment is usually about twenty pages long, and may include key dialogue moments (with temp dialogue—but this can still convey the scene in ways descriptions often can't).

Scriptments are excellent ways to create a document with enough depth to explore all of the nuances of the story and how it will integrate, support, affect, and react to the gameplay before committing to an actual draft.

THE FIRST FIVE MINUTES

We were on an awards panel in which we had to review thirty games in three weeks. We walked away with one huge observation: **You can't overestimate the importance of the first five minutes of the gaming experience.** Rarely do reviewers, or anyone else, actually finish a game before they pass judgment on it. Usually, they've done a couple of levels, often as not with cheat codes. There isn't enough time in this life to play every game that's reviewed. And maybe people don't have to. Malcolm Gladwell, in his book *Blink,* argues that we can pretty much "thin slice" whether a game is any good or not in a few minutes. (He doesn't talk specifically about games, but the principle applies.)

Your first five minutes had better be compelling. The gameplay should be tight. The player should be hitting buttons and having a good time in the first thirty seconds. Backstory can wait or get ditched all together. A game should be like life. You live it in the present tense. You worry and hope for the future and sometimes you look back in nostalgia or look back for a key to the future, but you can't go back . . . not really. Think about flashbacks. How often in real life do you suddenly think back on something that happened in the past and have it profoundly relevant to the present or future time? It happens, but it's rare. It should be the same way in games. In the first five minutes the player should be confident.

He should feel like saying:

"This game is for me. I don't want to show up in an empty ninja training room with some Bitching Betty telling me how to do stuff. Give me some credit. I've been playing games for a while now. Find some way to make it painless for me. Teach me on the run, and not all at once. Make it invisible. Nobody wants to learn and I sure-as-hell don't want to go to the manual or the Internet . . .

"In the first five minutes, I should feel like a star. I should feel challenged and yet triumphant. I should feel like I'm going to get through this without a lot of frustration. I should like being this hero. I should like the way the world works. I should be curious about what it holds for me. I don't have to know everything. In fact, it's better if I don't. But I should see windows into possible futures."

ACTION ITEM (BETA)—THE FIRST FIVE MINUTES

Play the first five minutes of an unfamiliar game. Then stop. Do you want to keep playing? Did the game capture your imagination? Did you even get to take control, or were you still stuck in the opening cinematic when the five minutes ran out? Write down as much as you can about the experience.

SCRIPTS

There are various scripts: cinematic, in-game dialogue, onomatopoeia. These are defined as follows:

* ✳ **Cinematic Script.** Your normal script document. It looks like a screenplay broken down with scene names and descriptions.
* ✳ **In-Game Dialogue Script.** Often as not, this comes in an Excel spreadsheet form. Make yourself familiar with Excel.
* ✳ **Onomatopoeia Script.** This may or may not be tied to the in-game script. It is endless variations on phrases like "Ouch, that hurts!" or "Take that!" or "Is that the best you've got?" and includes kicking sounds, hitting sounds, etc.

THE UNIQUE CHALLENGES OF GAME WRITING

Game writing has a number of unique challenges that make it unlike creating content for any other entertainment medium. To begin with, you never know what you're getting into. When you are writing a movie, you know that it is a linear product. Your script is going to be somewhere between 90 and 120 pages, give or take. It usually has one beginning, middle, and end. You often go in with a relative idea of the budget, market, audience, and chain of command.

Most often, the screenplay is a "gating issue" for a movie: a film rarely goes into production without a completed and approved script. Of course, that doesn't mean there won't be brutal tinkering with the screenplay later on, but the process of idea, to development, to script, to production is a fairly predictable trajectory for a film.

GAMES LIVE BY THEIR OWN RULES

Games, on the other hand, rarely go into production with a script. In fact, we've never heard of it. The "gating item" for a game is the *design document* (and that document is always being revised throughout the development of the game). In addition to all of the details regarding gameplay, the design document will usually contain a story, which is often broken down over levels and include some brief character bios that read something like, "Harvey Spank is an Ex-CIA Navy Seal pulled out of retirement when Mohammed Akaida returns from the dead to begin a reign of terror." The story is, more often than not, a series of missions punctuated with genre clichés. Nobody is really happy with it, but it got him or her past his or her first "milestone."

Now, you're faced with a challenge. Expand Harvey Spank into a real character worth caring about. Define the world in which he finds himself. Support the gameplay by working with the lead designer to find a compelling narrative that integrates with the core mechanics and characters. Work with the level designers to create *set pieces* that function as story anchors within the missions. Write scenes and dialogue for your hero, for NPCs (Nonplayer Characters), and for the main antagonist and his horde of minions. Then, generate potentially thousands of lines of incidental dialogue. And do it all in a constantly changing environment, where the deliverable may be thirty minutes of cinematics script one week, then an hour the next, then fifteen the week after that.

GAME DEVELOPMENT IS VOLATILE

The following is a short list of ways that your story can suddenly change on you.

* ✳ Ideas naturally grow and change: This is true of all mediums. As you get into the project, things happen. Sometimes you will be the engine of this change. More often than not, change will come from the producer or the lead designer. There may be a good, rational reason, or it may occur on a whim. Caprice happens a lot in game development. On a movie set, nobody much cares what the crew thinks of the script. Not so with development teams: it is not unusual to find yourself on a conference call with all of the leads, and they've all got story notes. In game development, everybody has input, though sooner or later, a clear creative leader emerges.

* ✳ Another game comes out that is similar to your game, or simply catches the eye of the team, and they react to it.

* ✳ Somebody, usually a marketing executive, does a "swoop and poop" (they fly in and change things to suit some usually misguided idea they have about content).

* ✳ The licensor has reservations about aspects of the game.

* ✳ You create more work for yourself by pitching an idea that everyone loves, and the team is determined to see it in the game.

DESIGNS LIVE AND BREATHE

Writers are well advised to see the game's design document as a wish list rather than a blueprint. It represents the highest hopes and best intentions of the lead designer (in fact, of the entire development team), but it has a very tenuous relationship with reality. We can't remember a project that didn't undergo massive revisions, usually cuts (Everything Always Changes), somewhere between the halcyon days of the first draft of the design document and the brutal realities of "crunch time" (when the team is trying to make their Gold Master deliverable).

The following things will all happen at one point or another while you are working on a game (we're making some more broad, but accurate, generalizations based on our experience):

✳ Levels will come and go (almost always go).

✳ Characters will be cut or collapsed into each other.

✳ Cinematics (narrative cut-scenes) are always shortened. Always. Every narrative-driven project starts out with this idea of endless cinematic storytelling and then ultimately boils down to somewhere around thirty minutes of narratives with some additional in-game sequences and lots of voice-over.

✳ The schedule gets collapsed. Now that we find ourselves in a world of huge licenses, with day and date releases (game releases tied to movie openings), developers and publishers are sometimes overwhelmed by the needs of players outside the development loop. And for an original title, marketing is always pushing for a Christmas release.

✳ The budget gets crunched (usually an indication that the publisher has lost confidence in the project).

✳ There is a huge technical blow (we can't do flying in our air-combat game).

✳ You suddenly get the attention of the "higher ups," and the game's profile rises within the publisher, putting all sorts of pressure on the developer to deliver a Triple-A title that meets the new expectations of the executives who have suddenly discovered what they believe to be their next hit.

✳ Some combination of all of the above.

✳ So how do you construct a story in a world where the only certainty is massive change?

BUILD 'EM TO BREAK

When you are writing a movie, you don't get a call where your producer says: "You're not going to get a leading lady." You might get a call that says you're not getting a specific star, but rarely will a producer call to tell you to remove a main character from your script. In games, some version of this situation happens all the time. You will always get what we refer to as *the bad phone call*. You might even get more than one. Elements leave. Levels are removed. Characters are cut. Features change. So, you have to build a story that can recover from the "damage" no matter where it comes from. You have to plan for the inevitable, and then be ready to implement your "fixes" when you get *the bad phone call*.

We refer to this as our *build it to break* theory of story construction for video games. Here are the core tenets:

✳ Never make the entire story dependent on a single element, whether it is a character, location, prop, set piece, etc.

✳ Write at least three major set pieces, with the expectation that one of them won't make into the game.

✱ Create at least one backup character that has similar motivations, skill set, and backstory to some of the minor characters in the narrative. If these minor characters get cut, your backup is ready to fill in the gaps created by their absence.

✱ Write at least one "universal bridging device" scene that can just as easily get you from Point A to Point B as it can from Point A to Point D (when B and C get cut). For example, stage action, such as a mission briefing, inside a helicopter that is flying to the next location, rather than writing the scene to take place after the helicopter has landed.

✱ Limit all of the main action to your core cast of characters. This will significantly reduce the number of permutations that may result if a character or level is cut.

✱ Preplan the optimal places within the narrative to "cut and paste" as you create the game story. Often, when the cuts come, the team will ask for your advice and input on how to solve the problem. Showing them how to cut two levels without creating any significant impact on gameplay (because you thought of it in advance in anticipation that this day might come) is great way to not only preserve the integrity of your content, but also have a "hero moment" with the team.

✱ Create a separate V.O. (voice-over) document of dialogue that can either be an internal monologue, or a recounting of some of the major action within the narrative, as seen through the eyes of one of the main characters. When all else fails, a few well thought out lines of voice-over can cover a whole lot of gaps.

"Not enough bandwidth" and "had to make cuts" is usually all the explanation you are going to get when it's time for revisions. For all bitching and complaining about big corporations, most publishers are actually fairly liberal about the power they give to the teams. Teams tend to function like democracies—almost to a fault. Everybody has input and, it seems at times as though everybody's input has to be acted on.

ACTION ITEM (ALPHA)—CREATE A CONTINGENCY PLAN

Imagine that tomorrow, your normal route to work or school has fallen into a black void, one that you will need to avoid lest you too become trapped. Now plan another way to get to your destination. What pitfalls must you avoid? How much time is your alternate path costing you? Is there a possible shortcut? As best you can, write it down.

CHARACTER (BY EXTENSION, PLAYER) NEEDS AND OBJECTIVES

As in real life, we often have multiple needs and objectives even in a single moment of a game. If you're driving to Los Angeles from Chicago, you might need all of the following things at the same instant:

* ✳ Gas
* ✳ Food
* ✳ New music
* ✳ A map with an alternate route past some nasty weather
* ✳ The phone number of some girl you know who lives in Chicago
* ✳ A bathroom
* ✳ A set of chains so you can drive through icy mountains
* ✳ An explanation from the Almighty as to why some places are so beautiful and some are so ugly

Okay, maybe you don't need the explanation, and you probably have different levels of urgency for these things, but before you can check off the "L.A. trip" objective in your life, you will need all the other things. You'll need some of them multiple times. All of them are part of your story, but not all of them are things you want to emphasize.

For instance, the trips to the gas stations aren't usually exciting unless you're in, say a *Road Warrior* world where gas stations are fortified and you have to fight your way to get gas. A trip to the bathroom isn't interesting unless bathrooms in this story are portals to alternate worlds (which, it could be argued, they often are on cross-country rides).

In his book, *Everything Bad Is Good For You: How Today's Popular Culture Is Actually Making Us Smarter*, Steven Johnson calls such things "telescoping objectives." That means they are objectives within objectives, some essential, some optional. (Let's say you've conserved ammo, so that you might not have to make that dangerous side trip to get more ammo.) While normally the writer is only concerned with the high level objectives in the game—in this case, the girl and why you need her mountain—the explanation from the Almighty (if this is happens to be a metaphysical motorcycle travel game) might actually be important.

INDUCTIVE STORY AND DESIGN

Along with wanting to evoke that type of mentality, it also has to be polished and professional. Frankly, as game writers, we'd better have the skill to do an assignment that sounds something like: "Tie these things together: Our hero is riding a bird towards a fortress as he's attacked by fire vultures and jousters on other birds; then, write a scene where he is in the water swimming down to get a key from a dead man's hand; then, connect that to a scene where we are in a trap-laden treasure room." If we couldn't make that work, with a little give and take from the developers and publishers, with the tools we have, we shouldn't be in the business.

Let's call our approach *inductive game making*. We believe in the premise of doing cool things and having your game be the sum total of all the cool things you're doing. This doesn't mean that you don't have a plan, but it contrasts with the much more common practice of *deductive game making*. That's the model in which you start with a 20-level massive world game and end up with a 4.5-level linear game. You keep deducting stuff from the game when it is either too ambitious, too hard or no fun until you end up with the essence of the game. We understand the theory, no matter how well it is couched in euphemism. "We're still at 135 percent," meaning: "We intend to make 35 percent more cuts, whatever that means," or "We're right-sizing the game."

There is always a bunch of frustration, disappointment, and retrograde action when the arbitrary cuts come through. Let's say we compromised and said, "Okay, we're going to design 50 percent of the game and let the other 50 percent emerge as we develop it. We have a creative road map with built-in flexibility. We'll seize opportunities and dump things that don't work. We'll constantly test and take advantage of emergent gameplay." With this approach, games would certainly be more interesting, and more about the vision of the creators, rather than simply trying to hit every checkmark of a genre.

Nevertheless, in fairness to the "locksmiths," there are points where things have to stop changing. Ideally, things should be locked (also called freeze—as in design freeze, code freeze, art freeze) at the last possible moment and the door should never be shut to innovation or exploitation of an opportunity. Fact of the matter is, the further you get in the process, the better the idea you have of what is fun and unique, what is doable and not doable. Hence our argument for an inductive, iterative development process.

THE HIGH-LEVEL DESIGN DOCUMENT

All games start somewhere, usually with a burst of creative inspiration. But once the initial idea has taken root, it is time to share it. That means creating documentation for others to review. Most often, the first pages generated in the development process come together in what is called a High-level Design Document (also referred to as a Concept Document). Here's the structure we use in creating ours.

THE ONE-SHEET

The *one-sheet*, also called the Executive Summary, is up front in your design document. You may even find that you create a separate one-sheet or executive summary document of your game. The reasons for this are numerous. First, this is a fast way to pitch the game to busy decision-makers. Secondly, it allows everyone else who might be interested, or have input, to see an encapsulation of your vision. Perhaps most important, it forces you to figure out exactly what is the core gameplay experience you're creating.

Often, we'll start by trying to write the manual. If you can do this, and communicate all of the ideas that you hope to achieve in the game, then chances are good that your design is solid. You'll find that the longer and more detailed the document gets early on in the process, the more "idea drift" you are likely to experience (A one-sheet can be anywhere from one to five pages in length. Go figure).

So start by trying to write the one-sheet. The elements of the one-sheet are as follows:

TITLE

The title of your game. If you are not yet settled on a title, it is a good idea to include (working title) in parenthesis. Spend some time on this and really think it through, because your title is your opening salvo. It should be something memorable, and should tie into the main theme, action, character, or genre of your game. Will a catchy title be enough to sell your game? Of course not, but at this point it can do two important things for you: It can set the title (and by extension, your game idea) in the mind of your audience and it can draw them into your document.

GENRE

Some common genres are FPS (First-Person Shooter), Third-Person Action, Stealth, RPG (Role-playing Game), Simulation (Driving, Flying, etc.), Survival-Horror, RTS (Real-time Strategy), Platformer (sometimes called Hoppy-Jumpy), and Sports. Sometimes, your game will include more than one element from multiple genres. If so, then call it a hybrid, so you have to list the genres that best describe the envisioned gameplay. Listing a genre is important, because, like film studios, developers often have a slot to fill, and they are looking for a specific type of game, or gameplay.

VERSION

Usually, we'll put a version number on our document, but not a date. Why? Anything with a date has a shelf life attached to it. If you submit a document in January, and it is reviewed by a publisher in May, it doesn't feel as fresh and new when a decision maker reads it. Also, it implies that a lot of time has fallen off the calendar since you first took the project out. By simply assigning a version number instead, you can keep track of the document, verify that your executive has the latest draft, but do so in a way that does not draw attention to how long you've been shopping the project. Remember, everyone likes to think that they are the first ones to see a new idea, and that the idea is coming to them "oven fresh." Don't put anything on your document that can make it look stale. Note: this same note also applies to any "Header or Footer" that you choose to put on your document.

THE BIG IDEA

Put a brief synopsis of your content (story, character, worlds) and your gameplay here. In one or two paragraphs, describe the essence of the game experience.

CATEGORY

Similar to genre, here go ahead and list a few games that compare to your title. You might say: *"Game X* (your game) is a unique experience that combines the fast-paced action of *Game Y* with the open environment worlds of *Game Z."*

If you have a unique gameplay or content "hook," this is where you should feature it.

Also, is your game Single Player, Multiplayer (local, network, wireless or Internet), Cooperative, etc.? If it's Single Player, do you have a "campaign" (a series of missions or levels with a possible narrative storyline that progresses as the player advances through the game)? If so, this is where to put a brief description, and if possible, compare it to other games in the marketplace.

One final note: Never badmouth another game in an attempt to build up your own. Always make favorable comparisons, never negative ones. And try to pick games that are successful in the marketplace. It should be obvious that you don't want to say that your game is going to be a comparable to another game that has failed; yet we see this done all the time.

PLATFORMS

List the target platforms for your game (PlayStation 3, Xbox 360, Nintendo DS, PC, etc.). Note that each time you list a potential platform for your game, you will need to explain why it is important to release the game for that platform. Some games are better than others as multisku titles. If your game is really optimized for a single platform, say so, and why.

LICENSE

If the game is based on a license (film, book, comic, etc.), describe the license here. Also, if the game is utilizing licenses (such as identifiable brands), name them. Finally, if this is an original intellectual property, briefly explain why it can become a license (lay out the foundations of the franchise). Remember that your reader is looking for more than a one-shot deal. Think about how can your game be more than a game.

PLAY MECHANIC

This is the core gameplay and control of the game. For instance, in a driving simulation, the play mechanic would be driving the car. However, this can go an additional step to include unique elements, such as crashing the car, upgrading the car, or using it to run over pedestrians. The play mechanic describes how the player interacts with the gaming experience, and how and why it will be compelling and fun for him to do so.

TECHNOLOGY

Provide a summary of the technology you plan to use for the game. If you are using middleware, list the engine and tools that will be employed. If the engine is proprietary, list its key features. Note that there are separate documents that will have to be included from the engineering team that will fully detail the technology for the game (often called a TDR—Technical Design Review). That is not anything that you need to worry about for this part of the document, though you should have an accurate description of the tech, and why it is the best solution to execute the game.

TARGET AUDIENCE

Who do you expect to play this game and why? You can describe a specific demographic, but it is more helpful to describe a type of gamer.

KEY FEATURES—USPS (UNIQUE SELLING POINTS)

Here, list the key elements of your game that make it unique. Think of these as the bullet points that would be listed on the back of the box. Keep this to about four to six features. You can describe more later in the document if you need to; for now, you are hitting the high points.

MARKETING SUMMARY

This is a quick list of why this game will do well in the marketplace when compared to others. Also, think of "hooks" that marketing people can get excited about because early on, they—more than almost anyone else—determine the viability of your project. If marketing doesn't think they can sell your game, it doesn't matter how groundbreaking you are, how many champions you have at the publisher, or how cool the lead character is. You're dead in the water if marketing is against it.

Describe how the player will control the game and advance. Is the game "twitchy"? Does it rely on combos that will take a while a while to learn? Are there "skill levels"? Does the game have multiple play modes, such as shooting and driving? Are there any minigames? Is there an inventory system? Can you "level up" the hero character? And so on.

As with the big idea, describe the core mechanics in as straightforward a manner as possible.

> ### ACTION ITEM (BETA)—EXECUTIVE SUMMARY
> Write an Executive Summary of a game you want to make.

THE HIGH-LEVEL DESIGN DOCUMENT

Now we are into the meat of the document. Everything that has come before should be no more than three to five pages in length (and separate it from the rest of the document so that, if need be, it can be a "leave behind" that is independent from the rest of the High-level Document). As we move beyond the one-sheet, we start filling in the details, and providing more specifics about the envisioned game we want to create.

PRODUCT OVERVIEW

Reintroduce your core game concept, this time fleshing it out. If you have a lead character, this is also the time to start filling in their details.

THE CORE CONCEPT

Describe the main elements of the game. Include any and all of the following things that are relevant to your title, but don't extensively detail them here (that will come later). Instead, show how each of these elements incorporates into the larger gameplay experience:

* Characters (Including the PC—Player Character)
* Worlds
* Gameplay
* Combat
* Hand to hand
* Weapons
* Movement
* Interactions
* Vehicles
* Story
* Realism versus Fantasy (Fiction)
* Controls

PLAYER CHARACTER

Now describe the player character in detail, and their journey through the game. Note that if you have more than one character that the player will control, describe them all here. What do you hope to accomplish in the relationship between the player and their character? How will you achieve this?

NARRATIVE DESCRIPTION OF GAMEPLAY—AKA THE "GRABBER"

In this section, take a key *set piece* from the game, and describe it as if you were telling a story. Often, we'll put the player-controlled actions in a different font, or bold them, to make them stand out from what the player is seeing on the screen.

What you want to impart is the interaction/reaction dynamic (cause/effect) of the game, and how that manifests itself on screen.

The Grabber is also referred to as the hook. By that, we mean something that is intended to hook (or grab) your audience's (or readers') imagination. This is where a cool, over-the-top element or set piece from your game should go. Think how can intrigue people with the Grabber and leave them wanting more.

ACTION ITEM (BETA)—WRITE A GRABBER
Write a Grabber for your game.

STORY
Here you provide a beat sheet of story and how it integrates with the key gameplay. Detail how the story enhances the experience. Key off the moments you explored in the Grabber.

INTERFACE
The interface is how your player(s) will interact with the experience. Describe the elements of the interface:Are they configurable by the player? Is the interface intuitive and easy to use?

OBSTACLES
List the main obstacles that the player as the hero must overcome to win the game. These can include:
* Enemies (thugs, cannon fodder, midlevel bosses, level bosses, end boss, etc.)
* Environment
* Scripted events
* Puzzles

INTERACTIONS
Describe how the player interacts with the game to advance through the experience:
* NPCs (communicating, controlling, etc.)
* Worlds (exploration, manipulation)
* Weapons (combat)
* Equipment (gadgets)

LEVEL WALKTHROUGH

Take the reader through one level of the game, describing all of the key action, and interaction that takes place. What will the player experience? How are gameplay and story integrated?

ACTION ITEM (BETA)—LEVEL WALKTHROUGH

As best you can, write a level walkthrough. This can be for a game you want to make, or if you prefer, your current favorite title. Include details where needed, but try to keep your walkthrough under three pages.

INTRO CINEMATIC (IF APPLICABLE)

Describe the intro cinematic that leads the player to the first part of the game, or to the shell screen.

GAME SHELL (FRONT END)

Detail the game shell (start screen, load screen):

* ✳ Options—List the options available to the player (widescreen, sound, autosave, etc.)
* ✳ Load/Save—Describe the details of saving and loading a game.

CONTROLLER CONFIGURATION

This has to do with button mapping (assigning buttons on the controller to specific functions you can perform during gameplay). Note that this will often change during the development of the game, so just lay out your best version of the proposed controls (everyone realizes that these will change, but mapping a controller will also show you if you are thinking about too many complex interactions—if you can't map it, you can't play it). Also, if the player can custom-map the controls, detail that here.

CHARACTER ACTIONS

List the actions your playable character can perform.

* ✳ **Movement.** Describe how you control movement.
* ✳ **Using Objects.** List how you interact with objects.
* ✳ **Character Interaction.** Describe how you interact with other characters.
* ✳ **Combat Description.** As precisely as you can, list the elements and actions of combat in the game.

✳ **H2H (Hand-to-Hand) Moves.** Include a list of the various fighting moves that the player can employ during hand-to-hand combat if it is part of the game.

✳ **Weapons.** Detail of the main weapons you can use.

✳ **Other Items You Can Control.** These are items such as combat within vehicles. If this is your primary gameplay, then it should obviously be listed first.

EXPLORATION

Describe how the player moves through the world:

✳ Linear versus free roaming
✳ Advancing through levels
✳ Advancing the story
✳ Manipulation
✳ Using/taking objects (items)
✳ Setting off triggers

INTERFACE

This is a description of the user interface for the game:

✳ Components
✳ Inventory
✳ Items
✳ Weapons

DIRECT EFFECTS ON CHARACTER

Describe how the player utilizes, maintains, gathers, and loses health during gameplay. Also, if they are affected by power-ups, which can increase their abilities, describe how this works:

✳ Health
✳ Damage
✳ Armor
✳ Replenishing health and armor
✳ Character death
✳ Power-Up

LEVELS

In this part of the document, create a list of the levels of the game. Include how the player progresses from one level to another. Often, the number of levels is a direct reflection of the size/scope (ambitions) of the game. Keep this as realistically feasible as possible for the schedule and budget you are proposing as you describe:

* Descriptions by level
* Key enemies, NPCs per level
* Story elements

ART

If at all possible, attach any concept art here, including:

* Character designs
* Level maps
* Weapon/Item concept art
* World concept art
* Sample textures
* Sample interface
* Sample front end (game shell)
* Cinematics storyboards

CUT-SCENE AND STORY SYNOPSIS

Include a breakdown of the main narratives for the game:

* In-game (real time)
* Possible pre-renders
* Incidental (in-game) dialogue
* Event triggers that are story dependent

SOUND

Describe the sound needs for the game in as much detail as possible:

* Character sounds
* Enemy/NPC sounds
* Dolby digital 5.1
* Music
* Streaming audio within gameplay
* Using music and efx to set moods
* Licensed versus original compositions
* Vocal recording (voice-over) sessions and wish-list stunt casting (ideal actors for the roles)

DEVELOPMENT SUMMARY

If you are able, this is where you want to put a summary of the development process needed to complete the game. The summary would include things like:

* Preliminary schedule
* Budget
* Engineering acquisitions and schedules
* Personnel bios and resumes (of core team members)
* Risk Q-and-A (a list of questions and answers anticipating the most likely issues that will be raised by readers and decision-makers reviewing the document)

LOCALIZATION

This is the process of optimizing the game for other markets. Describe the complexity (or ease) of localizing your game. Cover the following:

* Overview
* Languages
* Text
* Speech (full localization)

CONCLUSION

This offers one last chance to pitch your game, and describe why it must be made.

Hopefully, this gives you an idea of all the elements and planning that go into dreaming up and presenting a video game. Next, we'll get more specific about the steps necessary to get into a script for the game.

ACTION ITEM (GOLD)—CREATE YOUR OWN HIGH-LEVEL DOCUMENT

Utilizing the presented structure, write your own High-level Design Document. Fill in as many of the details as you can. If you are unsure about an item, leave it blank. During the process, think about how your perceptions of what you want to create are either affirmed or challenged by the task of addressing these elements of the game.

8

GAME PROPERTIES AS FRANCHISES

THINKING IN FRANCHISE TERMS

Any ambitious person who creates entertainment properties would like to see their creation last as long as possible. While not everyone is going to come up with a *Star Wars* or *Halo*, there are certain elements and qualities that go into a franchise property. It probably helps to think of every game in terms of a possible franchise, because game publishers do. When story intersects (you can decide whether it is a smooth merge or a collision) into the nitty-gritty of game design, this is where the larger franchise elements you develop for the property can really come into their own.

Think about the unique ideas in your game, and how they could be expressed beyond gameplay and story. For instance, if your Vampire Hunters have developed incredibly cool bullets with a "heart tracker" and "holy water centers," it is good to explicitly tell the player this in the game. It's a great piece of dialogue for your "Q" character (James Bond's gadget-maker): "You're gonna love these Silver Specials . . . pure silver and filled with holy water. Use them when you've got a sure kill, because they're expensive."

Now, your unique ammo has become a franchise component. You can envision how it could easily translate across your property. Other characters can be creating their own custom ammunition to fight various creatures and monsters, maybe even you. As the player, you may have the opportunity to make your own ammo, utilizing a pallet of ingredients you collect or earn, turning a fun idea into a core gameplay feature. Once again, think of how this becomes a franchise: a game in which you get to customize weapons' ammunition as you see fit—from explosive rounds, to poison, to spread versus accuracy versus power, to incendiary, to magical, to those with a unique signature that identifies you as the shooter, etc. A simple idea has turned into a franchise builder. Your game is moving beyond shooter toward something more.

This is the core of building franchise properties. You don't always start with something new. Instead, you see something familiar in a unique way. Sword fights had existed in entertainment for years. But say "light-saber duel," and only one franchise comes to mind.

THE IMPLICATIONS FOR YOUR PROPERTY

Oftentimes, publishers and developers are inundated with minutiae and are in such a hurry to get their project going, they don't have time to think all the way through the franchise. Here's a classic example: We were doing a project with a character that was a bounty hunter. We all know how a bounty hunter works. He hunts people down for money (or some other treasure). He's a form of a mercenary. He's not doing it out of ideology, though it is a common character shift in mercenary stories to have the character get sucked into the cause—Han Solo in *Star Wars* is a good example. For the time being, let's think of the character as a straight-out bounty hunter. What would that imply for the game design?

First, there's the obvious implication that if the player is working for money, that money means something in the game. Therefore, an economy is clearly in the story. He has to use his money to buy things. That brings a lot of other things with it. He has to have a place to spend the money. He has to have somebody who pays the money. It carries the deeper implication that he has to operate in a cost effective manner—after all, a bounty hunter, even a mutant orc alien commando type bounty hunter is, at one level or another, a businessman. He wants to carry out his mission in the most cost-effective way possible.

HOUSTON, WE HAVE A PROBLEM

The problem with economy is that it has profound art, code, and design issues attached to it. You have to have things to buy, places to buy them, and you might even have issues of debt collection (which can lead to fun and unpredictable missions as well as a very interesting and complex world).

What if the development team hasn't thought of this? This happens to us with regularity in the real world. Often, you get an answer back that says something like, "We don't have the bandwidth to install an economy." To an engineer, this seems to be a good enough answer. To a storyteller, this seems like a fundamental violation of the contract of a bounty hunter game. This is where you have to appeal to design to bring the obvious gameplay elements of the genre into play.

CREATING SOLUTIONS WITHOUT VIOLATING THE FRANCHISE

If you can't find a solution, then think of a different spin on the franchise—he's not a bounty hunter; he's an indentured mercenary working off an abstract debt. The bad version of this one is that he was released from prison to kill forty guys and isn't free until he does it. If he fails, remote control or some such thing will terminate him. In this case, the developer doesn't have to spend money on an economy, but they have to change the spin of the franchise.

There are all sorts of shades of these solutions, and somehow you get past it all, but you will have to learn how to send up alarms now and again when you see a problem coming. The first line of this conversation might be something like: "Look, I think we have an issue we have to deal with. I think it's solvable, but it's not trivial." Lay out the issues and potential solutions and work from there.

Remember that it is much easier to unify the vision, integrate gameplay and story, and avoid potential pitfalls, if you think the franchise through at the start. Because once the franchise is cemented, the resistance to change and revision only increases. And if your gameplay or story is at odds with your franchise elements, you are in for some difficulties.

ACTION ITEM (ALPHA)—ESSENTIAL ELEMENTS OF A FRANCHISE

Take your favorite game and think about what is the absolute essential franchise element of the title. For instance, could *Metal Gear Solid* exist without stealth?

ELEMENTS OF A FRANCHISE

There is usually a *big idea* behind intellectual properties upon which franchises are born. While there may not be any magic bullet or formula, here is our take on what goes into writing a franchise script; We feel there are four main components to keep in mind (we touched on these earlier, but here they are again). In order, they are:

* **Theme.** What is the reason you are telling this story? In *Star Wars* the reason is the son's need to live up to the father he never knew while seeking love, approval, and respect. This theme rings stronger than "power corrupts" (the movies that followed the original film).

* **Character.** Franchise characters are well defined. People can understand, relate to, and root for protagonists like that. It's just the opposite for the antagonist. For example, Sara Conner in *The Terminator* knows that she is Mary to her son's savior. She has the burden of the world on her shoulders, so we understand why she is willing to go so far.

* **Tone.** What is it? Light, dark, real, fantasy, straight, comedy. It should be easily defined. In our friend Frank Miller's *Sin City*, he says, "People take a lot of killing in Sin City."

* **World.** There is a distinct sense of place that anchors the story in the meta-reality beyond our characters. It influences look and feel. For example, *Sky Captain and the World of Tomorrow* offered a retro 1930s yet futuristic look.

Another thing to consider in writing for a franchise is what happens when things go off the rails. Let's take a look at a few examples:

* ***The Matrix* Sequels.** They spent more time in the grunge world than in cool, pseudo-reality fetish world that had everyone excited. There were guns, lots of guns. People ran across walls, and jumped from building to building, and Neo could see things in "bullet-time." It was all so sexy. Then, they explained to us the world we weren't that interested in and made us spend most of our time there. If they didn't put it on the movie posters (Neo in his torn sweatshirt), then why make it the focus of the movie? The story everyone wanted to see (Neo using his new found powers to take control of "reality" and wake up other important individuals to fight the machines) is hinted at but never shown.

* **Jar-Jar Binks in *Star Wars*.** Why was he so hated? Because he introduced a tone that didn't previously exist in the series. Comic relief had been the province of R2-D2 and C3PO. That's all anyone wanted in the series. When Jar-Jar appeared it looked like the creators weren't taking the property seriously.

* **James Bond in *Octopussy*.** Roger Moore (friggin' 007!) was dressed up in a clown costume. A classic tone element of Bond was destroyed for a lame joke.

...hen put together, and working in harmony, character, world, tone, and then
...d your mythology. With this nailed down, you can think about how the i...
...be best exploited.

ACTION ITEM (ALPHA)—VIOLATING THE FRANCHISE

Using the above as examples, write down a moment from one of
your favorite games or films where you felt that the franchise was
violated. Remember, this is not always a bad thing; in fact, it is
sometimes needed to keep a franchise fresh.

FRANCHISE IN PRACTICE

We really learned the lesson of franchise flexibility (or lack thereof) when we were
trying to turn *Mission: Impossible* into a game. It was a good thing we had the following mission statement:

Our mission (which we've chosen to accept) is to create a mass market, compact game that can ship on time while fully exploiting the *Mission: Impossible*
license (cue the theme music).

We knew that, in order to be mass market, the game should be easily grasped
and played. Our goal was a very high completion rate without external aid (hint
books, online chat, schoolyard talk, etc.). We weren't concerned about replay and
variable play as much as we were with giving the gamer a great single-player experience. We wanted an extremely limited learning ramp and a "learn on the run"
strategy—a disguised training level if you will.

With *Mission: Impossible* (taken from the film, not the TV series), we reasoned that Ethan Hunt is a spy, while Solid Snake is a commando. That was an
important difference. Hunt is dressed (most of the time) as a character indigenous
to whatever environment he's in. That's why he frequently uses disguises and carries disguised gadgets. That's also why he has limited resources. Hunt's technique
is stealth and interaction. Hunt does not carry big honking guns around unless
he's in an environment where other people are carrying big, honking guns, or when
a mission has gone pear-shaped and he is now functioning like a commando. In
that case, a big honking gun should be acquired opportunistically and cleverly.

WRITING TO THE MARKET

In developing any game, you must consider your target player, and your target
buyer. They are not necessarily the same.

Suppose you are assigned to a game called *The Squishies* based on a very popular preschool program called, you guessed it, *The Squishies*. It seems pretty obvious that this should be an "E" game and everything about it should be tuned for the heart of the market, which is preschool. What does that bring with it? Your market is going to be primarily parents. Therefore, you are making a game to be sold to parents and played by kids. So, in designing and writing the game, you have to look at what the market wants.

Parents are a tricky market. At one level, they want a game that is, if not nutritive, at least not detrimental. They also probably want a game that will serve as a babysitter. That means a lot of hours of playtime. Most important, they want something that their kids are going to like, because they want to know they received value for their entertainment dollar.

Now, think about your player. What does that preschooler want in the game? Can they control their favorite characters? Can they sing and dance along like they do with the show? Will they be able to understand the core mechanics of the gameplay? Which platform is best suited to reach them?

Somewhat obvious observations like this are the type of things people most often miss when they get deep in on the creation of a game. Why does that happen? Because it is part of human nature that we all tend to want to satisfy our own interests; teams make games that they would like to play. Game designers aren't preschoolers. Therefore, they have to tune their interests to making a game that they would have liked when they were preschoolers.

This is an acquired skill, but it is one you must master if you're working in a demographic to which you don't belong (such as, parents). You have to write to some part of yourself, but it doesn't necessarily have to be you in the present.

FRANCHISES AND THEIR CREATORS

It is not uncommon that the most popular media products are generated by a single individual with the power to spread, amplify, and realize his or her vision. Look at the biggest entertainment properties in history. Homer wrote *The Odyssey*. George Lucas is the master of *Star Wars*. Ian Fleming created James Bond. Walt Disney created Mickey Mouse. Bob Kane gave us *Batman*. All right, so two guys, Siegel and Schuster, created *Superman*. There is only one Oprah Winfrey, who is a product herself.

George Lucas didn't create mythology, a fact he is well aware of given his promotion of Joseph Campbell's "myth" scholarship that he says enabled him to finish writing the basic *Star Wars* story. Lucas did not realize his vision alone. He had help with the scripts, and talented actors brought the characters to life. Effects wizard John Dykstra made the ships fly. All the people involved provided important and even essential things, but at the end of the day, all of these contributions were to service a single vision provided by George Lucas.

It's much debated whether Walt Disney would have been qualified to be an animator at his own company (USB Iwerks was the fellow he relied on in the beginning). It doesn't matter. Steamboat Willie (aka Mickey Mouse) will forever be known as Walt's creation.

Bob Kane's original *Batman* is thin compared to the rich character we saw in Frank Miller's *The Dark Knight Returns*, but in just a few pages, Kane created all of the vitals for the franchise. The four-panel section where young Bruce is looking into a microscope, doing parallel bars, etc. should be ingrained in writers' heads as what makes the very essence of a franchise.

The same could be said for the James Bond moments where he's driving the Aston Martin, seducing Pussy Galore, pulling off his scuba suit and revealing a tuxedo, humiliating a villain at a game of cards, using gadgets invented by Q, and speaking the signature lines "Shaken, not stirred" and "Bond, James Bond." These are franchise icons that have become embedded in culture.

This type of familiarity was not invented in the age of electronics. How about these items: 221B Baker Street, a calabash pipe, a deerstalker cap, a houndstooth coat, Dr. Watson, gaslight, a hansom cab, a walking stick, a magnifying glass. Any one of these items would probably cause the name Sherlock Holmes to flash across your mental theater. While we can argue all day whether Sir Arthur Conan Doyle was responsible for Holmes or whether his college professor was the true inspiration, what we cannot dispute is that Conan Doyle's name is on the entire canon of Holmes books. While he did not create any of the icons mentioned above, or even first write about deductive reasoning, he certainly synthesized them in a way that somehow still resonates to people 130 years later.

Let's put this in a video game context. Imagine if Holmes's icons had been argued over in a development meeting. He might have ended up with a corncob pipe and a top hat, used inductive reasoning, ridden around on an Arab charger named Sinbad, and been a drummer instead of a violin player. Would such changes have led to a worse character? That's a matter of opinion. It is very difficult to argue that he would have been a more successful character, given that Holmes has been translated into almost every medium and language in history—including more than a couple of video games.

There's no doubt that James Bond changed a lot in his translation to films. The gadgets, the girls, the effects we saw in the movies had a lot to do with the success of Bond. At the same time, when you look to the core of Bond franchise, it was all stuff Ian Fleming had in there from the beginning.

The point of this discussion is not to celebrate the creators but, instead, to discuss a context in which everybody on the team can work.

Not everyone can be the creator. If the game is a licensed property, the creator might be dead and gone and a "brand assurance team" manages the creative vision of the property. If it is an original property, the creator might be on the team, which needs to understand that it is executing his or her vision. And that visionary better have some degree of creative control. More properties than you can imagine have been ruined by some marketing guy rushing in with a corncob-pipe idea.

LEVEL 9

INSIDE THE
CREATIVE PROCESS

It's called the creative process, not the creative act, for a reason. Imaginative, inspired and inventive entertainment, regardless of the medium, rarely, if ever, strikes from out of the blue. Instead, it builds . . . you sense it first on the horizon, and then the more you observe it, and contemplate it, the more the storm begins to take shape, until you find yourself in the center of it. Then, when creative lightning does strike, it's not a surprise; it is, in fact, expected.

GENERATING IDEAS

As writers, each of us has our own style, our own creative process. Flint is a long-distance runner who paces himself and writes every day. His process is one of discipline and structure. Flint is the ultimate multitasker, able to give productive, creative attention to a number of projects. John, on the other hand, is a sprinter, who writes in fits and starts during bursts of chaotic energy (our friend Ed Neumeier, screenwriter of *Robocop* and *Starship Troopers* once called this "binge writing," which is the perfect description). Ideas will simmer for days, and then suddenly, creatively boil over. John tends to focus his artistic energies on one project at time.

A big part of what makes our writing partnership work is that we have opposite, yet complementary, approaches to the creative process. And while each of us finds his own way to the finish line, we always reach it at the same time. We have creative rhythms that work for us. Inspiration needs to be nurtured if it is to flourish, and discovering a creative process that works for you is what we'll explore in this chapter.

It is important to note that all writers have a unique approach to any artistic endeavor. But as professionals, it is our job to make sure that regardless of how we get there, the end result is a script and/or design that will excite and entertain. And if you choose to be a freelancer, you have an additional burden: No one is going to give you credit for just showing up, or always being on-time, or making a fresh pot of coffee when one is empty, or keeping your cubicle neat, or answering the phones when the receptionist is sick, or bringing bagels on Friday, or fixing the copier, or coming in on the weekend.

No, instead you are going to get paid for making approved deliverables on time. That's it. Your entire livelihood depends on your ability to do so. Fail this, and your career will be short and not very sweet.

To make sure that you are hitting your deadlines with quality material, you need to get to a place where your creativity flows. That means you need to have a method that allows you to generate and explore ideas.

Everyone has ideas, but your job as a writer is to exploit them, to build upon them, to mold them to fit the project you are working on, and ultimately, to document them in a way that communicates clearly and emotionally with others. Writing is the tangible expression of ideas. And just like the old saw about being too rich, or too thin, a writer can never have too many ideas.

RECORDING AND MINING IDEAS

KEEPING A JOURNAL

We have different feelings about keeping journals. John does not do it, while Flint keeps one and writes in it every day. His journal is a junkyard of writing warm-up exercises, half-baked ideas, laundry lists of what was done the day before, and a recounting of interesting moments. It's a written warehouse that has been growing for decades. For Flint, writing in it each day is a warm-up for writing everything else; like stretching before exercise. Flint limits writing in his journal to about twenty minutes or so. The journal's real value is that it's a safe place to keep thoughts about projects and the people involved in them. It's a place to not only organize ideas, but to free form them. There are lots of good reasons to keep a journal:

✳ It gets you primed for the day's writing by "running water through the pipes."

* It creates "writer's discipline" by giving you a self-imposed daily assignment.
* It's a safe place to vent any frustrations, which means you don't bring them with you into the project and your writing.
* It's a place to make note of any useful observations you've had.
* It can be a repository of random ideas about characters, set pieces, dialogue, etc. that may prove useful later.

If something good does come out of your journal ramblings, you can cut it out and paste it into its own document, something like what John calls an *Idea Mine*.

ACTION ITEM (BETA)—CREATE A JOURNAL

Create a personal journal, and for one week, write in it for twenty minutes a day. Remember that this document is something that will only be seen by you, so don't worry about trying to make it perfect. Misspell words, use sentence fragments, link thoughts, or mush them together into interesting non sequiturs. Each day, write about at least three things: how you're feeling and what you hope to accomplish creatively for the day, an observation that has artistic value, and an idea you have for gameplay or story, no matter how raw it may be. Whatever you choose to write about, limit yourself to twenty minutes. No more. Put yourself under the pressure of time. When the twenty minutes with your journal is up, ask yourself, "Is there more I want to write? More I'd like to add? Are there details that I want to fill in? Am I thinking about what I'm going to write about tomorrow?" If the answer to any of these is yes, then good, the act of keeping and nurturing your journal is awakening your creativity. Consider making it a habit.

THE IDEA MINE

While John doesn't keep a journal, he does keep what he calls his Idea Mine. This is his storage area for any interesting or worthwhile thoughts or observations. This lives as a separate folder on his computer, with a document that he just keeps adding to. For example, John may get an idea for an action set piece, and not know anything about how it connects to a story. That's okay . . . it gets written and placed in the Idea Mine. Or perhaps he hears a unique speech pattern from someone in front of him at the supermarket—the way they speak, maybe an accent, or even the turn of a phrase that catches his ear. It, too, gets written and goes to the Mine.

After a while, a body of work—disjointed and unfocused, but full of golden little nuggets—begins to develop. And when the time is right, that gold can be "mined" (hence the name) to help fill in the blanks in a project that we are working on. Many characters that have found their way into our scripts started this way.

Start your own Idea Mine to:

✳ Build a body of stock characters, set pieces, locations and dialogue that you can utilize in your work.

✳ Have a place to write down ideas while they are fresh in your mind, rather than lose them because they don't connect with the project you are currently working on.

✳ Practice your skills of observation.

✳ Refresh your memory of a specific event that may prove creatively useful at a later date.

✳ Have a creative sandbox where there is no pressure to have the scene, or character, or dialogue, or concept nailed down, but instead, have a place where you are free to experiment, maybe attempt multiple takes on the same material, and yes, even fail, in a risk-free environment.

ACTION ITEM (BETA)—WRITE FIVE CHARACTER STUDIES

As an exercise, go to your local coffeehouse, bookstore, or fast-food joint, and consciously observe five people. Think about their behavior, listen to the way they speak . . . observe their clothing, their carriage, how they interact with the world. Don't let your subjects catch you watching them, or, if you think you might get caught, wear a large trench coat and cough a lot. Now, with your observations fresh in your mind, write it all down. Create a *character study* that is a few paragraphs long for each. Fill in as much of the details as you can, and then create the rest, imagining their backstory. Finally, give them a reason for being where you saw them. Your Idea Mine now has five characters waiting on deck for your next story. Do this once or twice a week and soon you'll have your own unique cast to call upon when you are creating your fiction.

A final note: Don't overorganize your Idea Mine. Part of what makes it work is the random, hodgepodge nature of many ideas crashing into each other. Weird juxtapositions often lead to inspired bits of creativity that would otherwise be crushed by structure.

RECORD IT, OR LOSE IT

The point is, regardless of how you do it, whether through the structured and disciplined approach that Flint takes, or the more free-form and moment-of-inspiration style that John prefers, as a writer, you must be an observer of the external stimuli around you, as well as an introspective stenographer of your own internal dialogue. And when you think of, or witness something, that has "story value," you must first recognize it and then record it. There is nothing worse than having that great idea, or making that great observation, only to have it forgotten because you didn't get it on paper.

KEEP A GAME DIARY

If you're in it for the long haul, start keeping a diary when you're playing games. Write down what you like and what you don't like. Refer to it each time you start a project. Try to capture the immediacy of what is happening. Later on, go back and analyze it. Things like, "I can't get past the Creeping Blorch. It's really pissing me off," might sound stupid when you're writing them, but they're very revealing later on. Did you quit the game because you couldn't beat the Creeping Blorch, or did you have a great life experience when you saw him die a hideous death? What was the moment you were hooked on a game? You may have to go back later on to figure it out. Or, conversely, when did you *Frisbee* a game? Where were you when it came out of your machine, never to go back in?

A lot of the content in this book came from our game diaries: from notes and letters on builds, and from design documents. So start your diary now. If you don't like jotting stuff down by hand or keying in ideas, get a portable voice recorder and record your thoughts for transcription later on. Pay attention to your impulses. Bring your subconscious feelings to the conscious level. Before long, you'll feel like you're in the business.

THE CREATIVE KICKOFF

The project kickoff is all-important. That's the moment when there is a lot of opportunity to influence it in profound ways. You must pay close attention to the various obsessions (idée fixes) that those involved with the project may have. If people keep mentioning certain games or movies it does a lot of good to have the group look at the relevant materials together. Oftentimes, it's extremely valuable to spend a couple hours (or days) studying your competition. You want to know what they're doing right and how you can improve on it. And if you aren't going to improve on it, you might ask yourself why you're doing this game.

An approach like this gives you a good opportunity to get everyone on the same page by having good team-building moments: You are sharing common experiences, everyone is looking at any references or influences in a group setting, and concepts are being riffed while everyone is primed to create a vision for the project. Ideas are worth nothing if they aren't shared with the whole team. In fact, once a project really gets going there is often a great deal of *idea bounce*, in which a written description turns into artwork (or vice versa), both of which influence the design, which in turn then influences the code. Or a piece of design can influence the game story, or a piece of code can change the way the characters are textured or animated. And so on. When this happens, the team starts working like a well-oiled machine.

ACTION ITEM (ALPHA)—ARGUE FOR A CHANGE

Take a game that you really enjoy playing or admire and identify the one thing that you'd change to make it better. Then, write a compelling and persuasive argument for why this change should be incorporated into the game as if you were a member of the development team.

Another important reason to be as open and inclusive as possible during these *whiteboard* or *spitball* sessions is to make sure that all of the ideas and assumptions that are the foundation for your design and story filter through as many members of the team as possible. You will hear a number of differing points of view, some more nuanced than others, some in agreement, some hostile to the direction the game is taking. As a creative, it is your job to take that diversity of opinion and filter it into content that works for the project. Is that to say that you must run every idea by a committee? Of course not. Sometimes the most powerful and compelling content comes from the inspired vision of a single creator. However, being open to all ideas early on can only enhance the project, even if you later choose to reject most of them.

THE GREAT IDEA THREE MONTHS TOO LATE

This will also help you avoid one of the most tragic things that can happen in game development: the great idea that comes three months too late. More times than we can remember, a game will be in various states of chaos, maybe six weeks from Alpha, with milestones and budget crushing the team, when someone will say the most horrible thing you can hear . . . something like: "Wouldn't all of these problems just go away, and the gameplay be so much tighter, if we added a jetpack to the hero?"

What makes it horrible to hear is that they are right. The answer to making your game great, to truly making it sing as you'd always intended, has just hit your ears, and because of the schedule, and because of the budget, there's not a thing you can do about it. The best way to avoid "the great idea three months too late" is to hear as many ideas as you can upfront. And that leads us to timing.

TIMING

Timing is an important factor. Sometimes you want to let your idea germinate for a while and wait to present it to the team until you have fully thought it through. Conversely, the excitement and immediacy of the moment when inspiration hits can be contagious, and spread like wildfire through the entire production. Part of your job as a creative person is to know when to present your ideas, and how to do it in such a way that causes the most excitement and the least panic.

Don't go out of your way to avoid a little pain; most great games have an acceptable level of panic involved in their development; they challenge you to move beyond your comfort zone, and that's where the real magic often occurs (we discuss creative panic later in this chapter).

It would be nice to just generalize, but there really is no hard and fast rule; every situation and team is different. However, we believe the more you can front-load your ideas about the game, and share them and vet them with the team, the better off you and the project will be.

TOUCHSTONES

Wherever they start, whether it's in journals, Idea Mines, random musings, inspiration from other games or mediums (films, books, music, graphic novels, anime, etc.) or on a computer screen, all projects have beginnings, even if minimal.

When we were working with Andre Emerson on *Dead to Rights*, we started with the vague notion that we wanted to do a film noir themed, story-driven game set within the surreal physics and hyperreality of Hong Kong-style cinema. Andre didn't really know what noir was, but two months into the project he could have written a Ph.D. thesis on it. While both the game and story development took a lot of twists and turns, it is safe to say that the final project was indeed film noir meets Hong Kong.

The following "beginnings" are some touchstones we've encountered, as well as a few we've created to help inspire our imagination.

THE WAR ROOM

Strategy is all-important. The first time we saw a war room was while working with the Electronic Arts "Edge Team" on a project called *Soviet Strike*. In the open-

ing months of the project, the team began collecting every form of physical documentation available to make the project feel realistic. Mike Becker, the creative
director built hundreds of models of the military hardware that was going to be
used in the game. Artwork went up on the wall—at first it was just inspirational
stuff and then it was replaced, bit-by-bit, with artwork generated for the game. We
had a small sand table with which we planned out different levels. Eventually, huge
maps of the levels started going up on the wall.

What was once a forgotten little conference room became the creative nerve
center of the project. You walked in there and you were in Strike World.
Incrementally, what was known as "the Ozproject" began feeling important. The
producer, Rod Swansen, started bringing in high-tech interface designs. In no
time, we truly felt like we were in a war room. You could *feel* the game in that
room. Marketing felt it. So did sales. A game that started out as a marginal project turned into a major corporate effort. One trip into the room and everybody
"got it." If they didn't get it, they realized that everybody else did and it was time
to get with the program.

THE MOCK-UP POSTER

With *Fear Effect*, we had an entirely different situation. For this game, there were
a multitude of strong, creative opinions among a number of very talented individuals. Stan Lui, the owner and artistic visionary of the developer, *Kronos*, had been
playing with the idea of a Chinese-mythology morality tale for years. A number
of skillful artists, including John Pak and Pakin Liptawat, had created character
and environmental images that were beautiful on their own, but didn't convey the
property in a way that captured the imagination of the publisher. So we decided
to make a mock-up of a poster of the game, with our heroine, Hana, out front,
and her sidekicks Deke and Glas behind her. We took a chance and used character designs that had previously been rejected by the publisher because we felt that
they were the strongest, and closest to the vision we had for the game.

Combining John's characters over Pakin's backgrounds, and adding our title
in a unique font that captured the gritty, anime feeling we were after, did the trick.
That moment when we saw the final poster come out of the plotter was electric;
everyone—representatives of the publisher who had rejected the elements indi-
vidually wanted posters for their offices when they saw the elements combined—
suddenly grokked what we had been fumbling around trying to communicate;
from that moment, the vision for the game was, for the most part, unified. The
poster image became one of the dominant influences on the entire production. In
fact, when *Fear Effect* was released, the cover art for the game was a variation of
that poster, and it even used the same font for the title.

BOX COPY MOCK-UP

If it seems like you're missing something (originality or energy)—maybe it's a feeling that the game is going to be monotonous, or hasn't yet found its *voice*—try something as simple as writing the box copy (the maybe three-paragraph sales pitch on the back of the box that will be the "come-on" to the consumer—the "buy me" text) to see if you can generate that creative spark.

When writing your box copy, consider the following:

❋ Core gameplay and features (often referred to internally as USP—Unique Selling Points)

❋ The Grabber (or Hook)—the one-sentence summary of the project that grabs the imagination of that potential player and hooks them into buying it.

❋ Hero characters, creatures, vehicles, weapons, powers, worlds, etc.

❋ Story

❋ Depth of experience

As previously discussed, use temp artwork, either that you've had created, or snag images from the Internet that communicate your ideas. You are simply taking a first stab at what you're going to be selling. Later on, your ideas and editing can be done on the basis of whether or not they fit your box (or mission statement if you want to think of it in traditional business terms).

ACTION ITEM (BETA)—WRITE YOUR OWN BOX COPY

Using the elements outlined above, write the box copy for your original game, or an alternate version of the box copy of a game you have played. Think like the marketing department. Ask yourself, "What elements would they punch?" Keep it short and to the point (it's got to fit on the back of the box).

WRITING THE GAME MANUAL FIRST

Another technique that we employ that is similar to the box copy technique, but is a little more in-depth, is to start by writing a mock manual for the game. By that, we mean that we write a sample manual, including as much detail as we can about gameplay, controls and story within the format of a console game manual (since some PC games can have manuals that run into hundreds of pages, we stick with the console manual format for this exercise).

Because it is a manual, the text must be focused and to the point. This forces a lot of the clutter around your ideas out, and helps you get to the core of your content.

Take any game you admire that is within the genre, or reasonably comparable, to the game you are creating, and use its manual as a template to generate one of your own for your title. As you write, make sure that you are communicating to that potential player, that reader who has no history with your project and is coming to the game without any notions or knowledge of the experience he is about to embark on. It is your challenge to explain to him how the game works, and why he should pick up the controller and be jazzed about playing it.

Think of it this way: if you can't explain your core gameplay, or your fiction, to a reader within the confined structure of a manual, then you may want to revisit your design or story. As an exercise, writing the manual first is a great way to the get the essence of the game experience you intend to create.

MASTER COLLECTED NOTES

As the writer, you need a place to collect your ideas: Your own war room . . . or your *one-sheet* of inspiration.

We use what we call a Master Collected Notes document for each project. It contains all of the material that hasn't made it into the project yet, or might never make it. In many ways, it is a more focused version of the journal that Flint keeps, or the Idea Mine that John utilizes. In this case, however, it is very much project specific. We suggest you use one, and refer to it regularly. Keep it current. Give it regular feeding and care and it just may get you out of creative jam.

If there are other games, or graphic novels, or books or films that you see as being influential or inspirational for your title, start collecting them in a central location. Make sure everybody has seen them, or at least the parts relevant to the game. Burn references onto a DVD: moving pictures, even those created by someone else, are worth more than a thousand words.

When you use an idea from the Master Collected Notes, highlight it. Remark within the document why you used it. This will help you to create your own running commentary, a self-reflect critical eye on your own ideas. You'll find that certain ideas you continually reach for often form a pattern, and within that pattern, you may discover the core strengths of not only your story and game, but your creativity as well.

When an idea no longer fits, or has been rendered moot by events, delete it from the Master Collected Notes, but don't discard it. Send it back to your journal or Idea Mine; someday, you'll use it.

DON'T OVER-EGG THE SOUFFLÉ

Just as a script (or a book, natch) always needs editing, game concepts need editing as well. Throughout our careers, we've discovered that games can be just as hobbled by too many ideas as they can by too few ideas. Don't get us wrong: Having too many ideas is an embarrassment of riches. That is never the problem. However, trying to jam every single idea into a project is a recipe for disaster.

Don't over-egg the soufflé is a saying you'll often hear in the entertainment business (an over-egged soufflé doesn't rise so, by definition, it is no longer a soufflé). It's also called *gilding the lily*. Either way, it means don't add more than you need . . . it means finding the right balance . . . it means not losing your best idea among a sea of other ideas . . . it means creatively focusing in on what really matters. There's no hard and fast rule for the right number of ideas; you have to develop a sense of what to pursue and what to send back to your journal or Idea Mine for the next project.

In general, fewer concepts that are fully fleshed out are better than more concepts lacking detail. One strong hook that can capture the imagination is more powerful than a laundry list of features.

STRATEGIES FOR BREWING AND PRESENTING IDEAS

Ideas don't usually come out fully formed. Often, they are a fragment or an instinct or a vague notion in search of structure and meaning. It's okay if you don't always have ideas fully figured out before you start working with them. If you can boil an idea down to a visual or a tagline—something simple—it may be easily presented and accepted. Of course, it might also be easily rejected. Still, the main point is to get it out there, from your mind to the page, so you can start working with it.

THE BAD IDEA

As we mentioned at the beginning of this book, one trick we use for presenting a concept is what we call *the bad idea*. This is not a judgment on anyone's creative process; for us, it is a term of art.

When we are in a meeting and say, "Okay, the bad idea is this . . . ," what we are actually saying is, "I want to give you something I think is pretty good, but I don't want it shot down because it isn't thoroughly thought out." This is our way of limiting our vulnerability while freeing our imagination, and hopefully opening minds to the idea. We want to softly put something on the table for discussion. We call it a "bad idea" so that we can divorce it from our ego.

If it falls flat, well, it was a "bad idea," what did you expect? But if it inspires creativity, then everyone will quickly forget it was a "bad idea" and instead, begin to invest in it and find ways to make it their own. "Bad ideas" can often be springboards to some of the most amazing creative breakthroughs: think of them as imaginative icebreakers. "Bad ideas" are very valuable to the process, so get used to presenting them and try to encourage others to share them with you.

CASTING YOUR CHARACTERS

Characters can be easily illustrated with an archetype. For example, you might say your hero is like the actor Jack Black or maybe he's John McClane (Bruce Willis) from *Die Hard*. In the first, you are going for the entire persona that the actor has created through a body of work. In the second, you are honing in on a very specific fictional character created by the actor for a very specific piece of entertainment. However, both instantly bring a sense of the character to mind.

Comparing your character to a well-known actor or fictional character is a way to very succinctly express a notion to people in shorthand. For example, with both of the above examples, we know instantly that our character is going to face danger with a certain degree of humor, and that he will be cracking wise while facing overwhelming odds. One is more likely to talk his way out of trouble (Jack Black); one is more likely to shoot his way out (John McClane).

As you're writing, think to yourself, "Who would play these roles?" If you have some actors, or characters from other games, films, television, or books that you feel would be right, compile them in a cast list. When you are writing, imagine those characters or actors speaking their lines to you. Even if you never show your cast list to anyone, you'll find that your characters will be that much more alive, that much more real, because in your mind's eye, they were fully formed.

ACTION ITEM (GOLD)—WRITE A SAMPLE SCENE WITH YOUR DREAM CAST LIST

Do you have a favorite actor, actress, musician, politician, celebrity or fictional character that you'd like to perform your material? Well, cast them in your story. Take a scene with two siblings arguing over what to order for dinner. Now write that scene the way you'd see it play out with actors from your cast list. What are their dialogues, their mannerisms, and their blocking? Now, rewrite the scene with two different members from your cast list. Be conscious of the changes your make, and how a definable personality can affect dialogue, actions, and motivations. If you are adventurous, ask someone you trust to read your scene and see if they can identify the actors, and why. Their answers just might surprise you.

COMMUNICATING THE TONE OF YOUR IDEAS

When ideas for a game and/or story are initially presented, the first emphasis is usually on tone. The tone of your project should be firmly established before you get too far into the process of developing your ideas, as it will form the foundation upon which much of what is to follow is based.

If you are doing a franchise you might find that you have to pick and choose between various interpretations. For example, if you're doing James Bond, are you doing the Sean Connery Bond or the Roger Moore Bond or the Pierce Brosnan Bond? Each has its own unique tone.

In approaching your own project, you might begin by thinking the game should feel like the opening scene in *The Matrix*: a world where unreality is superimposed on reality, a world that is mysterious, fantastical and yet somehow grounded in a logic of its own; our world, but not. Once again, getting the tone right is essential if your content is this ambitious.

When we discussed *Dead to Rights* earlier, we said that it was film noir (tone) meets Hong Kong physics (tone). So in one sentence, you are already getting an overall sense of the creative direction of the project:

- The world will be dark and brooding (noir).
- The hero will speak to us in voice-over (noir).
- Most of the game/story will take place at night (noir).
- The action will be over the top (Hong Kong).
- The violence will be a blood opera of choreographed mayhem (Hong Kong).
- Gravity and physics are surreal (Hong Kong).
- Saying film noir and Hong Kong has allowed us to encapsulate the entire tone of the project, and it flows throughout the entire development, affecting design, art, and code.

Don't be overly broad when it comes to defining the tone of your project. Let's say you see your characters taking their situation seriously, no matter how preposterous the events might seem. So you tell someone your game is real world. That could mean that the dialogue should feel like real people are saying it, but to someone who doesn't yet understand what you're trying to communicate, real world could be a dangerous concept.

Games by their very nature are extremely unreal, so instead focus on how a real world tone manifests itself. For example, you might explain that everything happens in real-time, or that the world will be an exact model of five city blocks that actually exists or that if someone is shot, then the damage he sustains is life threatening. If your heroes are soldiers, explain that the characters utilize real

THE ULTIMATE GUIDE TO
VIDEO GAME WRITING AND DESIGN

world weaponry, operate on actual battlefields, and use authentic jargon rather than talking like a bunch of slackers who suddenly discover themselves in a Special Ops squad.

As we always tell ourselves, we're not in the game business; we're in the entertainment business. Video games are our primary expression, but here's a case where filmic references really do help everyone get on the same page and allow you to clearly communicate the tone of your project.

ACTION ITEM (BETA)—GENERATE A TONE BREAKDOWN DOCUMENT

In a page or less, breakdown the tone of one of your favorite games, films, or books. Think about how the tone of the piece affects your reaction to the work. Does the tone influence your emotional connection to the content? Ask yourself what would happen if the tone changed, but the content remained essentially the same. For example, if *Star Wars* was a serious, dark tragedy rather than an action-adventure with tragic elements, how would that manifest itself within the journey of the characters, the on-screen violence and the science-fiction universe that was created? Describe how a few tweaks in tone can have profound influence on the property you're writing about.

RESTARTING AND KEEPING FOCUSED

As a writer, ideas are your currency. Being able to effectively and compellingly communicate your ideas through the written word is what this is all about.

Obviously, there are aspects to the art and craft of game writing that are different than other mediums. One thing you'll encounter repeatedly is the stop/start nature of game writing: you'll have brief, labor-intensive times working on a project, and then there will be long periods in which you'll do nothing at all.

Game projects tend to gestate over an extended period, normally between eighteen months and two years, though development cycles can be shorter. That's a long time to maintain a vision and maintain your enthusiasm, particularly since both are likely to undergo all sorts of changes in that period, and, if you're like us, you will be working on many different things.

Restarting on a project has two aspects. One is to gain clarity of vision on what has changed since the last time you worked on the project. Have levels been cut? Have assets been cut? Has the focus of the game shifted? The second aspect is getting into the headspace of the project again.

GETTING BACK UP TO SPEED

We've learned over the years that usually nobody but the designer and writer knows how much work is engendered by a change in the project. Producers are notoriously bad at predicting such things. A trivial change for them might result in an amazing amount of work for you, and a huge change for them might end up with the cutting and restructuring of a couple of scenes. It's all an individual perception.

Remember that the producer, in addition to creatively overseeing the project, is also responsible for delivering the game on time. It can, and in fact, usually is, a crushing burden. Also keep in mind that they are seeing all sorts of moving parts that are outside your view.

Good producers insulate their creatives from the business machinations that are part of any game's development. We've been privileged in our careers to work with, and for, some of the best; they are our friends. We've followed them into battle, and gladly will again. And yet, these very same producers still drive us crazy. It's part of their job description. We don't take it personally and neither should you.

And so, the way of dealing with revisions is to take a deep breath and listen to the proposed changes. No matter how bad it sounds . . . don't panic. Panic is your enemy (we discuss creative panic later in this chapter). The best approach is to listen carefully to the changes and take notes. Create an assessment document in which you restate the revisions, and your approach to addressing them.

At this point in the process, it is time for you to let go of the things that are no longer relevant. This is where *creative amnesia* is an asset. You must will yourself to forget the great ideas that are no longer part of the project. Figure out the scope, scale and time frame of the next steps. Get sign-off on your approach. If you can't get a full sign-off, get approvals on your first steps. The point is that you want to become actively re-engaged in the project. You want to become part of the solution.

HEADSPACE

When the word *headspace* first appeared in the 1960s and '70s, it caused some people to wince, but it isn't a bad word. For our purposes, it as a technical term meaning: A particular state of mind that one is or desires to be in. You get the idea.

Let's say you worked on the first phase of a project and at a certain place and time you tuned into the project well enough that they kept you around for the second phase. In restarting, your goal is to be able to recapture and build on that initial headspace. The best way to achieve this is to move forward.

It doesn't matter how small the step is; you simply need to do something that reflects the new direction of the project. You have to get your hands dirty even when restarting seems so devastating you don't want to work. You have to make yourself do it, even if it is only a half-hour a day until you can work up a head of steam. Invest the time, and if nothing happens, walk away, collect your thoughts, and then attack the material again.

Try isolating all of the relevant documents you need to revise. Open them up, skim through them. Edit the old document, and even start adding some of the issues you need to deal with as notes within it. You are simply trying to get the project fresh in your mind again. It won't be long before you are rolling.

REVITALIZATION TRICKS

We call the following methods *Pavlovians*. They are little jump-starts that we use to get back into the headspace we had when we began a project. They work for some people and not for others.

MUSICAL CUES

When you are working, it is sometimes helpful to create a musical play-list relating to your project—as if you were making your own sound track for the real game. As a rule, instrumentals tend to work better and are less distracting than vocal tracks. Your custom sound track can be on the money (for instance, if you're doing a game that is *Aliens* meets *Lord of the Rings*, you can mix those sound tracks together) or you can choose music that is completely off the wall.

The idea is that the music is playing softly in the background and is subconsciously imprinting on you as you write. (You can also play it at full blast on your headphones if you work that way; word has it that Stephen King listens to blaring rock-'n'-roll.) The trick is to use this sound track only for this project. Then, days, weeks or even months later, when you're reopening the project, you'll be keyed into it.

> ## ACTION ITEM (ALPHA)—CREATE A WRITING SOUND TRACK
> Using your computer's media player, burn and create a custom sound track that you'll use only for writing. Use anything that works for you, but try and choose music that you believe will inspire your creativity, and is invocative of the gameplay, characters, place or arc of the experience you are working on. Then see how the music affects you creatively as you write. Make a note of this in your journal or Idea Mine.

VISUAL CUES

If you have reference artwork, keep it on your wall or on your computer to take you back to the headspace of the project. It can be artwork actually generated for the project or inspirational artwork from other areas. It doesn't matter. If your project references another game, a magazine, a book or a film, go back to that material. Play the game, watch the movie, re-read the article, and so on.

TALISMANIC INFLUENCES

If there's a place you go to work on a project, go back when you re-start the project. As it so happened, this book began at a Starbucks when a coffeepot was broken and we were waiting for the replacement to arrive. Going back there grounds us to the project (no pun intended).

SIGNATURE LINES

Often with characters, you'll want to isolate a block of dialogue that encapsulates their persona. For instance, if you were doing a Dirty Harry game, start your writing sessions with a signature line for that character: "I know what you're thinking, punk," or "Do you feel lucky?" If it is your own character, write something that only that character would say. This gives you something to key his or her dialogue from. After you've been away from that character for a while, by simply re-writing their *tag*, you'll find that character is suddenly back in your mind, fresh and ready to start spewing new lines that are consistent with their previous dialogue.

Writing characters and dialogue this way lends authenticity to them, and also tends to make good material for audition pieces (character sides for your voice actors).

HARD CHOICES

KILLING YOUR BABIES

Revisions. Just typing the word brings back a flood of painful memories. However, you must be willing to *kill your babies*, or your career was a writer will be arduous, frustrating, and short. This means letting go of your ideas when they no longer fit the project because of either creative differences or production realities.

This is one of the hardest parts of being a writer: to do your best work, you must be emotionally invested, but to survive professionally, you have to be coldly detached from your creations. It is one of the paradoxes of our craft, and unless you have total creative control over a project, you'd better prepare yourself to deal with it. Things are going to get cut: levels, characters, worlds, features, set pieces, cinematics . . . everything is subject to revisions and deletion. This is the cold reality of the video game business (or any entertainment-related writing, for that matter), and having a mature attitude about it will help both your career and your sanity.

Does that mean you simply roll over and play dead when faced with a creative decision you disagree with? No, of course not. If you truly believe in something, then fight for it. Explain why it matters, and why the game would be better if it stays.

But also remember that the world is full of unemployed idealists, so be a realist. Don't pick battles you can't win. In fact, an executive with a major publisher once told us (regarding a game we were working on that was in complete and total chaos) that, "it doesn't matter who's right, it matters who wins." In this particular situation, he was correct. We were right, but it was for naught, because somebody else won.

So don't plant your flag in the ground over a minor issue when the larger game, the larger entertainment experience you are creating, can still be creatively and financially rewarding. Part of your job as a professional, is to find a way to get back what you've lost, and if you're really on your game, to turn that loss into a net gain for the project.

Ultimately, look at the difficult process of killing your babies as an opportunity. Sometimes, the best ideas come when you are forced to part with the ones that you really loved. And that leads to the next issue with ideas that have overstayed their welcome.

CREATIVE AMNESIA

Whole industries and professional disciplines have been built around helping people to "let go" or "move on." Instead, when faced with difficult revisions, we practice *creative amnesia*. As a writer, forgetting is a skill to develop. What do we mean? Precisely this: when an idea has been cut out of a project, learn to forget about it. There are few things more tedious than some guy who is trying to force something back into a project that's already been tossed out. To keep yourself from becoming such a person, learn to practice creative amnesia.

ACTION ITEM (ALPHA)—PRACTICE CREATIVE AMNESIA

Think of something really cool. Now forget all about it. It's harder than it sounds.

10

THE TEAM AND THE DYNAMICS OF DEVELOPMENT

THE DEVELOPMENT TEAM

The following is a graphic that we've created to show how video game teams work together from the writer's point of view. It isn't chiseled in stone; it is simply our description of how it has worked for us. While you will want to learn the different job titles on your own project (and they seem to be different everywhere), we're trying to illustrate a process here, because most games function in a parallel manner. By that, we mean that all of the wheels are moving at the same time, as opposed to a serial manner in which, perhaps, the programmers would do all of their work and then the artists would come along and do their job. Take a look at the following illustration to get an idea of the various territories that exist in this collaboration.

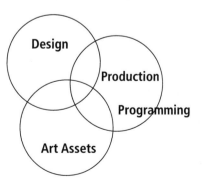

There are four main departments to any video game development team:

* Design
* Programming
* Art
* Production

DESIGN

Design covers both the overall game design, as well as the design of the individual levels. The design team is usually led by the lead designer. He or she is responsible for much of the creative vision of the game.

Design deals with all aspects of the game in which the player interacts, including core game mechanics, play patterns, controls, character attributes, health and damage, weapons, power-ups, interfaces, game shells, enemies, puzzles, and vehicles to name but a few.

Level designers are responsible for laying out the individual worlds (levels) for the game. They work under the lead designer. Level designers place enemies and collectables such as inventory items and ammunition, they set event triggers (which cause specific things to occur when an objective has been accomplished), design environmental hazards to be overcome, and work closely with the lead designer to make sure that the core gameplay for the title is being fully exploited within the level. They are also responsible for *tuning* their levels (optimizing the gameplay and polishing the details). At each increment of the development process, Design interfaces with the other departments.

PROGRAMMING

Programming (also called Engineering or Code, depending on the developer/publisher) is responsible for integrating all of the assets of the game and making sure everything runs. They develop, or optimize, the engine for the game. They build or maintain the tools that are used to create the game. They code things like particle effects. They deal with the game's physics and breakable environments. They build the hidden data bases that support things like hit points and weapon's damage. They tweak controls. They program when to trigger sound effects and music cue. In short, if it must be implemented to run in the game, Programming is responsible.

The department is usually run by the lead programmer. Depending on the size of the game, the lead programmer will have a number of programmers working under him. These programmers will usually be responsible for a specific aspect of the game (physics, optimization, effects, animations, etc.). When it comes to making the game do everything that it is supposed to do, it is the responsibility of this department/group.

ART

The art department is concerned with all art assets that will have to be created and implemented in the game. This includes character and world designs, building 3D models of characters, creatures, enemies, weapons and interactive objects, generating textures, creating the lighting schemes and overall mood for the game, and producing artwork for elements of the game, such as the interface and game-shell.

Art departments employ artists with a variety of skills in traditional sketching, Photoshop, and 3D CGI. Art is usually led by the game's production designer, who is in charge of all of the imagery for the project. A lead artist will work closely with the production designer, and help to coordinate the work among the various artists.

PRODUCTION

Production is the area where all of the departments overlap, because production has to be aware of developments in all areas of the project. This is the home of the producer. Producers usually have some level of creative control over the project. They are also responsible for keeping the game on schedule and on budget. Production interfaces with the publisher's producer, as well as their marketing, public relations and sales departments. Production handles the day-to-day operations of the development, including human resources, scheduling, and accounting.

Production is also where you will find the sound and music departments (although we've also seen them as part of the art department—it varies by developer and publisher). It is the job of the producer and his team to keep their eyes on the ultimate goal of delivering a successful title. If the other departments (design, programming, and art) can be described as "detail-oriented," then production is the "big picture" department.

During game development, production is constantly trawling for opportunities to improve the game while trying to head off any potential problems. Production must remain the eye of the storm during the chaos that is game development: The most successful producers we know make *Spinning Plates* and *Whack a Mole* look effortless.

As a writer, your primary contact will be the producer and the lead designer. You may also interface with the creative director (who, for your purpose functions like a movie producer, and is often the owner of the development company) as well as the sound designer/recording engineer. During the course of the project, you will often work directly with various members of the design and art teams.

Your job is to deliver a gripping story that gives meaning to the gameplay, engages the player emotionally in the overall experience and adds to the immersion the game is creating. You accomplish this through all of the tools that any writer uses: setups and payoffs, character journeys, dramatic tension through plot twists, believable dialogue, clear motivations for the characters, and structuring the emotional highs and lows of your narrative while utilizing irony and pathos, joy and exhilaration. The tools of the writer's craft are at your disposal, but how you choose to use them will determine whether your game story is a success.

THE COLLISION OF STORY AND GAMEPLAY

Games are not, at the current time, a story-driven medium. As we've discussed, narrative exists to support the gameplay. And for many in the game community, there is a serious ambivalence about story in games in the first place.

Many of the top designers in the game business would, if they could, dispense with story altogether. Fortunately for game writers, this isn't going to happen anytime soon—not in a world of movie tie-ins, licenses, and a growing awareness among publishers and developers of the value of the value of intellectual property (IP). And some of the best lead designers have embraced games as new medium in which to tell compelling stories. All of that having been said, there is still a great deal of resistance to story in games: often, story is viewed as a necessary nuisance.

More than once we've gotten calls from producers that sound something like, "We need to throw some dialogue at this." Many game producers perceive scriptwriting as the insertion of dialogue. They don't realize that dialogue is the tip of a much larger iceberg—most notably that you have to have to have something for your characters to talk about and, above and beyond that, you need interesting characters with interesting motivations that can talk about that something in an interesting way.

To be fair to all involved, there's a very important flipside to the argument. A lot of writers think that the game is all about their story and they either aren't suited or aren't willing to make the compromises with reality necessary to function in this medium. Every publisher and most developers have a story about hiring an expensive novelist or screenwriter who, upon being confronted with an Excel spreadsheet of incidental dialogue for a 150 characters (each needing twenty variations of such thrilling lines as: "Look out!" or "Nothing here," or "What was that?"), rapidly calls his or her agent in an effort to get out of the project. That won't work, and it does a disservice to other writers with traditional backgrounds that are trying to get assignments in the games' business.

If you're going to write games, regardless of your credentials (or lack thereof), you have to accept the unique demands that the medium places on a writer. Often, this has less to do with egos and more to do with a lack of communication: clearly defined expectations and deliverables would go a long way toward solving this culture clash.

ATTITUDE IS EVERYTHING

As a writer/designer, try to keep the following things in mind about the game business.

GAME WRITING IS A NEW MEDIUM AND WE'RE MAKING IT UP AS WE GO

We are constantly torn between knowing what we're doing and trying new and exciting things. We're an immature medium in an increasingly mature business. Huge strides have been made in the area of hardware and code; storytelling and game design are racing to catch up with the opportunities that have been presented by this advance in technology and software.

THE GAME BUSINESS DOESN'T LIKE RISK

Today, the business is extremely risked adverse, existing mainly on licenses and sequels (we are discussing major publishers—there are a number of independents making quirky, interesting games that the big boys would never consider supporting). Building an original property in the game space requires more than great content: It also requires an A-List developer capable of delivering that content, and a publisher willing to support it both financially and creatively. It is a far cry from that multimedia period in the early '90s when developers and publishers were willing to try almost any cool, new idea.

WRITING IS HARD

It's hard to write a short story, a novel or a screenplay, much less a multidimensional, flexible storyline for a game.

PUBLISHERS OFTEN HAVE WEIRD EXPECTATIONS

Somewhere along the line, someone asked us if it was possible to create a game that would make somebody cry. You might as well be asking how many pins you can stick into the head of an angel. It may be possible, but would it be worth it? Do players want that kind of emotional connection to a game? We can argue both sides of the issue.

Why can't there be games that have the pull of powerful dramas? A huge segment of fans rush to see the latest tearjerker. Whole cable networks have been built around the disease-of-the-week movie. Why can't we make games that appeal to this audience's desire for a good cry? On the other hand, does our core market for video games really want to be that emotionally invested in the characters they play?

IT NEVER GETS EASIER

You can do a hundred games and every one of them will have moments of elation and moments of horrible frustration. You're going to be dragging a lot of design documents into the recycle bin. You're going to have brilliant breakthroughs (or at least things you think are brilliant breakthroughs) eighty-sixed for a myriad of different reasons, most of them having nothing to do with the underlying virtuosity of the idea. It's a pretty good rule of thumb that you're in trouble every time you think you're safe.

SUIT UP LIKE IT IS YOUR FIRST TIME—EVERY TIME

If you are constantly talking about the past, it usually means you're cheating the present. No matter how many times you've done this before, when it comes time to write, you have to dig down inside yourself to find that creative spark that allows you to approach a project with wild-eyed enthusiasm and optimism.

SUFFER FOOLS OR YOU'LL BECOME ONE

In video games, even if you have the best idea in the world, if your team is either unwilling or unable to implement it, it doesn't matter how good your idea is. Accept that there are some battles that are simply un-winnable.

DRIVE THE HARDEST BARGAIN WITH REALITY THAT YOU CAN

Somewhere, hidden by the best of intentions and a lot of techno-babble is cold, hard reality: What the project can be, given the allotted time, budget, talent, and will of the team. A good writer will always have an eye to this reality and try to work with it. Remember, you're a part of the team; how vital a part is up to you.

EVERYTHING ALWAYS CHANGES

Okay, we're going to make a blanket statement (and one that we believe with our many years of experience is totally defensible, not very controversial and hard to argue with). Here it is: *In game development, everything always changes.*

Let's walk through that statement and how it affects you:

* ❋ **Everything:** Refers to schedule, game design, art capabilities, marketing direction (and subsequently creative direction), licensing expectations, producer whim, budget, technological limitations, controls, personnel changes, and a myriad of unexpected, and unanticipated problems with almost every aspect of the game's development. In short, everything: all of the components can impact the content of the game in catastrophic, bizarre, and amusing ways.

* **Always:** It is not a question of *if*, but of *when*. And that *when* usually happens soon after development begins and doesn't stop until the game goes gold.

* **Changes:** The dreaded revisions. Throughout the development cycle of a game, every aspect of the game is subject to change. Making a game is an iterative process, and sometimes the only way to see if something works is to try it. And then revise it, and try again. Development functions on a constant feedback-loop. Ideas are explored, then promoted or demoted. New concepts come in; old ones are abandoned. Levels are built and then abandoned. Feature creep (slow, unintended evolution) enters the process, challenging the very core elements of the design. Someone on the team discovers a cool bug, and suddenly it becomes an essential part of the game mechanics.

Remember, change it is not always for the worse—sometimes its makes things better. If you are the kind of person who can't handle change, and a lot of it, stop reading this book now and abandon the video game industry until it is several generations more mature, because this is the reality of game development, and you need to be ready for it. Anticipate it, accept it, embrace it, exploit it, and utilize it to your advantage. The dictum of *Everything Always Changes* is what makes games a unique medium in which to explore creativity.

ACTION ITEM (BETA)—EVERYTHING ALWAYS CHANGES—PART 1

Okay, here's the setup. A young girl named Sara has just magically acquired the ability to fly. She's late for school and there's a storm outside. She needs to get to school in the next ten minutes without anyone realizing that she can fly, but flying is Sara's only chance of getting there in time. If she doesn't get there in time, a bully named Karl will steal the magical orb she needs to continue flying. This is the source of her unique power. Now, write a one-page description of this sequence. What challenges will she face? How can she use her power of flight to her advantage? Will the storm affect her as she flies? How can she stop Karl? Don't look at the next Action Item until you have this written for reasons that will become obvious.

FIRE DRILLS

Fire drills are a fact of life. Get used to them. Every major project has at least one. There's that day (usually you see it coming, sometimes you don't) when you have to do three days of work in just one day. There are all-nighters, broken commitments, and hassles. Tempers flare. Everybody knows that fire drills happen. Learn to see them coming. Everybody gets one fire drill; sometimes, two are excusable; three means that something has to change.

Fire drills happen. However, when they happen too often, there's a serious problem, which usually involves an inexperienced producer or at least a producer who's not in control.

The first fire drill is on you. In other words, you've got to make the heroic effort, somehow get the work done or, at lest, get him to *safe*. Isolate what needs to get done in order to get him out of trouble (after all, fire drills don't happen unless there's a fire somewhere) and be a hero. That's why you get paid the medium bucks. Once the crisis is over, you are well within your rights to, without lecturing or browbeating, draw some fair boundaries. You can then say something like: "Look, I'm going to need some warning," or, "What's the next thing like this that's coming up and how do we get out ahead of it?"

We worked on one project where the creative team and the development team sat on opposite sides of the world, with twelve hours of time difference to deal with. The creative team would come up with new ideas, or the developer would discover something about a level and want to make revisions, but the physical structure and time difference meant that every revision was a two day event, just to let everyone know what was happening.

It wasn't long before fire drills became the norm on that one, with late-night (and sometimes all-night) phone calls and hours-long Instant Message sessions. When a team has six weeks scheduled to complete a level, and you spend four days just getting and acknowledging revisions, you can see the impact this can have on development. Add a few new ideas per level, and suddenly, the schedule might as well be printed on toilet paper, because that is what it is worth. This creates a situation where everything becomes an emergency.

The main problem with fire drills is that they are usually reactive, rather than proactive. You are dealing with problems (putting out fires), but you aren't building something, so much as keeping something else from burning down.

In the end, the way we solved our problem was we put everyone on a timer. If you had a new, great idea, you were responsible for staying up all night (regardless of what side of the Atlantic you were on) and communicating with the rest of the team during their workday. That cut the two-day process down to (sometimes) immediate feedback.

Amazingly, when people were forced to stay up all night lobbying for their ideas and changes, we suddenly started to see less and less of them. And the ones that did come in were important, and presented with passion, because you had to sacrifice your time and sleep first before you could ask others to do the same. We were able to coil the fire hose pretty quickly after that.

GETTING TO SAFE (DEALING WITH STRESS)

There's something we call *getting to safe*. This isn't a well-defined place; it is a feeling you engender with people—the feeling that it is all going to be okay. They feel safe. They'll meet the deadline. Their stuff is going to be approved. The ground is familiar around them. They're not on shifting sand. They can see a way to the end.

When you're doing a project, you want to surf between that wonderful, exhilarating feeling of, "We're doing the coolest thing that anybody has ever done. This is going to be a breakthrough," to the other place, "This is nuts. What the hell is this project all about, anyway? This is turning in to chaos. This is falling apart!"

At some point, we all need to feel safe. Getting to safe is relieving the pressure, getting everyone out of jeopardy. Safe is your comfort zone. People either have to be in their comfort zone or they have to know how to get to their comfort zone. If they aren't, they'll eventually start thrashing around like a drowning swimmer and start taking people down with them. Often, project treachery comes out of people who are out of their comfort zone and struggling to get back there.

DON'T LET IT FESTER

Getting people to safe can take many forms, but usually it involves giving them something they can hang on to, a life preserver for that drowning swimmer. During the course of the project, there will be times you'll have to juggle deliverables and dates to make this happen.

For instance, we were working on a recent project that has some complex cut-scenes early in the first level of the game. Schedule-wise, we didn't have to get to them for a while. Instead, we were doing level-beats for the rest of the game. But the cinematics director was flailing around, unsure of whether the sequences would work or not. His doubts began to affect other members of the team. So we knew that we had to work with him to write these cut-scenes, and quickly.

By generating completed pages, we gave him what he needed. He could see the task he had to accomplish and had even been our partner in creating it. He had gotten to safe, and could now happily schedule, assign artists, and begin boarding the cut-scenes. An unknown element that was making him anxious was back under control.

YOU NEED TO FEEL SAFE AS WELL

Occasionally, you'll find that you need to get yourself to safe as well. If some part of a design or a script is gnawing away at you and you've decided to put it off because you don't have the solution, but you can't let it go because it has become a fear-object that has you doubting yourself, then you can't ignore it. If you do, it will slowly begin to seep into all of your other work.

To do your best work, you must be confident that what is hitting the page, and eventually the screen, is creatively correct. Someone can always fly in later and tell you why you are wrong, but when you are generating content, you can't be filled with doubt. If that means getting yourself to safe by solving a problem now that you'd hoped to put off into the future, so be it. In the end, your design or script will be better for it. If you're capable of generating compelling content, born of frustration, than you have a skill set we don't have . . . and frankly, wouldn't want.

A LITTLE STRESS IS A GOOD THING

All this is not to say that we strive for a stress-free creative environment. In fact, stress is not only expected, but at times, can be beneficial. Stress is a necessary part of the process. Without pressure, decisions never get made, deadlines are never reached, and creative breakthroughs never become implemented.

Stress is a desirable part of the project, but only as long as it is relieved by periods of relaxation, rebuilding, and most important, progress. In other words, people don't mind working eighteen-hour days if they have fair warning and they have a good idea of when it is going to end, and if they know there is a reward on the other side of it.

When the pressure goes on relentlessly, the project nearly always ends up a disaster. People can work hard for long, magical periods of time, but there must be light at the end of the tunnel. And when your game is a hit, a fascinating thing happens. All the struggles, tribulations, and impossible hours seem to fall away, replaced by the warm glow of success.

ACTION ITEM (BETA)—EVERYTHING ALWAYS CHANGES—PART 2

So, in the previous Action Item, you wrote up a one page description of young Sara flying her way to school to stop a bully named Karl from stealing the source of her power. Good. Great. We hope you love it. We think we'd love it too . . . but for one small problem. Apparently, we can't get flying in the game. Sorry. No flying. We realize that this was a core mechanic, but it's just not feasible based

Continued on next page

> *Continued from previous page*
>
> on the schedule. Instead, we can have ball lightning as Sara's power. And we're cutting down the level, so Sara will start outside the school. Now, rewrite the sequence, with Sara still having to stop Karl, who is now trying to steal the source of her lightning power. Think about what changes you need to make and what can you keep from your previous draft. Oh, and sorry again about the flying . . . but that's the game business.

MAKING SENSE OF BASTARDIZED FICTION

With this approach, all too often you end up with *kitchen sink* projects. A game called *Blackwatch Island* was once a Nazi lab, but before that, it was a Druid shrine, and before that it was an alien landing zone and the site of a colossal battle between the Vampire Overlords and the Exiled Babylonian Gods. Only now it is a voodoo-laced narco-terrorist Special Forces camp. You get the idea—everyone got involved, and it ended up a chaotic mess.

At the end of the day, as much as some might believe in the wisdom of crowds in terms of making decisions, the creative process is not an open market or a democratic process. In fact, it is precisely the opposite; it is a small, esoteric vision that, if properly constructed, can influence the crowd, or at least a segment of the crowd.

FINDING THE CORE IDEA

One way to cut through a convoluted idea is to try and get to the underlying motivation for why the idea was presented in the first place. If you have a wild survival horror game with a story that is going in twenty different directions, get to the core of the experience. "Why survival horror? Because we wanted to create the most terrifying game anyone has ever played." Good, now you've got the foundation. This can become your mission statement. If you can get people to sign off on something as simple as this, then great. It helps to have a focus.

Suddenly, all the ghosts, zombies, werewolves, vampires, undead, aliens, and mutilated creatures that were crowding the content and fighting for attention are now in service of the mission statement. And it becomes much easier to start pruning ideas, to cut through the chaos and get at what really matters to create a compelling gameplay experience. Another great side benefit of a mission statement: nobody can go back on it without at least admitting that they have changed their mind or changed the focus of their direction.

GETTING SIDETRACKED

Let's say we're doing a Space-Marines-Attack-Cartoonia story. You might frame it as *Starship Troopers* meets *Who Framed Roger Rabbit?* You might have a million issues to decide later, but everyone agrees that the further the team gets from Blasting Toon characters, the further we are from the target.

Now let's suppose that somebody in the process (we'll call him Billy), has always wanted to do a cartoon character game (let's call it *Creatoon*) in which you create your own cartoon characters in a virtual, identi-kit kind of a way. This is Billy's winky, the thing he really loves and wants to see it brought to fruition. While *Creatoon* is somewhat in the ballpark, it is still far from Space Commandos attacking Cartoonia. It's sort of related. It might even be a USP (Unique Sales Point—a feature of the game), but if marketing were like hunting you'd be hitting the hand, not the heart.

This prompts a decision crisis. In order for this controversy to get this far, Billy and others on the development team have to be heavily invested artistically in *Creatoon*. Maybe Billy could care less about the Shooting Blabby Bunny level. To him, the whole project is *Creatoon*. The problem is, the mission statement for the game is clear: Space Marines Blasting Cartoon Bunnies. That's what marketing says they can market; that's what sales says they can sell.

Billy doesn't care. He's the champion of *Creatoon*, and he also happens to be a great Artificial Intelligence programmer. He might walk off the project if *Creatoon* is cut, and he might take a couple guys with him. Billy is so angry he might leave and sue the company for the rights to *Creatoon*. He's talking to his higher-ups, who view him as one of the company's biggest assets. The team has a horrible problem.

In the end you (and probably everybody else in their heart of hearts) know that *Creatoon* is a fun little product add-on for a juvenile "edutainment" product, but it is not the game that you, or most of the team, or the publisher, wants to make. If too many resources go into *Creatoon* at the expense of Space Marines Blasting Cartoon Bunnies, you'll end up with a flawed project.

How do you reconcile the two? Who gets the resources and who doesn't? What do you do about Billy? As the writer, do you side with *Creatoon*, because Billy is your buddy? Or do you point out to him that it's not really appropriate for your project? Suppose that the problem with *Creatoon* is that when the player designs his own cartoon character, it is supposed to have a unique personality that is reflected in customizable dialogue.

At this point you realize that executing the *Creatoon* design is going to mean ten different alts for every line the custom-designed character is going to have. Your work just increased exponentially. This is suddenly a serious problem. Your one-hundred-page cinematic and incidental dialogue script just jumped to a one-thousand-page script. (You might think this is an exaggeration, but this has actually happened to us and it's not funny.) In addition to the added work, you have a scheduling and money problem.

The other issue, perhaps the more important issue, is that the idea is creatively flawed.

GETTING BACK ON THE RAILS

What to do? You have a legitimate business issue. Your work has increased exponentially. Somebody has to deal with this: They either have to pay you more or keep the work relatively the same. The notion that the idea is creatively flawed is a well-founded opinion, but an opinion nonetheless. If things have gone this far, the compromise solution is usually to try it and see if it works. Remember when we were discussing the iterative model for game development? Not every iteration moves a project forward. Sometimes, a build is just as useful at proving what doesn't work as it what does.

In our example, the team implements a small sample of *Creatoon* within the larger game. Now, Billy's pet idea gets a fair shot, and he has an opportunity to realize his vision. This also eliminates the possibility that other people "just aren't getting it."

Of course, moving an idea through to implementation costs time and money, but this is part of the process of developing any game. If Billy's idea is good, the build will show it. If it is time to move on, the build will show that to: It's hard to argue with a playable that doesn't work.

11

CHANGES, REVISIONS, AND CREATIVE CRITICISM

Games, like most creative works, go through many changes on their road to fruition. However, a unique aspect of the video game business is that it embraces the process of iteration. That means that development of a title doesn't necessarily have a gradual ramp upward to completion. Instead, there will be starts and stops, wrong turns, missteps, reversals and retreats, a refocusing of ideas, features-sets that are abandoned, levels that are cut, and new ideas that come flying in at the last minute, which may make everything better, but may also make everything that much harder.

Because games can be in this constant state of flux as they are being created, you will be dealing with revisions to your work throughout the process. Sometimes this will be out of necessity as the game comes together, and other times, it is for creative reasons.

Almost everyone on the development team will deal with criticism at one time or another. Designer and writers are usually in the position of giving and receiving the bulk of the criticism on a project; it's one of the brutalities of being a creative.

DEALING WITH CRITICISM

In the movie business, hearing criticism is called *getting notes*. It's usually the least pleasant part of the entire process. It means a lot more work. It means juggling a thousand elements in your head until your brain overloads. Remember that, unless you're working with a sadist, it is awkward for everyone. When you receive it, just take a moment to remember that you're a professional writer.

Being a professional writer means that you're getting paid to write. You are writing for a *market*. You are producing a *product*. None of this is meant to sound disparaging. It's a cool way to make a living, but it means that you have to park everything you were taught in your Introduction to Creative Writing class about "following your bliss" or whatever. This isn't about your feelings or your ego; it's about getting the job done. Think of it as a goal-oriented exercise. When getting notes, someone else is setting the agenda. Someone else is holding the cards. Someone else has, for the time being, control of your life. How bad can this be? Let's take the worst-case scenario.

A WORST-CASE SCENARIO

Your executive isn't happy. The first sentence out of his mouth is, "I've got a lot of problems with the script," or "To be honest, we didn't like the script." There is one, and only one, correct response to this: "Let's fix it."

If you have a great producer, he'll be able to articulate what the flaws are and how to fix them. Unfortunately, great producers are rare. In fact, the minute you hear this kind of a note, you probably already know that you don't have a great producer, because it is hard for disasters to happen if you've taken all of the steps mentioned earlier to get the script in shape. After all, if you've laid the ground-work, how much can really be wrong with the script? You're working from an approved outline, presumably you agreed on what the scene would be, where it would start, where it would end, and what would happen in between. So it follows that all that can really be wrong is staging and dialogue. Yet often, this is the first stop towards three words you never want to hear "back to premise." Back to prem-ise means starting over (the only slightly less devastating revision is called a "page one rewrite").

One of the best ways to understand how best to deal with receiving criticism is to look at how you should give it. Of course, in an ideal world, everyone would understand how to give you notes (usually a laundry list of complaints and fixes). However, by taking a moment to see how it should be done, you'll have a better handle on how to deal with getting notes and moving on to addressing the revi-sions they spawn.

P.O.I.S.E.

No one likes getting critical notes of their work, especially if you've invested a great deal of time, effort, and emotion in creating it. The saying that "everyone is a critic" is indeed true. However, not everyone is a good critic. In fact, most people are lousy at it. The art of having a critical eye is more than identifying what is wrong, or what you don't like, but also knowing how to put the artist that created the work back on a path to getting it right.

You may have dealt with criticism before. It usually goes something like this: "I don't know what I like, but I know I don't like that." This is the absolute hardest kind of note to deal with. It identifies a problem, but offers no solutions. Instead, you are expected to go back and flail around in the dark until maybe you get lucky. You aren't even expected to try to read the critic's mind; because they themselves don't have an idea you'd be able to lift if you could.

There is an art to giving and taking criticism. Remember that the goal of being critical is to create improvement. It is not to give someone a beat-down. If you are asking for revisions, you are more likely to get the result you are after if you give criticism in a way that will achieve that desired result.

Remember that you are criticizing the work, not the person. Don't take it, or make it, personal (leave those issues to management or human resources). We are talking about creative criticism, and that involves a very clear distinction between criticizing the creation, and not the creator.

When giving notes, the lazy thing to do is just whine about everything you didn't like, usually without even acknowledging that a lot of work was done. But when you give feedback in a professional way, it's your chance not to get revenge against the existential unfairness of your fate as a creative, but to set an example. We'll give it to you in five words and a spiffy acronym: P.O.I.S.E. (Praise, Overview, Issues, Strategy, Encouragement). We know this sounds a little bit like Management-Speak 101, but trust us, it works.

* **Praise.** The first words out of your mouth should be something positive. It doesn't matter what your overall feelings were. Find any aspect of the work that you can identify for praise, no matter how inconsequential, and then do so. If you can't think of something good to say, then there is really no point in continuing. Instead of offering criticism, it is probably best to simply mark the work as rejected, and then consider finding someone else to do it.

* **Overview.** After you've given praise and the person that created the work being criticized is feeling okay, that is when you should create the context of your comments. Think broad strokes here. Are the problems to be addressed minor or large? Is this going to call for massive revisions, or

just a change of some of the details? Is the tone wrong? Have others expressed their concern, or is this criticism coming just from you?

✳ **Issues.** This is usually the main body of the talk. Detail the specific things you want to see changed. Any loser can whine, but since the goal of criticism is to get things to the next level creatively, this is where you have to know what it is that you'd like to see changed. Don't criticize something if you yourself can't identify what is you don't like. "It's not working for me" is not productive; in fact, it's just the opposite, setting up problems and conflict without offering a solution. You need to explain in tangible reasons *why* it's not working. You should also have suggestions. Put yourself on the line. The person being criticized is extremely vulnerable. Your job is to join them in the fight.

✳ **Strategy.** Try something like this: "Here's how I think we can approach the next draft . . ." This is your chance to get the project going in the direction you want. Offer a clear and concise road map to achieving the desired revisions. Discuss how long you think that this will take to accomplish. Are there some initial changes that can be made that might give everyone a clearer vision of the ultimate revisions? For instance, if you want to revise a level, is there a set piece within it that can be focused on first? When this is squared away, it then becomes the template for the rest of the revisions to follow. If the changes are massive, they can sometimes be so intimidating that they lead to inaction. Instead, show how to fix the problem one step at a time.

✳ **Encouragement.** Projects live or die on this one. Return to praise, but now with a forward vision. "I just need to see more of this (whatever it was you liked)." If you value their work (and you should, otherwise, why are you even bothering to be critical?), say so, and let them know what they are doing right. Tell them you're confident they'll nail it on the next round, and then let them get back to work.

And then stop. Don't drag on. If they have any questions, answer them, but at this point, you've given your notes, and done so within a context that will lead to positive results. The one thing that you definitely don't want to do is begin arguing, and this is where it is most likely to happen. Don't let it.

ACTION ITEM (ALPHA)—EVERYONE'S A CRITIC
Using P.O.I.S.E. as your guide, be critical of something you think needs work, whether it is a story, a movie you've recently seen, or even what's for dinner.

DEALING WITH REVISIONS

Okay, so in an ideal world, P.O.I.S.E. is the way that you'd get notes. Unfortunately, the vast majority of the time, you're more likely to get critical comments on work in the form of a drive-by mugging: fast, unfocused, sometimes random and often harsher than necessary. Even when this happens, it is important to remember that in almost all instances, people are responding to what has been created, not to you. So first and foremost, when this happens, don't take it personally. Separate your creations from yourself. Every idea you come up and every word you commit to paper can't always be pure genius, so accept the fact that they may be right.

When you get notes, consider the following:

CLEARLY IDENTIFY THE ISSUES

Clarity is key: Don't try to read between the lines. If you are unsure of what changes need to be implemented, ask.

AGREE ON THE NEW DIRECTION

If you don't agree that the changes are for the better, now is the time to lobby for your position. Take a moment to explain why you believe the initial idea was best. Explain your reasoning for the choices you've made. If you truly believe you're right, here's your chance to lay out your case. But be careful of planting your flag in the ground, especially if larger forces are in play. If you agree that the changes are for the better, find a way to invest in them now. Pitch an idea that ties into the new direction.

CREATE A REALISTIC SCHEDULE TO IMPLEMENT CHANGES

This is where optimism can be your enemy. On a macro-level, almost every game development suffers from overly optimistic projections about schedule, budget, features—you name it. Everyone wants the best-case scenario. It is extremely easy to fall into this trap, especially when the exuberance and excitement surrounding the game they are creating are prime movers in helping to sustain and motivate the team. But revisions can often lead to unforeseen ramifications. So if you have any suspicion at all regarding the extent of the changes, it is better to say so. Set a realistic target to hit, and be prepared to adjust if needed.

KNOW THAT NOTHING YOU CREATE IS SET IN STONE

Every idea is subject to revision. You have to be mature enough in your attitude and confident in your creativity that you are willing to part with your favorite elements. If it was a great idea and it's going away and there is nothing that you can do to stop it, then bank the idea for another day and move on. Be assured that you'll come up with an even better idea tomorrow. After all, what is sadder for a creative than thinking all your best ideas are behind you?

REMAIN POSITIVE

This is the hardest one of all, but if you are to successfully implement the changes, probably the most important. Don't let negativity affect your ability to deliver. Find something in the changes to get passionate about and invest yourself in them.

EXPECT THIS TO HAPPEN AGAIN, AND AGAIN, AND AGAIN

Don't kid yourself into believing that if you nail the changes, you'll be done. If you do, you're setting yourself up for heartache and heartburn. Chances are, you're going to do this many more times before the idea becomes locked. Revisions are part of the process; they are a sign that things are progressing. Look at them in this light, and they are much easier to deal with.

THE BIG CRITICAL SECRET

When someone is criticizing your material, often, the truth is, he or she has an idea of how to fix it. And that idea is to use his criticism as a way for his idea to come into the mix. Nothing good will happen until he gets his idea out. This is a very important point: An idea will not go away until it is given a fair hearing.

Someone, your producer or the lead artist, has an idea. You instinctively don't want to hear it. You fear it could unravel everything. It is probably going to be a bad idea because he's the guy who's been trying to angle his pet monkey into the project from day one. You want to blow past the criticism. You want the idea to go away. The problem is, it won't. It will be the invisible elephant in the room until it gets expressed. Your job is to park your ego (difficult as that may be) and hear them out.

Once the idea is in play, there are a number of possible outcomes:
1. **Great.** It will be a great idea and solve all of your problems.
2. **Okay.** It will be an okay idea that is just another way of doing what you were trying to do and will necessitate additional work to get you to where you already are.
3. **Has merit.** Some of the idea will be good and some of it will be bad.
4. **Great, but . . .** It is a great idea that will mean a whole lot more work.
5. **Rejected.** The idea doesn't fly in the room, and pretty much dies an ignoble death right then and there.
6. **Rotten.** It will be a terrible idea and unravel the entire project. And everyone thinks it's pretty cool.

GIVE THE IDEA A FAIR HEARING

We don't need to talk about Outcome number 1. It is a win all the way around. Outcomes number 2 and number 3 are issues of analysis. You listen to the idea and implement what works and ditch what doesn't. Bear in mind that you don't have to pass judgment on the spot. Think of twenty hip ways of saying, "'Let me think about it." Take the pressure off, because at that moment there's an excellent chance of a creative implosion. Work your way through the entire idea and the ramifications of implementing it.

One of the best reasons to take some time to think about it is that often there is an *itch* there that is legitimate. Itch is the idea that requires you to read between the lines. When someone says that they have an itch, pay close attention. Usually, the only way to deal with an itch is to scratch it, and that means figuring out how to do so. The idea might not work, but somewhere in there is a problem he or she is addressing or an opportunity they want to seize. If you go away and think about it, you might be able to find a way of using what is good and getting rid of what is bad. You can almost always defer decisions on big ideas.

Outcome number 4 is the toughest one. It almost gets to be a moral issue. If someone comes up with a great new idea in the middle of the process and that necessitates a lot of new work, who pays for it? If you go out and redo a bunch of approved work, you will have to pay for it with your time and labor or the company will have to pay for it by giving you more money. Or, you may decide that the revisions will be so dynamic and have such an impact on the final game that you believe you're now working on a certain hit, and therefore, weigh the value of that against the amount of new content you're suddenly going to have to create. Everyone wants a hit on his or her resume, so you'll have to make a judgment call on this one.

Outcome number 5 is pretty easy: it's a deflated trial balloon. There is not much more to do than nod sympathetically while breathing a sigh of relief.

Now we get to Outcome number 6: the fear object. That's the reason you were trying to edge the guy out of the conversation and seriously considered chloroforming him. It's the idea that you hate that will topple everything, the idea that has just enough merit that people will like it, and nobody at the table will see or care about the catastrophic ramifications it can cause. Your first instinct is to do the obvious, natural thing for any sentient being to do: come out, all guns blazing, and tell the guy exactly how stupid the idea is. If you haven't experienced this, you might think this never happens much. We're here to tell you that it happens all the time. Development, often as not, is a contact sport. Everyone starts yelling, things spin out of control, and the project is in trouble.

The only way to deal with option number 6 is coolly and calmly. Talk the idea through. See where it takes the project. See what the idea does to the game: what does it add, what does it take away? Discuss its impact on the development. If ever there was a time to suggest a compromise solution, it is now. Can you get to the essence of what the idea is trying to accomplish? If so, you may be able to come up with another solution that will get to the same goal with less splash damage.

If it's not going the way you hoped, retreat. In war, armies have to do that. You have to retreat and regroup. Your best approach for the rest of the meeting is, "Let me get my arms around this one." Then you spend the rest of the time listening and taking notes, which is a great way of subtly disengaging from a situation. You are involved and are busy, but you can avoid eye contact and not show what you think. Besides, the notes might be valuable later on. Write everything down. Really try to get it. Realize that there may be something very wrong with the project and accept that if you really aren't getting something that has everyone else excited and thrilled, that something might be you.

DEALING WITH VOODOO THEORIES

Every once in a while somebody will pitch you a voodoo theory about game design or writing or story or God knows what. In movies you'll get voodoo theories like: "Quill-pen films don't work." Then, of course you'll challenge the theory with, "Well, what about *Pirates of the Caribbean*?" The likely response would be, "Based on a theme-park ride." This can devolve into a stupid argument like, "So what are you saying? Quill-pen movies not based on theme-park rides don't work?"

In games, you get voodoo theories like, "People don't like voice-over," or "We can't keep any secrets from the player," and so on. While we agree that people don't like badly executed voice-over, they are usually fine with good V.O. And if you can create a satisfying game moment by surprising the player, why not try it.

Could you make a game with Bruce Willis's character from *The Sixth Sense* and not tell the player that he is dead until the end of the game? There is an excellent argument that you could, and that the shocking resolution would be both compelling and a huge payoff for the player who figures it out. But many game producers will simply make a blanket statement such as, "The player must know that he is dead, otherwise we are cheating him." Well, okay, but you've just eviscerated the idea so as to render it useless. What killed your great idea? Voodoo.

In games you might hear, "People button through cinematics." There is truth to this. People button past leaden, overlong, overwrought, bloated cinematics about subjects and characters they don't care about. Nobody buttons past the glorious reward cinematic unless they've seen it a whole lot of times or they're so *twitched* that they need more adrenaline.

People like good cinematics as long as they know their place in the game. That's why we have to admit to being a little amazed and appalled by the length and incoherence of the opening cinematics in a lot of modern games.

A moment about why that happens.

The vast majority of games start out very ambitious. Then stories sprawl, there are numerous different types of gameplay, etc. Endless cinematics are written, levels get collapsed, and a story that was going to be told over a number of different levels now needs to be set up. We have often confronted this problem ourselves. All of a sudden, four scenes, which seem necessary to the further telling of the story, are clogging up the beginning of the game.

We have a problem, so we bang our heads against the wall until we fix it. One possible solution is to break into some of the gameplay and put in new scenes in places we hadn't expected. There will be various types of resistance, and under normal circumstances, you would probably lose your arguments; either the scenes would be cut, leaving the game story making no sense and the developer mopping his brow, or the scenes would be shortened by people who have no business making editorial decisions. This is the kind of situation that leads to voodoo theories; you just have to be creative in trying to solve it.

CREATE AN ACID TEST

The IMF (Impossible Mission Force), if you know the franchise, is a precise organization. For that reason, the character Hunt enters a mission with exactly what they think he'll need. Nothing more; nothing less. Hunt's inventory, at the beginning of every level, should be extremely limited to mission critical devices. In fact, the very presence of an item in the inventory should be a clue to the player as to how the level is to be played. In a mass-market game, we don't want the player fumbling with four hundred inventory items to try and figure out how to get through a door. We want him on the move. If an item is mission-specific, he uses it and tosses it. Therefore, we reasoned that every decision had to go through this acid test:

* Is it Mission: Impossible?
* Is it Mass Market Console?
* Will the casual gamer get it without cheats?
* Does it create suspense?
* Is it producible within budget and time frame?

If an idea couldn't produce a "yes" to each of these questions, then it failed the acid test and was rejected.

ACTION ITEM (BETA)—CREATE AN ACID TEST
List the five items that must be considered for the game you want
to create. These will become the core elemental markers that will
define your title, so think it through carefully.

WHEN YOUR CREATIVE VISION IS OUT OF SYNC

You started with the best of intentions, but somewhere along the way, the team decided to move in a different direction creatively, and despite your best efforts to convince them otherwise, they're sticking with their new course. So, what do you do? Well, that depends on how badly you want (or need) to stay on the project. From your point of view, something has gone horribly wrong. It is going to take a lot of fixing and it is unlikely that the project will come to a happy conclusion. You have to decide whether you are going to try and stay on the project or not. If you're going to stay, you have to regroup and reform in a defensive position. The more orderly your retreat, the more likely you are going to be able to reform. If the conversation becomes heated, you have only succeeded in adding personal acrimony to professional assault. Be very careful not to say something offensive.

The orderly retreat, whether you're leaving or staying, involves a lot of sincere listening, a lot of praise, and a lot of humility. The best thing you can do at this point is honestly say, "I'm not seeing this . . . let's walk through it." If you're a great poker player you can skip the "I'm not seeing it" part. In fact, if you can conceal your contempt for what is going on, it will serve you better in the long run. Once you know all you need to know, get to "Let's think about it" as quickly as you can and get out of the room with a smile. Once you're out of the room, you have do decide whether to stay on the job. This means weighing the practical considerations (paying the rent) and the abstract considerations (I don't want my name on this thing).

Your decision making process will include a multitude of personal and professional considerations. But you'll need to come to a decision. If you decide to stay on the job (assuming it is your decision), then you have to fully embrace the new direction. In other words, you have to behave like a pro (some might say prostitute; we say mercenary).

With any luck, in time, you may see the same value in the new direction that everyone else does. This is even more reason to not be rash in your decisions, as oftentimes, even major changes aren't nearly as catastrophic as you feared, especially when everyone else realizes the cost of unraveling the old idea. Sometimes it takes a few days for everyone to realize that an idea that sounded good in the room cannot be implemented.

If you decide to leave the project, comfort yourself with the fact that you, no matter who you are, are not right for every project. Shakespeare probably couldn't write *SpongeBob SquarePants*. You are not suited for every team. You don't have to be a big sports fan to know that some players are stars on one team and then flame out on another. It's not a reflection on your talent, or your moral character, or your personal charisma.

Maybe the team really was composed of idiots. Maybe there's some hidden factor you didn't see, like an office romance that led to bad judgment. Whatever it was, it is just a project that didn't work out. Get out as gracefully as possible and avoid future damage.

UNSOLICITED REVISIONS

Usually your job during development is to enhance and improve the game without breaking things. Many times during a title's development, it enters an extremely fragile state, with a multitude of moving parts. At these points in the process, ideas function in one of two ways: either as lubricant that suddenly gets all the gears meshing together in unison, or as sand that fowls the gears and eventually clogs the system, grinding everything to a halt. Even a good idea can shut down the machine if it can't be integrated without causing major problems.

It is important to realize this, because if you choose to put yourself into the mix and offer ideas and suggestions that aren't being solicited by the team, you need to understand the possible consequences of doing so. You may be the hero, or you may be the goat. So think very carefully before deciding whether or not to inject your ideas into the mix.

If you honestly believe that your revisions will make the project better, then you have the obligation to bring them to the attention of the team, and deal with the implications that may arise. Remember, criticism is not usually your job. There are times, however, when you might feel, morally, that you have to say something, clearly and concisely, to people who can decide on the issue. But if you are simply trying to introduce your own pet ideas, ones that will not significantly enhance the game or the experience for the player, take a moment and consider not only what is best for the game, but also what is best for yourself and the team's perception of your contributions.

CREATIVE PANIC—THE IDEA YOU DON'T WANT

No matter how emotionally stable and experienced you are in your career, there are going to be times when you will panic. The feeling starts when you don't know what to do and you imagine the elaborate structure you have built in your design and/or script is collapsing around you. All you see on the road ahead is a ton of work on something that won't be any good. Panic happens when you don't quite know what to deliver and no matter how many times you rephrase the question to yourself, you can't get a clear picture of what to do.

THE INSIDIOUS NATURE OF CREATIVE PANIC

The worst thing about writer's panic is that it leads to two equally unproductive places: a lack of interest, or a lack of activity.

In the first, you stop caring, and it is reflected in your writing. Passion has been replaced by an overwhelming desire to just get it done, slam it out the door, and ship it. There is nothing wrong with being a mercenary. In fact, we highly recommend it. But you can't be a mercenary when it comes to your creative output. You must find something within the project that you can hang onto, that fires your imagination and reinvigorates your interest.

We've been brought into so many projects where the first writers, or designers, had clearly given up. You can almost point to the exact page where they stopped caring, and just wanted to be done with it. Don't let this happen to you.

The second result of panic is inactivity. At this point, you're angry and confused. Your beautiful toy is being broken by other hands, and you just don't want to play with it anymore. So you stop. This is an easy pathway to the old writer's block excuse.

Well, you must ask yourself: If a writer is not writing, then what is he or she? One of the hardest things about our craft is that everyone believes he or she can do our job. Remember that the world is filled with aspiring wordsmiths: If you stop generating content, you create a vacuum that is just waiting to be filled. And it will be. The result will be more chaos, not less. So don't ever let frustration lead to inactivity.

Times like these are where you must let your professionalism overcome your need to be a difficult creative. In the long run, you'll find that you'll get more respect from the team, the producer, the publisher, and the developer by accepting the situation, and then aggressively becoming part of the solution. And, believe it or not, oftentimes, the revisions make things better, and it isn't long before you realize that the new direction is actually pretty exciting, and that toy you didn't want to play with is suddenly looking shiny and new.

HOW TO REGROUP

The best way out of the panic is to regroup and plan your next right move. Like a good general, you want to plan an orderly retreat, and then your next attack. Write up your notes on where you think you are and where you want to go. Start in the comfort and privacy of your journal, if you keep one. To regroup:

* **Clearly identify the problem.** Often, what you think is the problem is only a symptom of a larger issue. For example, everyone may be criticizing the hero character's animations, but the real problem is that nobody likes the model. Or the game feels sluggish, but it really is the controller mapping that isn't working. Or no one likes the incidental dialogue, but the problem really is the performance of the team member who did the temp vocals being used as placeholder . . . and so on.

* **Create a consensus on how to solve the problem.** Make sure that all of the team members who will be affected have their say. Then create a contingency plan in case the first solution fails.

* **Generate a timeline to get the game back on track.** Nothing is more frustrating than a problem that goes on indefinitely. Don't let panic fester, or you'll jeopardize the entire project.

* **Be prepared to accept defeat.** This is the hard one. If the issue can't be resolved in a reasonable timeframe, be ready to re-design, re-write, re-conceptualize, and re-code your way around the problem. Make the hardest bargain you can with reality, and then, get the project moving forward again. Further in development, there may be time to revisit this battle, but right now, you have a war to win. Clear, decisive action will always reduce creative panic.

In his book *Deep Survival: Who Lives, Who Dies, and Why*, Laurence Gonzales says that the best thing you can do after a catastrophe like getting shipwrecked or lost in the woods is to regain your bearings and figure out "the next right thing" to do. That is particularly true when you are in a project situation that prompts you to panic.

The brutal truth is that a game writer has very little institutional power and even when you do, you probably don't want to use it. Instead, the next right thing involves meeting your team's needs—getting them to a safe place, because when there is a problem, they aren't in a good place to begin with and the environment is ripe for real trouble.

Even if you control the project, very rarely do blatant displays of power have the desired end. More often than not, power plays tend to make enemies.

ACTION ITEM (ALPHA)—REFLECT ON YOUR OWN CREATIVE PANIC

Write down an experience you've had with creative panic and how you overcame it. Think about what caused it: insecurity, fear of failure (or even success), lack of desire, loss of interest, confusion about the deliverable, feeling overwhelmed or maybe even friction with a collaborator. Be brutally honest, because one day, you can almost be assured that you'll find yourself in a similar situation again. Here's your chance to get out in front of a problem before it occurs, and maybe even avoid it.

CREATIVE STRATEGIES FOR GAME WRITERS

While the act of writing is not voodoo, sometimes the creative process behind it can be. There are as many idiosyncratic methods to getting *word to page*, as there are writers. Still, as a general rule, you want to create a transparent environment. That means no hidden agendas, no off-the-record conversations, and no secrecy at all.

OPEN COMMUNICATION

A major part of transparency is constant communication. You want the team to see what you're doing at every possible increment. Like we said, "No surprises." Sometimes you'll get clients who, right after your turn in the outline, will say: "Okay, so send me a draft when you've got it done." Don't wait. You want to send the client the first few scenes when they are finished. If there's a problem with your interpretation of the characters, with your format, with whatever, you want to know ten pages down the line, not one hundred pages into the project.

Lawyers often refer to operating in this fashion as "acting in daylight." In essence, by keeping everyone informed during the process, you are doing two simultaneously positive things: making sure that everyone is in sync with the content that you're creating, and already establishing a feedback loop to modify and revise the content as it comes together.

Notice that we didn't say that this is also an excellent way to CYA (Cover Your Ass). We didn't say it because it should be self-evident.

SMALLER DELIVERABLES

Instead of one big deliverable, create a series of smaller deliverables with weekly or bi-weekly targets. Usually, this is the way the team will want to work anyway, so offer to be flexible and define a structure that allows you to stagger your workload.

Keep the team on the ride with you from beginning to end. Let them know what you're doing and why you're doing it. If you are encountering problems, tell them. If you need help, ask for it. And ask them that they do the same thing for you, even if transparency isn't always possible. Weeks or months down the road, if there's a problem, you're in a much better position to help solve the issue,

THE DECISION-MAKING PROCESS

During any creative endeavor, your goal is to turn an utterly subjective truth into an objective truth. That is to say, take an idea that you think is "cool," and get everyone else to agree that the idea is, in fact, "cool." Persuasion and force of will alone will not get your there. Passion helps, but it, too, is not enough. Persistence can be a virtue; it can also be irritating as hell. In the end, all of these come into play, but the merits of the idea itself ultimately determine whether or not it is worth pursuing.

When subjective truth has become an objective truth, it is like the difference between polling and an actual election. The view of the team (or those who matter on the team) is no longer an opinion; it is shared truth. Everyone has signed off; there is no going back. The idea is deemed worthy of implementation and the team is moving forward. If anyone wants to go back and change something that's fundamental to what has been agreed to, they will have to deal with the repercussions that go with it.

RUN IT THROUGH THE RINGER

Let's say a member of the team comes to you with *SpankLords from Neptune*, a new high-concept game that fuses together women in bikinis with aliens. In their mind, it's a good game with a good story. If you like it (with some ideas and reservations perhaps), then you can define it as having "potential." Now it's time to run *SpankLords* through the decision-making process and see if we have a project or not.

The process has a few parts, and even if you think you know the content, you can be amazed by how often projects are torpedoed by the fact that people refuse to recognize the necessary steps or skip one altogether.

Here's the process we've used successfully:

✳ **Air Conflicting Views.** There come certain points in every project where people of good faith disagree. In fact, there are lots of points like that. Most of the time, these conflicts resolve themselves as the game comes into focus; sometimes they don't. Conflict is part of the process. Defending your ideas and arguing points is part of the give and take that ultimately leads to better projects. This may take three minutes, it may take three hours, or it may take three days. The main consideration is that everyone gets a chance to speak. Central questions should be answered, and prompt decisions should be made. If delays for more information, or executive approvals, or opinions, etc. are absolutely necessary, schedule the first available time to get them squared away. However, such delays can't lead to inaction. Time is your enemy here.

✳ **Discuss the Idea in Bright Sunlight.** Once again, keep it transparent; no back room stuff. There is a need and value for back-room discussion in some creative endeavors, but game development isn't one of them. Involve as many people in the decision process as possible. This usually means all of the key leads on the team, the main creatives within the company, as well as the producer and possibly representatives from management. Be inclusive: if someone doesn't want to be part of the process, they'll let you know. Note that just because you are including many people in the process, this doesn't necessarily mean that everyone will have a say in the final decision. In fact, giving everyone veto power will probably lead to chaos. However, letting everyone who is going to be affected by the decision have some say in the outcome, even if is just a chance to express their opinion, goes a long way toward getting the team's support behind the eventual conclusion.

✳ **Everyone Gets a Fair Hearing.** Everyone involved in the fight should have a chance to present his or her alternative or addition in its best possible light, without mockery. This is a variation on conflicting views, in that not every option that is presented will clash with every other one. Sometimes, you'll have an embarrassment of riches from which to choose.

✳ **The Need for a Timely Decision.** Whoever is ultimately responsible for pulling the trigger needs to be ready and willing to do so. Whether there is a formal time (such as a weekly meeting) or an informal time, there has to be a straightforward and fair process. The decision should be clean and clear, and be announced in such a way that everyone hears the result at the same time.

MOVING FORWARD

Once the decision is made, the team has to reunite. Most likely, someone has just lost something and is not happy. That person will be even less happy if the team member who won is not sportsmanlike. If you don't want introduce unnecessary chaos and friction in the project, you'll need to get past this as quickly as possible.

If a decision does not go your way, don't keep trying to force things back in your direction. Do not whine. Do not put a moustache on your old idea and bring it up again. It is over. There is nothing more tiresome or counter-productive than a person who is still trying to push an agenda when everyone else has moved on.

Conversely, if you win your point, skip the victory dance. You do not want retribution from the person who lost, and there's plenty of room for that. Your job is to make sure he or she walks away from the meeting enthusiastic about the project overall. That is the best possible outcome.

APPROVALS

In almost every case, once something is approved, it can't be unapproved. This is especially true with licensors: you usually only get (or want, for that matter) one bite at the apple.

The approvals process varies greatly among the numerous developers and publishers in the game's business, but all have some sort of "sign-off" methodology in place. Understand what it is, how it works, and how it affects your deliverables. As a practical matter, almost all approvals within the team are done verbally, whereas executive approvals and licensor approvals usually involve a paper trail.

Keep in mind that just because something has been approved, that doesn't mean that it is finished and you can wash your hands of it. Things do have a habit of changing or being revised after something has been approved. However, it is a more serious issue to revise something that has been approved, so these changes are not trivial. As a general rule, avoid revisiting approved work unless it is absolutely necessary.

THE GAME WRITER'S PLACE WITHIN THE TEAM

Just as game designers don't go from a game design to a completed game overnight, writers don't go directly from an idea to a finished script. They do story premises, beat charts, outlines, character breakdowns, etc. This means generating a great deal of content over time, and doing so within the context of ongoing development.

If you are brought into the project from the outside, one of the first things you have to figure out when you're hired onto a team is what everyone else on the team's attitude is toward the fact that they're not the writer. Does anybody on the team think that he's a writer? Many times, a designer or someone else on the team may have laid out the initial story and characters, so you may be replacing and/or supplementing someone else's work. Even though everyone agreed when they started that it was "temp," their creator has become invested in his story content. If so, you have an issue to deal with. If you are fortunate, the initial game story, while raw, is filled with great nuggets that you can use and build upon. If that is the case, then the best thing you can do is turn any potential competitor into a collaborator.

In fact, the best thing you can do with everyone involved in the project is to turn each of them into a collaborator. Video games, more than just about any other entertainment medium, are a collaborative art form. You'll never hear the key grip comment on an actor's performance on a film set, but in games, the 3D modelers are more than willing (and, in fact, encouraged) to comment on the creative elements of the game, whether it directly affects their department or not. If you hope to survive in the game business, you'll need to embrace the collaborative spirit: There are very few successful loners making games.

BOUNDARIES FOR GAME WRITERS

In any creative endeavor, it is important to have boundaries for everyone, either explicit or implicit. Depending on your situation, a game writer can be a temporary and tangential member of the team, or fully integrated into the entire project's development process. Regardless of your level of involvement, you'll need to have a sense of where your boundaries are.

Boundaries are present at all different levels of the team and the development process. There is the hierarchy of the team (whom you can talk to and can't without creating offense). There are also creative and production boundaries.

TEAM HIERARCHY

As loosey-goosey as the game business pretends to be, there are formal and informal hierarchies in every organization involving people. Development teams are no exception. As a writer, you touch a number of different parts of a project, so you don't fit easily on the organizational chart. That means, theoretically, you can talk to anyone. You are dealing with the core content that goes into making the game, and that means that you will potentially interface with all the leads on the team. Make sure that if you are pitching ideas, or working through creative issues, that you aren't inadvertently going over someone's head.

In almost all cases, you should check in with the producer of the project, and keep him or her informed of whom you are talking to, and what the discussions are about. If any issues arise, let the producer decide the best way to proceed, or what actions should be taken to solve any territorial disputes.

CREATIVE BOUNDARIES

If you are brought into the project as freelancer, rarely do you start with the rest of the team at ground zero. Usually, there are some givens. For instance, *Red Ice* is a military adventure set in the Arctic. That's how it was sold, that's what the design document says. That means, nobody wants to hear your "tropical" take on the project.

Nevertheless, it is very possible that people on the team have certain "winkies" that they want to hold on to. As previously mentioned, a winky is our term for some little idea that you just love and will have a hard time letting go of. We all have them whether we like them or not. It might be the fact that the game is set in Detroit, it might be that the hero has a girlfriend named Raven; it might be that the guy uses a flame-thrower in the game. It can be anything.

The point is, if you inadvertently trash someone's winky, you will at best have an alienated collaborator. At worst, you might get your self kicked off the project and never know why. That's why you need to do your best to know what you can touch and what you can't, and that means delineating what is important to people.

Identify the winkies of the various team members, and if you can do so while keeping the integrity of the content you are creating in tact, incorporate them into the content you are writing. While it may seem like you are playing politics with the creative elements of the game, the fact of the matter is, often, finding creative ways to include everyone's winky actually makes the game and its content that much better. There is a reason people fixate on certain ideas, and winkies often add immeasurably to the final gameplay experience when they are judiciously and elegantly incorporated into the design and story.

As with the team hierarchy, turn to your producer for guidance and advice. Also, the lead designer is often the last word on creative issues, so be sure to seek out his or her input as you are working through how to best creatively interface with the team.

PRODUCTION BOUNDARIES

Try to separate business from creative issues as much as you possibly can. You (or your representatives) will inevitably deal with someone from business affairs who will handle your contract and arrange for getting you paid. Unless there is a major issue to be addressed, don't bring any business-related issues to the team. For the most part, they've made their hand-off to business affairs, and at that point, they assume that things are being squared away. And know this: Deals take forever to get squared away. Don't expect to start today, and cash a check next week. Generally, we anticipate an eight-week window from when we make a verbal agreement until we make a trip to the bank.

While complaining to the producer that your deal is taking too long can be effective, it can also be counterproductive if you've created friction between the team and the business elements of the project. As with all of the other boundaries we've discussed, common sense is really your greatest ally. If you have any reservations about talking to someone about an issue for fear of causing problems, then that alone should be enough to set off your internal alarms. Proceed with caution.

WHEN THINGS GO WRONG

When things are going right, problems are fairly easy to address. However, games often live by a variation of the old saying, "If it ain't broke, don't fix it." It usually goes like this: "It's working perfectly, let's break it." This can lead to things going wonderfully right, or horribly wrong.

SPIN

We live in a world, whether we like it or not, where we have to deal with spin. Spin is often interpreted as lying, but we don't mean it that way. Instead, it is putting the best face on what could be seen as an otherwise negative situation. Spin doesn't work unless it is based on something true. In most cases, the reason that things don't work out can best be explained by "creative differences."

Everyone in the business can agree that great minds often think differently. Spin is competency neutral. Nobody was right or wrong. It protects all parties involved from darker implications. Why do you need spin? Because no matter what you do, you are going to have competition and enemies. And the reality is that the game business is a fairly small community, where everyone has one or two degrees of separation.

COMPETITION

Contrary to popular opinion, your competition is not necessarily your enemy. In fact, competition and enemies are two wildly different things. Your competition is simply another person who does the same thing for a living that you do. Often they are competing for the same job. Sometimes there is acrimony, although we can report that it is amazingly rare. This can lead to people being enemies, but just as often, competitors get together to form guilds, trade contract strategies, and share writing tips.

In some ways, that's what's happening here. We're active writers/designers in the industry; you are likely to become our competition. We feel that there's a big enough pie for all of us. Besides, some good competition keeps us on our toes. And bad competition doesn't make our job any harder (actually, it makes it a lot easier).

ENEMIES

Everyone makes enemies—even if you're not trying. You can do everything you can to avoid it, but it is still going to happen. Anyone who deals with creative endeavors will make enemies at some point in time during their career. It is the nature of working in the realm of ideas, where subjective opinions matter, and passions can and do occasionally run very hot.

Often you make enemies on failed projects when everything falls apart. Sometimes you make enemies on projects that go extremely well when everyone tries to snag the credit for success. Success can be much harder to manage than failure, and more than a few hit games have created bitter acrimony. Some of the more successful developers are breakaway teams that decided to go their own way following a hit title.

What is fascinating is all of the strange bedfellows this makes, especially when various colleagues and competitors team up with former enemies and end up creating a monster title. It happens more often than you'd think: At the end of the day, the desire to make great games is something that everyone in the business shares. And the amount of people capable of doing so remains relatively small when compared to other forms of entertainment.

Navigating the development process without making enemies is an art in itself. But remember that first and foremost, you want to make a great game. If this means stepping on toes, then you have to learn how to tread lightly. Balancing creative needs with social necessities is a big part of being a member of a game development team. Learn to do it well and it will make a big difference in your career, your credits, and possibly your mental health.

12

GETTING DOWN TO BUSINESS

ART IS COMMERCE

We work in an exciting business. We work on exciting projects. We're excited about them. People want to know about them, and they ask you questions. You don't want to be a jerk and say, "Hey, can't tell you." If you do that, the subtext says, "You're not in the in-crowd. This game is more important than my friendship with you." At the same time, you don't want to violate your agreements. So legally you should be sure you are released to talk about any subject of a game you are working on that has been publicly announced. You can talk about what is obvious. Otherwise, you can say, "Look, I'd love to talk about it, but I just can't." Or you can just dodge the subject with, "We just don't know yet." It's a lame answer, but polite. More often than not, they'll take it.

THINGS TO CONSIDER

Talk to your lawyer and accountant about whether you should incorporate. There are complex legal and tax implications to incorporation and you should tune your strategy to your situation. Memorize your social security number and your Federal I.D. number. Knowing it on the spot can save you faxes and emails. Know your date of incorporation. Write down your bank number for money wiring instructions (foreign companies often like to pay that way). In the company you work with, who is your deal with? Is it with the developer, the publisher, or some third party? You need to know who is paying you because this is with whom you negotiate.

Odd as it may seem, you need to know the name of the project, even if it is a working title. Who has creative control? Is this project a work-for-hire or is this project an original that you've sold the company? If it is a work-for-hire, it is very unlikely that you will be able to get creative control. If you have a reputation to protect, however, you might be able to get the ability to be consulted when changes are made to your material. If this is an original, or based on a book or screenplay you've written, you might be able to maintain some approval over the project (which is great if you can get it).

WGA

You need to know if this company is a signatory of the Writer's Guild of America (WGA). If so, you should make it a WGA deal. Writing games can get you into the guild and get you health insurance and a pension fund. This may seem irrelevant when you're twenty-two years old, but there's a day when this will matter. See the WGA website to learn the details. Presently, the WGA has a one-page sample contract that is in no way onerous to the developer and helps you. See if you can get them to go for it.

MAKING THE DEAL

Manners come in handy once you get a job, because that's when it is time to make a deal. We could write a book about this alone. If you can, get an agent or lawyer who is experienced in this industry to help you with your deal. Even then, making your deal isn't a "fire and forget" concept. You should pay attention to your deal, because a good one can mean a lot of money and benefits down the road. A bad deal can mean a lot of heartache. There are many moving parts in a deal, and you will want to have as many of them move in your direction as possible.

SIZE AND SCOPE

Your scope of work is a huge issue in interactive gaming. More often than not, nobody really knows how much work they are asking of a writer. Expect a lot of give and take here, as the project becomes reality. That means, be prepared to give. Also be prepared to draw lines if the project escalates beyond any anticipated size. (Remember that a small change in the design can have huge implications for you.)

Go for a ballpark number, such as forty minutes of cinematics and one hundred pages of in-game dialogue as well as outline, bios, etc.

Take some time on the math and ensure that if things change dramatically, then the gentleman's agreement with your producer will be open to another conversation.

PAYMENT

You need a schedule for payment. Obviously, you will want to frontload it as much as possible. You can expect that they'll want to pay you on acceptance only because this is how they tend to deal with developers. A writer should not be paid on acceptance because he can't control whether or not people will like his work. He should be paid on delivery for the work coming in to a professional standard and the developer should have the right to terminate the contract; paying for work completed and in progress. There is a good argument for a commencement payment and incremental payments along the way.

In the case of a freelancer, the developer wants you to do their project with their money. If the money is back-loaded, all their money is really paying for is your job hunt after you finish their project. That's not the best way to get the best performance out of a writer, given that he'll be scrambling around trying to pay the rent while doing the project.

It is usually fair enough to say that half of payment is received at the beginning and half at delivery. Sometimes, the nature of the project is so amorphous, and there will be so much need for the writer's services, that the writer will want a weekly fee.

As a freelancer you will have other projects going on, but you must be absolutely fanatical about meeting deadlines. You can never let a developer or anybody else think that they are suffering because of your other commitments. As a general rule, you can be open about other work you are doing, but it should remain invisible to them at a practical level.

AVAILABILITY

One of the things you are selling to a developer is your availability. They should expect to pay for that. Projects are often slowed down or delayed through no fault of yours. You should not suffer for it. An *outside* date means that you get paid on a certain date as long as you have met your part of the obligation. Expect to owe them some work.

APPROVALS

Even if you are paid on delivery, you should have some kind of approval notification, or an approval period. The idea here is that you limit the risk of endless drafts before you're paid, or an endless wait before you know whether or not your work is approved. Once a deliverable is approved, changes happen out of their pocket, not yours.

The corollary to this is that we all know that there are going to be endless changes outside of your control, and you can't go back and renegotiate your deal every time this happens. You have to mentally budget several free revisions, but you do want to have an "enough is enough" stake in the ground.

It also doesn't hurt to have your approval person named in the contract. You have to know who makes the decision. More often than not, this won't be in the project, but it helps to have a person identified, one-way or the other. Not only do you need to know whom the person (or persons) in line on the approval decision, you need to know the process. Are they people outside of the company? Licensors? You can save yourself a lot of heartbreak if you can be in sync with the totality of your approval train.

CREDIT

Credit is a form of compensation. Having your name on any game, even a flawed game, is usually better than no credit at all. Negotiate this upfront.

If they won't guarantee you a specific credit, get yourself a "favored nations" status credit. What this means is that if anyone else doing work similar to yours on the project is getting credit, at worst, you get a credit comparable to theirs.

To you, a credit is money and it is something to be taken seriously. Where is your credit going to appear? In the game? At the beginning of the game? At the end of the game? On the box? In the manual? On the website? Find this stuff out and do the best you can for yourself.

Credit doesn't cost anybody any money—at most it is pixels and ink. It is unfair to see other people's names on your work and not yours for months or years of work. We've been there. Obviously, fairness goes both ways. If somebody has contributed a great deal, figure out a way to keep him or her happy. If disputes occur, look at the WGA's criteria and pitch your case as best you can. Credit matters.

ATTACHMENT TO FUTURE PROJECTS

With regard to attachment to future projects, people are often loathe to give that away upfront, but it is an ideal thing to ask for if you find that you've been giving a lot more than expected. "Listen, I know you don't have any more money in the budget and you need this stuff. I want you to give me right of first refusal on any sequels that get made." It's hard to say no to a request like that when you're bailing them out.

If they can't give you money, but it is evident that they have to make something up to you, know what to ask for.

It's often to your advantage to work on things before the contract is negotiated. You own your stuff right up until you sign it over. Your bargaining position is wildly different when people are negotiating to buy your intellectual property than it is when it's work for hire. This is not a call for deviousness; this is a call for risk and return. If you start working on something before it is a sure thing, then you took a risk. If they weren't obligated to buy your stuff when you did it, they took no risk. It is totally legitimate that this be balanced at deal time.

ROYALTIES (GOOD LUCK)

If the game becomes a runaway hit, the people who made it so should benefit. Backend: bumps, bonuses, and royalties are hard to get on a video game for complex reasons having to do with the industry, but it is often legitimate to ask for them. If their sales exceed projections, you should be rewarded.

ANCILLARY MARKETS

It is very unlikely you will participate in merchandising profits unless you are a deal element or you created the intellectual property, but they are certainly worth asking for if you can justify it.

For example, if you create characters and those characters end up being licensed by a third party as action figures, why shouldn't you get a taste of the profits? Smart companies give this out.

We have a theory, supported by a surprising amount of evidence, that when certain publishers started cracking down on royalties and stopped giving them to their programmers, designers, writers, and artists started doing "idea withholding." That's when people have great ideas, but just don't want to give it to their company, because they realize that the upside isn't worth it. So instead, they'll hang onto the idea until the climate at the company changes, or more likely, until they are somewhere else. We're not advocating idea withholding, and have never practiced it, but it happens.

PUBLICITY

Publicity is like credit. Unless you're a wanted criminal, it's never bad to have your face seen around. Some people have publicity built in their contract. The most basic form of this is something along the lines of, "will appear in similar likeness and manner and for similar time period," as other players in the process, like the producer, designer, and/or director.

TRAVEL

The WGA and Directors Guild of America (DGA) insist that their members fly first class. You won't get that deal from a game publisher or developer. Instead, you'll be traveling coach, and probably on the red-eye. Still, it doesn't hurt to ask for business-class travel if you'll be doing frequent trips. This is one of those areas where you have to use your best judgment, and read the situation accordingly.

Also know that many developers and publishers like to have you travel on a moment's notice, and sometimes expect you to pay for your flight, hotel, and rental car. You then submit an expense report for reimbursement (which often takes a month or more to find its way back to you). If this is going to put a squeeze on you, let them know in advance. It will save you a lot of scrambling around.

WHEN TO START WORKING

How much work should you do before a deal is made? That depends on many factors. On almost every project we do, there is an initial "good faith discussion," and then we are usually off and running, with the formal agreement chasing us. Game development simply can't wait three weeks while the lawyers hammer things out.

BEFORE THE DEAL

If you really want the deal, do what you have to do. If the deal falls through and you still own your material, that's an incentive. If it is intrinsically tied to the hiring company's material, be careful. In general, the rule we've adopted (and violated numerous times) is after three meetings and/or five pages, something significant has to happen.

BEFORE THE CONTRACT

How much work should you do after a deal is made, but before the contract is signed? It's time to be generous, but to a point. When you're asked to do a job, it is fair to say: "Look, I know how this stuff goes. Let's all plan that it's going to take a month for the contract and two months to getting paid." That's always a good thing to say in the room or in an email. It seems very reasonable and is easy to refer back to if you need to say: "Uh, guys . . . it's getting about time for your business affairs people to get off their butts and get me something I can sign."

BEFORE THE CHECK

How much work should you do before you are paid? It is funny how people can expect you to write fifty pages of a document faster than they can fill out two pages to get someone to cut you a check. If we're all honest here, we will acknowledge that people don't like writing checks and usually only do so when they must.

That, combined with the fact that companies have a lot of safeguards and government regulations to adhere to, all add up to a slow payment process.

In this situation, you have to use your best judgment. If you've signed the deal, the check is coming, eventually. However, if it becomes uncomfortable or awkward, then mention it to your producer.

GETTING PAID

Ah, tracking down your check. It goes something like this: You send the invoice, the check doesn't come so you call. "Oh, we never got your W-9," you're told, or "You have to get a purchase order." Where do you get that? From them, but they never told you. "Okay," you say. "So let me get this straight. You didn't pay because we didn't have a purchase order number, but you sat on the invoice waiting for us to ask for one?" Hmmm . . .

Here's how you get around it. Stay on top of the paperwork. Don't let the W-9 get lost in your in-box. Offer to go in and "get it all done." Stay on top of the following "games":

* **Nondisclosure Game** (usually you won't be doing much actual content related work until this is squared away)
* **W-9 Game** (and any other tax/government-related documents such as proof of residency)
* **Signed Deal Game** (your contract)
* **Invoice Game** (send an invoice for payment and ask if you need a P.O. number)

Call somebody the minute it feels like nothing is happening. Whenever possible, avoid dealing with the same person in a business context and in the creative context, and vice versa. If you can stay away from the check chase, let your agent earn his or her money. Some are good at that, some aren't. A good agent will use guilt, shame, badgering, and anything else at their disposal to get it done.

Dealing with the business aspects of the game is one of the most frustrating aspects of working on a title. Whatever is happening on the deal front, never let it interfere with the creative content in development.

LEVEL 13

CAREER CONSIDERATIONS

EVERYONE HAS TO START SOMEWHERE

"How do I break into the game business?"

It is probably no accident that the most common question we are asked is the most difficult one to answer.

If there were an easy and obvious way to get started in video games, you wouldn't have to ask that question, or even read this book. There are no sure routes into the game business; training, desire, and connections all factor in. Being in the right place at the right time helps, as does dumb luck. Persistence and determination can also increase your chances, so the more often you try, the more likely you are to get what you want.

GO WHERE THE ACTION IS

This means you need to be where the action is. While the Internet is a growing force, location matters. When you're starting out, you have to physically be in a place where they make games. That means places like Silicon Valley, Austin, Los Angeles, Seattle . . . any place where there is a healthy developer and publisher community. If you manage to get a start somewhere else, great, but at the end of the day, you have to be part of a community to succeed in games.

ATTEND TRADE SHOWS

The easiest and most obvious place to meet developers and publishers is at various game conventions: E3 (Electronic Entertainment Expo), GDC (Game Developers Conference), the D.I.C.E. Summit, hosted by the Academy of Interactive Arts and Sciences, and the AGC (Austin Game Conference) to name a few of the more notable ones. Also, game companies have become active at events such as ComicCon. Search the web for information on game, film and pop-culture conferences, trade shows, and seminars.

SEARCH THE WEB

All of the major publishers, and most developers, have active websites that you can visit. Look for career page links where you can submit your resume or inquire about job opportunities. Also check out some of the main gaming websites. Many include job openings that publishers and developers are looking to fill.

READ GAMING AND CGI PRODUCTION MAGAZINES

Toward the back of many of the most popular gaming magazines, you'll find developers with help-wanted ads. You'll find similar ads in magazines specializing in 3D Graphics and Photoshop. While they won't be looking for someone with your talents in these ads, their contact information will be there. You can then email or call them and inquire about openings they may have outside of artists.

EXPLOIT A PERSONAL CONTACT

An overwhelming majority of the jobs available in the game business are never advertised. Instead, information about who's hiring is usually a word-of-mouth affair passed around people already in the business. If you know someone in the game business, become his or her best friend. Or if you know someone who knows someone, don't be afraid to ask.

CONSIDER A HEADHUNTER

Headhunters make their money from the employer after they set up one of their clients with a contract. If you are new to the business, you won't have enough credits and experience for them to take an interest in you. However, they do have their ears to the ground when it comes to knowing who is staffing. It's a long shot, but you might be able to swing a deal, especially if you offer to work exclusively with them in the future (once you're an established commodity, of course).

GENERATE CONTENT

If you find an interested party that wants to know more about what you can bring to their company, then you'll have to be able to show your work—which, of course, means you have to have work to show. You'll need a sample game script, a preliminary design document, or a concept document. You'll have to write one of those and have it illustrated. Whatever you do, it must appear professional. You only get one chance to make a first impression.

BE READY FOR AN ENTRY-LEVEL POSITION

Getting "in" should be your first priority. If you can start as an assistant, or as a game tester, or even helping out in major publisher's mailroom, you are that much closer, and perfectly positioned, to make your move when the opportunity arises. Many of the best producers and designers we work with started in Quality Assurance (in other words, game testers). In fact, game testers, in our experience, tend to be some of the most insightful members of a development team.

If you get a job at a developer or publisher, expect to start at the entry level. You will probably not be paid much when you begin. That's okay, because the experience and contacts you'll be gaining will make up for the financial shortcomings.

TAKE FREELANCE WORK IF AVAILABLE

Don't worry about starting as a freelancer. At the rate games companies come and go and reorganize, just about everyone is a freelancer. We sometimes sift through a stack of business cards and discover that almost no one has been in the same job for more than three years. People who have held five jobs in ten years are the norm, not the exception. Even people who stay at the same company find themselves moving from project to project and team to team at a rate that makes them not dissimilar from freelancers.

BE PERSISTENT WITHOUT BEING A NUISANCE

If you can establish an email correspondence with someone within the company, you may be able to gain insight into what they are looking for. Be polite, be honest in your intentions, share your desire and your enthusiasm, but don't be a nuisance. Game development is hectic, and if someone on a team is kind enough to share their time and experience with you, and perhaps offer helpful suggestions on how to join their company, be grateful, and then stay out of their hair. There is no guarantee that you'll get work, but if you become a nuisance then you can be guaranteed that you won't.

> ### ACTION ITEM (GOLD)—CREATE A CAREER GAME-PLAN
> Think of your career desires as if you were designing a game. What objectives must you accomplish? What skills do you need to practice? Where are you going to find your goal? Now, generate a plan of three things you can do today to start making it happen. For example, that idea that you've had for years . . . today is the day you write down a one-pager for it. Is there a trade show coming up that you can attend? If so, make plans to go. Perhaps you want to make a list of companies that make the kind of games you like to play, and start making email inquiries of job openings. The point is you are the hero of your own career. Whether you win or not is entirely up to you.

EDUCATE YOURSELF
"So how do I learn what I need to know?"

This is another frequently asked question. A decade or so ago, people learned by doing. Now, there are schools for game design. Game companies are, more and more frequently, recruiting from schools, because an academic credit is better than nothing. Realize this: The game business is growing and everyone is always looking for new talent.

In addition to formal training, you can also gain knowledge by doing it yourself.

READ
Reading books such as this one, studying games, subscribing to game development and trade magazines, and attending game conferences are ways that someone outside the business can begin to learn the inner workings of game development.

JOIN MODDING COMMUNITIES
On the PC (and coming soon to your next gen console), many of the more popular 3D engines have healthy *modding* communities where you can join other aspiring game designers and writers, and using a preexisting engine, modify it with your content and art to create your own unique game. In fact, some of the most successful games for the PC have started as mods. Created by small teams of fans, a few have ended up rivaling the titles of major publishers. Many of these mod communities have morphed into actual game developers. Similar gaming mods will become more commonplace in the console market with the next gen-

eration of platforms like the Xbox 360, PlayStation 3, and Nintendo Wii, as connectivity and multiplayer capability are part of each platform's core strategy.

ACTION ITEM (ALPHA)—PLAY A MOD

There are a number of great game mods available for download, many free of charge. Play a few. Have fun.

FIND AN INTERNSHIP

If you're a student, do internships. You'll gain invaluable experience and contacts.

A FORMAL APPROACH TO LEARNING ABOUT THE GAME INDUSTRY

We taught a course at the Art Institute of California, Los Angeles, that was titled "Survey of the Game Industry." It was designed to familiarize students considering a career in console games with the creative, technical, and business issues of the game industry. The course attempted to answer four basic questions about the game industry:

* Where did it begin?
* Where is it now?
* Where is it going?
* How can I fit in?

Much of the homework was "hands on" as students were assigned to play a number of games and record their experiences in a journal. Guest speakers discussed various subissues of the game industry ranging from "how agents work" to "how designers come up with their ideas" to "why marketing departments decide which projects to support." Students of the eleven-week course were asked to demonstrate their knowledge of the industry by creating a video game concept document, which could be pitched (explained) to a game company. This document included: High-level Concept, Marketing Concept, Unique Sales Points (USPs), Gameplay Overview, Player's POV (Point of View) document, artwork as necessary, and other categories as defined by the Pitch Document Template (which is provided in this book).

The class was organized into groups of four or five, to provide real experience akin to working on getting a game to the public. This helped in teaching students the roles of different players in the video game production process and their responsibilities and powers. As you study this book, it might help to have people to work with. While you might not want to organize a video game creation team, it is still important that you learn how to work with others in creating games, because you'll learn just how different viewpoints can be.

At the end of this course, students possessed the basic "big picture" knowledge needed to begin a career in the games industry. As you may have deduced by reading this far, this book takes a similar approach. What we cannot do is enforce the type of homework assignments in that course. They are:

* Two hours gameplay and game journal
* Two hours web research and miscellaneous homework
* Two hours working on final project

Obviously, your own final project might be a game you come up with by using the resources provided in this book. We should also emphasize that if you are not already heavily into playing games, you should start now. You must understand the medium if you hope to develop content for it, and there is nothing more valuable than playing a variety of games to understand not only how games work, but also to get a sense of what content is selling and popular.

Students in the course were expected to get their hands on any games, game systems, books, etc. They were also encouraged to collaborate on various parts of their projects and to include acknowledgments in their work to other students who helped. On that last note, never forget that this is a collaborative medium, and that people remember who did what. It is an old show-business maxim that you meet the same people on the way down that you saw on your way up, so treat people fairly and you'll probably be treated more fairly yourself.

RULES FOR FREELANCERS

Mea culpa: We have broken every one of these rules. Even if you know them, stuff just happens. However, if you choose to be a freelancer, follow these guidelines and you'll find yourself in a much happier and financially rewarding place.

MEET YOUR DEADLINES
You cannot blow deadlines. Ever. Period. The end.

DELIVER QUALITY
Your work must always be of professional quality. That said, you can send in drafts that are clearly marked "draft" or "rough" or "notes." If you choose to deliver everything only if it squared away, though, do that. It's a matter of style and of personal preference. The trick is to assess your client and see what it is he or she wants to receive. Some clients want to be part of the process; some just want the results.

COMMUNICATE

Be open about the fact that you are doing other projects, because everyone should feel that their project is the highest priority when they need you. Even if you're writing movies for Steven Spielberg on the side, you can't let people think that you view their project as anything but equally important. There is nothing more damning to a freelancer than to have a reputation for not taking projects seriously.

BE ACCESSIBLE

Never go *off the grid* unexpectedly. Even though you are not an employee, the people who have hired you have the right to expect that you will be responsive. Imagine the frustration of trying to reach someone who has gone incommunicado. Don't ever put yourself, your client, or your fellow team members in this situation. Answer emails and calls promptly, even if you're *head down* or *in hiding* (terms we use when we are buried with work and entirely focused on making a deliverable). If you must go off the grid, either because you have to go out of town or for some other reason, always notify your client ahead of time.

UNDERSTAND THE ISSUES

You must understand technical and artistic issues. No one expects you to write code, but you do have to understand the programmers' needs. And the team will expect you to have a working knowledge of basic game design. Fortunately for you, this book will get you there. In fact, there is often a mighty thin line between game design and game writing.

HAVE THE RIGHT TOOLS

Be reasonably tech-savvy. Obviously, you should have a functional laptop computer. Other than your creativity, this is your most valuable tool. Note that the game business runs on PCs (by and large) and you will be fighting City Hall if you use a Mac.

Also, make sure you have broadband Internet access with an email account that can accept large attachments, Microsoft Word and Excel (incidental dialogue will often be written in spreadsheet format), a screenwriting program (we use Final Draft), and FTP software (you'll be grabbing larger files off of the publisher and/or developer's website). Perhaps most important, own, or have access to, the various game platforms you will be writing for. You want to play as many games as possible in the genre relevant to your project. You may also get a *Dev Kit* (a modified console) from the developer or publisher so that you can play *builds* of the game as they become available.

CREATE A BUSINESS FIREWALL

Do not mix business issues and creative issues. If possible, do not talk to the same people about the creative and business aspects of the project. If this isn't possible, always keep a clear firewall between the subjects. Ideally, have someone else handle the business issues related to your work. This can be your lawyer, a manager, or an agent (or in our case, all three). If you are just getting started, at minimum, you'll need an experienced lawyer to look at your contracts. This is the cost of doing business as a freelancer, so find someone you trust and can communicate with on a regular basis. Your lawyer should deal directly with someone in business affairs at the publisher or developer on your behalf, which allows you to remain focused on the creative aspects of the project.

FREELANCING SUCCESS

Everything your parent ever told you about watching your finances, or should have told you, is true when you are a freelancer. It is important that you live below your means and have a cushion. If possible, you should be able to survive for six months with no additional income. After you start working, you need to start thinking about your retirement. This might sound silly to somebody in their early twenties, but the years roll by faster than you think.

When freelancers get in trouble, they start taking projects that they shouldn't take based on two factors: greed or need.

* **Greed,** because someone pays you too much money for working on a bad project.
* **Need,** when you're flailing around simply trying to make ends meet.

If you don't believe in a project or are in desperate financial circumstances, chances are you won't do a good job. You'll waste time and more often than not, your reputation will suffer.

How do you know if a project is right? Try the *party test.* If you can go to a party with colleagues you respect and happily tell them about the project you're working on without a qualifier like, "You won't believe how much they're paying me," that's a good sign. You should also be comfortable telling them whom you're working for and with. Of course, this is assuming you're not NDA'd (Nondisclosure Agreement) out the wazoo, in which case, you won't be saying much of anything.

FOOTBALL STRATEGY FOR A GAMING CAREER

Games are expensive to produce. Any title can be a huge risk for a publisher and with risk comes caution. Publishers have to consider licensing, gameplay familiarity, limited ambitions, and the classic marketing bugaboo of trying to predict the future based on the past. By the very nature of this situation, innovation is limited. Nevertheless, most break-through, breakaway hits are innovative. So what to do? Do you do something new and take the risk or not? Do you do a whole lot of work on spec (risking your time and maximizing your potential for return) or do you do take a paying job, limiting both your downside and your upside?

It might help to look at it in terms of good ol' American football. Consider the following as the quarterback (team leader) of your own career:

THREE-YARDER

These are short, quick projects that pay the rent, keep you current, and sometimes allow you to break out. For a project like this, you might have to simply waste a down. That's okay, because you have three more. We always like to have a few of these going. The projects tend to be fairly low stress and are usually well organized. You can earn a very good living just making "three yards and a cloud of dust" plays.

TEN-YARDERS

These are good, solid projects that provide you an opportunity to hone your skills and pad your resume. They advance your career down "the field." These projects tend to be longer, and more intense. They are usually higher profile, higher stress, and more chaotic than the short play. The also tend to be more creatively rewarding.

HAIL MARYS

Like long forward passes that could result in a score, these are projects that fundamentally change your professional standing and career. The best of these are projects that you initiate. That means you have to initiate your own idea, write the concept document, and beg, borrow, or steal your own artwork. Hail Marys have three potential outcomes:

- ✳ An incomplete pass, which means you're a no-go.
- ✳ An interception, in which someone likes your idea, but finds a way to take the ball from you and make the project his own.
- ✳ A touchdown, with both creative and financial rewards that make taking the chance worth the effort.

There is a reason that this play is named after a prayer. The reality is most Hail Marys don't make it in the end zone. But the upside to successfully making the play makes it worth the effort, even if it takes years (and often, it does) to complete. We always like to have at least one Hail Mary that we are working on.

STAYING ON TOP OF TRENDS

Entertainment fashions change, too. In Hollywood, a low-budget horror-film trend might give way to coming-of-age films, then science fiction. Whether it is games, movies, or anything else, if you really want that to be your business, then trends matter. You have to know what is hot: what is and isn't selling. Does that mean you should abandon an idea that you're passionate about because it is out of fashion? Of course not. But it does mean that you should look at how you can massage the idea in such a way that it's not fighting against the hot trend.

Remember that the game business has become as much of a "me too" industry as film, television, music, and book publishing. A successful game will breed many imitators. Some may be good; some may even be better than the original. Any doubts? See how many World War II first-person shooters you can find that all have three-word titles, with the middle word invariably being either "of" or "in." This kind of thing doesn't happen by accident. Realizing this gets you ahead of the curve creatively when it comes time to pitch your Hail Mary idea.

ACTION ITEM (BETA)—STUDY THE TRENDS

What are the hot trends in gaming? Read a few gaming magazines, and visit some websites where games are reviewed, and see if you can pick up on the current "big thing." Is it content or gameplay related? Is there a game that has everyone else saying "me too"? What elements of the trend can you improve or expand to create a game you'd want to play? Write it down, including what you like or hate about what is "hot."

So, how do you know you have a project worth pursuing? We'll cover that later. You could be working on a stinky little project that has little chance of success, or on a project that has what we call "the glow." It's hard to tell the difference unless you have a strong understanding of the business of games, and even then, it's not easy.

BEATING OPPONENTS WITH REPRESENTATION

In our experience, truly bad guys in the game business are pretty rare. Obviously, we have to define the term. Let's say a *bad guy* is someone who intends to cheat people. He enters into agreements that he doesn't intend to fulfill. Such people are rare and are easily detected by a "karmic odor" that seems to surround them. They have a lot of enemies and they are routinely derided. The best way to deal with them is to not deal with them at all. In the real world, however, we all have to deal with unsavory characters. It is wise to tread with caution and protect yourself as best you can. This usually means that you need to have a lawyer and agent, and not overextend your own negotiating efforts. The more that the digital world begins to resemble Hollywood, the more important such personnel become. We'll discuss how to get them in a moment; for now, let's look at what they do.

THE AGENT

An agent usually gets paid 10 percent of everything you make even if they haven't made the deal, unless you negotiate a separate agreement with them. In California, for example, 10 percent is mandated by law. However, this varies by location, so be sure to check the laws in your state or country if you have any questions about business arrangements with agents. Sometimes you get a *package deal* which means that they take their percentage not from you, but from putting together all of the elements of a deal. This is uncommon in the game world, but is increasing in popularity.

An agent:
* searches for work for you;
* negotiates your deal;
* advises you on your career;
* helps you make contacts;
* gets you paid;
* gets your name out there.

Agents may also gain prestige in representing you. The bigger you are the more prestige they get.

THE LAWYER

In contrast, a lawyer handles your contract. He or she can negotiate smaller, but important points in your deal. A lawyer can also deal with nastiness that might arise from your deal. However, most lawyers will not litigate for you; if required, that takes a separate type of attorney. Lawyers are paid either a percentage (5 percent is a place to start), or by an hourly rate or a job rate. Be sure that you go into a deal with a ballpark idea of what your lawyer will cost you. Sticker shock can be astounding with legal fees. Don't be one of those people whose eyes gloss over when they see a contract—study the deal.

Just as with an agent, the more prominent you become, the more prominently a lawyer is seen within your field.

THE MANAGER

So how about managers? These folks operate in the twilight zone between agents and lawyers. Unlike agents and lawyers, they do not have to be licensed. Make sure you have a clear deal with a manager. Sometimes they want to be attached to your projects, which can be problematic when setting up a deal. That said, it is better to have anyone out there spreading the word about you than no one. Be careful, but trust your instincts. We've been very lucky to work with one of the best managers in the business.

GETTING REPRESENTED

There is no set formula for getting an agent or manager. The bare knuckles way of gaining representation is to get a list of agents and send a query letter or email to them telling them who you are, that you want representation, and you would like them to see some of your work. Many agents will only consider representing and looking at submissions from potential clients who have been recommended to them, so make sure and vet your list before you start, and remove these agents from your list (unless you have an "in," which you should then exploit to the fullest extent possible). This will save you a lot of unnecessary rejection.

The critical thing here is that you have some good work to show them. If you are a game writer, you should be able to give them a sample script, or a sample concept or preliminary design document. Send them any work you have done and mention any credits you have.

Again, everyone is looking for the next big star. In finding representation, your work should be well presented and professional. It should be something that an agent will be proud to pass on, if not actually sell.

If you meet an agent (or agency) that is interested in representing you, be sure to take the time to get to know them. You might go on quite a long ride together. Ask yourself the following questions:
* Do you like them?
* Can you talk to them easily?
* Do they seem to have valid contacts?
* What have they done?
* Can you trust them?

✳ Who else do they represent?

✳ Do they answer your calls?

Ask about the future of your relationship. Ask about career planning ideas. Ask about what they think you're worth. These are uncomfortable questions, but necessary.

Often, agent relationships are not immediately formal. More commonly, you could be a "pocket" client—someone the agent has unofficially taken on while seeing how your success develops. If that sounds odd, take a moment to look at yourself from your agent's eyes. No matter how much your agent might want to treat you like "family" and offer you free counseling, the agent has car payments, a mortgage, and (most likely) more expenses than you do. It's in an agent's best interests to see real possibilities of making money with you before making a commitment.

If you can't decide about representatives, do a web search. The Internet is full of information.

✳ Try to remember your first impression. Did you like them? Did it feel right?

✳ Any time you get into business with someone, it's worth a moment to do what we'll call the "karma test." This means using your personal network. Make a few calls. Ping people with emails. Ask questions like: "I'm thinking about making a deal with Howard Spank; what do you know about him?" You'll get a lot of stuff back. Your job is to sift through it.

✳ Put pride in your back pocket. Some agents can be brutally truthful about your talent and marketability. The good ones will offer constructive criticism. Remember, it's in their best interest for you to be successful: if they didn't think there was a way to make money off you, then they wouldn't be talking to you.

Bear in mind that people who are unhappy squawk a lot louder than people who are pleased. See if you find a pattern. Use your judgment. Say a prayer and go.

WRITERS AND THE GAME INDUSTRY

Let's rewind the clock thirty years. Many games were written by a single guy in his bedroom, after school. Let's call him Mikey. He sold his games in plastic bags at computer hobby shows. He passed them out to his friends. Mikey was creating an industry, though he didn't know it at the time; he just wanted to share his creativity and passion with others. Maybe make a buck or two. Games were his medium of choice, and the reality was, some of Mikey's games were pretty damn fun. That meant that more people wanted to play them. Suddenly, Mikey finds himself in business. Now, he needs an artist and maybe somebody to answer the phone. Since the phone didn't ring that often, Mikey found a receptionist who'd also taken a creative writing class in junior college and was able to cobble together whatever sparse text dialogue was needed, or help with the story, or edit the writing of the lead designer.

This cottage industry would grow by leaps and bounds, eventually becoming the game industry we know today. But the mentality that the script and story could be done by the development team didn't change until the outside world demanded it. Two main forces drove the change:

❋ **Sophistication:** As games began to rival other forms of entertainment in their complexity and visual appeal, players came to expect that the standard of the writing and the story match the quality of the rest of the title. For a story-driven game, this meant that traditional elements such emotional investment in the characters, realistic and compelling dialogue and an engaging plot now had to be factored into development.

❋ **Licensors:** As the business began to rely heavily on licensed properties (games made from films, television series, comic books, etc.), it found itself interacting with many in the traditional entertainment community. Licensors were used to working with professional actors, musicians and writers. When a game is being built around one of the crown jewels of a major, multinational entertainment conglomerate, licensor approvals become an issue. As the budgets for these games increased, and the involvement of high-profile talent became more common, it was only natural that professional storytellers would factor in the mix. Licensors demanded that their characters and franchises, some worth billions of dollars, be properly written and represented within video games.

What is great about the industry today is that the mind-set is changing. The value of professionally constructed narratives is being recognized. We are working with some highly talented teams that embrace the challenges of raising their storytelling skills within games to the next level. If we do get resistance, it can inevitably be traced to one or more of the following:

❋ **Cost:** A credited writer is more expensive than a level designer.

❋ **Control:** Developers are about control. Who isn't? Having a huge creative element in someone else's hands is a shock to the system.

❋ **Developer Coddling:** There exists a complex and semi-poisonous relationship between developers and publishers. Publishers don't like to offend developers or shake them up. And if a writer is being added to the project at the instance of the licensor, there will be unavoidable friction.

- **Natural Resistance to Story and Character in Games:** This exists for a number of reasons. When games began, stories were thin to the point of nonexistent. Many veterans in the video game industry believe that it should have remained that way. After all, doesn't everyone button through cinematics?
- **Not Made Here:** In the past, developers looked to the team to write the story. The desire to keep things internal still exists, although this attitude is changing as developers and publishers are starting to see the value of having a strong, professionally written content. While a big part of our business is licenses, we are now seeing much more work in developing original IPs (Intellectual Property) with developers and publishers. It's not enough to have a game anymore; you have to have a franchise. And this is where opportunities for writers abound.

Once you know the realities as a writer in this business, it's easier to avoid the pitfalls. And with that in mind, let's look at some traps you will hopefully circumvent.

FOOL'S ERRANDS, SUCKER CHASERS, AND THE LONG VIEW

The dead-end journeys go by a number of names: fool's errands, snipe hunts, sucker chases, wanks. All writers go on the occasional wild goose chase, but there are ways to avoid them, or at least minimize their damage.

We generally look for the following markers if we have a suspicion everything might not be on the up and up. Let's call these our "sucker chase signposts":

- If the person who is allegedly funding the venture has never been in the business before.
- If there is no evidence that cash has yet changed hands.
- If there are inappropriate people attached to the situation.
- If it just plain feels wrong.

We've been on more monkey missions than we can remember. Some of them took up extraordinary amounts of time and effort and came to nothing. Sometimes they were worse than nothing—relationships were ruined and great ideas were wasted. Fool's errands come in all shapes and sizes. They usually go something like this:

- "I know this guy who is loaded and has always wanted to make games (or movies, or albums). All we have to do is bring him a design (or script) and we're in. We can control everything. All he wants is a producer credit."

* "There's this Japanese developer that just had their game cancelled six weeks from Alpha, and they have a full team just sitting there. We can put a moustache on the game, add some new content, maybe change the player character model, and we'll be able to set this up with another publisher. No problem."

* "It's a great license, and it can be ours if we are willing to do the design for free."

* "Okay, the schedule is crazy, and the initial money's not great, but hey, we're all friends. And the upside is huge. What could possibly go wrong?"

HEY, JOE

Believe it or not, even experienced writers fall for these come-ons (ourselves included). We do so because Just Often Enough (aka JOE) they might actually bear fruit.

Here's how a typical JOE might go. You take some meetings and write a few pages. Maybe you meet the person who writes the checks. He is inevitably a dubious character who pays just enough for your lunch that you believe him. You want to believe him, anyway.

Months pass. Nothing happens. You ask what's going on with the project. You get strung along and then finally you hear (from someone else): "Oh, he was a flake."

As your career progresses, you meet a higher grade of flake and go on classier fool's errands. You'll meet real people with real credits and real offices that want you to do free work. A lot of times, you have to do it. After all, if he wants to sell a project to his boss (and everybody has a boss), he needs to show the boss something. The issue is how to wrangle the situation so that it doesn't get out of hand.

As we mentioned, there is only one reason to pursue that JOE project: sometimes, something real happens.

If you spend any time working in creative endeavors, you'll find that there will be many interesting and amusing characters populating your life. Some of them will want things out of you . . . and what they mostly want is money, but not the way you'd imagine it. Instead, they want you to work for free. They want you to write, to generate ideas and content that they can use in their projects. And against your better judgment, you'll do it, because JOEs occasionally do pay off in ways you didn't see coming. For example, the project never goes, but a guy you worked with on a ridiculous JOE is now a producer at a major publisher and has just been told that a team is looking for a writer. Does he know anyone? Suddenly, your phone is ringing.

Here are some basic guidelines we use in evaluating whether or not to take a JOE:

* Don't do a project that you wouldn't do if there were no dangling carrot.
* Keep pressure on the situation. If you get the feeling that you're the only one who's working—stop. Many long-time successful writers will tell you that nothing happens until there is a script.
* Give the potential employer a budget of your time and effort. In our experience, any potentially interesting project is worth three meetings and/or five pages. After that something has to happen. This should be stated up front.
* The more that a situation feels like money, the better. Try to have meetings with the guy who can make a "go-forward" decision. When is the potential to see some financial reward realized? Get a commitment on when you can expect to see some green, and be comfortable with the answer.
* Make sure that it is clear to everyone that you own your work until somebody else pays for it. In other words, the content you create remains under your control until you cash a check. This can get very tricky when it comes to known properties, collaborations, etc., but you can work it out.
* When it is time to walk . . . walk.

Another way to profit off a JOE is to come away owning something. You'd be surprised how often old projects just keep coming back. Truth is, a good idea is a good idea and ideas have an amazing habit of maintaining a shelf life.

TAKE THE LONG VIEW

Until you reach the stratosphere of success you are going to have to work to get work. There's no shortcut. That means you are going to be a mercenary one minute, a difficult creative the next, then maybe a visionary, then a gun for hire, followed by being a consultant, then the third writer in the room, then maybe the go-to-guy until, if you are lucky and talented enough, you eventually become the eight-hundred-pound gorilla.

Conversely, the minute you put your time and effort into something, your fingerprints are on it. So you have to ask yourself if you want those fingerprints there. Throughout any writing career, including in games, it pays to take the long view and try to think about what your career will be like in a few years. Unfortunately, not enough people do this, and often, a project they did years ago comes back to bite them in behind.

In games that's doubly important. The shelf life of your credits in Hollywood might last for decades, reputation-wise. In games they last for months. Nobody wants to hear about a credit over five years old. Two years is usually the most a game credit will remain impressive.

PAYING DUES

If you want to be a game writer, you need a sample game script. In order to have any real credibility you have to show that you are able to do the job. The game script is your calling card into "the club." This club requires you to pay your dues, which means gaining experience. Nobody likes paying dues. Everybody tries to find a way around it. By our very nature, we always search for the shortcut. Just by reading this book, you've gone the additional step, made a commitment that most aspiring writers aren't willing to do. If you've also been doing the various Action Items we suggest, you've even gone a further step, and are that much closer to becoming a professional.

Numerous are the designers, producers, executives, and marketing personnel who suddenly turn into writers the minute they install a copy of script formatting software. The interesting thing is that these guys are often able to control the script, and even get their stuff made. Sometimes it works brilliantly (there are some great writer/designers in the game business that have never worked in any other medium), but more often than not, it fails miserably. As you'll learn when you start your first script, writing is hard work. Professional writers know that practicing their craft is often lonely work in a subjective world where they are at the whims of other people's opinions. It's frustrating yet immensely satisfying.

Curiously enough, the same rules that apply to playing a good game—balancing frustration with satisfaction—also apply to the work of developing games. So expect to be frustrated, but also to be satisfied, and don't lose track of the necessity to pay your dues when getting started.

14

END GAME: WRAPPING IT UP

THINKING OUTSIDE THE SOAPBOX

Game stories and cinematics all too often look amateurish because, frankly, amateurs are making them. Not every guy who came out of film school with a beard in the late 1960s was a great filmmaker. Similarly, not every guy with a copy of Adobe Premiere on his computer is a great editor. Editing really is a skill and it takes years to learn it. If you have amateurs involved you will get amateur results. Likewise, if you have amateurs do your voice acting, it is going to sound like you have amateurs doing your voice acting. If you go with amateur production designers, or writers, you will get similar results.

The problem is that people pay fifteen dollars or so for a DVD of a Hollywood blockbuster film, so when they pay fifty dollars for your game, they don't expect amateur. They expect their money's worth. We, as an industry, are better off cutting scope and scale than cutting quality. If people are willing to pay twenty dollars for seventy minutes of movie and maybe another hour of interesting features, they'll probably pay fifty dollars for eight great hours of gameplay with maybe some online or multiplayer and replay value. (One consolation in the comparison is that people probably spend fifty dollars for a movie night for two, and that may not even pay parking, dinner, babysitter, and popcorn.)

The point is that we need to make sure our product is top quality. The day and age of the one-dollar-per-hour of gameplay are long gone. That was back when we were competing with babysitters. The kids have grown up, they're still playing, and they value their time. They want quality, not quantity. It may seem weird and counterintuitive, but often the best compliment a game gets sounds like a complaint: "It was too short." That means you left them wanting more, which is rare from experienced gamers. Normally, they drop a game when they get frustrated or bored or something better comes along.

Gameplay and content should always strive to get better, not necessarily longer or richer or deeper (these are not mutually-inclusive). Nobody minds their fifty-dollar investment if they get a great few days out of it—particularly more sophisticated gamers who have a life beyond the screen.

After all, as an industry, if games don't expand beyond twenty-somethings with too much time on their hands who can play all night and all day with no supervision, we are going to have a small, marginal industry indeed. Of course we still want that audience. They are our core demographic, and pleasing them with great games keeps us all rolling. But as the film and television industries will tell you, the young demographic dollar is tapped. They're buying cars, TVs, stereos, iPods, and DVDs, paying rent, downloading ring tones and music, going to pro sporting events and movies, and maybe even dating on their meager incomes.

Frankly, we're hoping to attract other players. Here's a new demographic to consider: An audience of guys who have probably ten times the disposable income of the teenagers, who have time on their hands. Seniors! Some of them actually fought in World War II. You think maybe somebody would try tuning a version of *Call of Duty* for them? It would be interesting to see what happens.

Another group that is almost ignored and also has both an engagement need and cash: fathers and young sons. We both have kids aged five to ten. It's fun to play games with them, but there are amazingly few that are suitable. While we're sure that some guy in the marketing department will give you some lame excuse as to why you can't hit this market, it doesn't seem that the film industry has any trouble reaching it. Who wants to try and deny that the boom in CGI movies like *Shrek, Finding Nemo, Madagascar, The Incredibles, Over the Hedge,* and *Cars* finds its roots in the fact that Mom and Dad want to take the kids to a movie that they won't find nauseating? Where is the game industry? Forget *Reader Rabbit.* It is very hard to find an E game or a soft T to play with a kid. That means hundreds of dollars aren't being spent in our homes every year.

So what does this have to do with game writing? Plenty. We need to do more experiments. Let's accept the premise that we're an immature industry that is finding its way. We are where movies were when sound was invented. We've learned enough to know that we don't have to keep the camera eighth-row center as in a play. We've learned that we can tilt, pan, maybe zoom, dolly or truck a camera. We've learned about close-ups and wide shots. We've got an audience that can probably still be transfixed or shocked like early film audiences.

Games have made incredible leaps in technology and in art. However, as a general rule, design and storytelling, which are the content center of the game, haven't yet reached the same level of sophistication. Games are still being designed around "break the crate" mechanics, and game stories usually have the equivalent of a cliché for a hero: the strong-jawed, broad-shoulder, ex-mercenary loner with a cool sounding name who has discovered a conspiracy that will destroy the world—and only he can stop it. Still, we can't stand too tall on the soapbox, because we've paid the rent writing this character over and over and over again. The challenge to do something creatively different that will be both a commercial and critical success is the holy grail of the game's industry, and we are optimistic that we'll see more creative risk-taking as the business continues to mature and bets on new talent.

And we hope that talent includes you.

ACTION ITEM (GOLD)—THE ULTIMATE CHALLENGE— YOUR CALLING CARD

Take a risk. Create a game document for something that you've never seen or played before. Put everything that you've learned together into a game concept that must be made because it's just that damn good. Invest the time, effort and passion and you may be pleasantly surprised by what you'll discover about your talent and yourself. And once you have it together, use it. You have something tangible to give people. This is your calling card. And know that if you can do it once, you can do it again, and again, and again.

WHERE YOU GO NEXT IS UP TO YOU

Where are we as an industry going? We have a lot of ideas, and there are some obvious directions the video game business is headed in: extreme realism, episodic content, and the online delivery of the same. But when it is all said and done, games are still about entertainment. And what is fashionable today won't be tomorrow. Game genres fall in and out of favor. And just when everyone has it all figured out, some amazing game comes in out of nowhere and turns the whole thing on its head.

So we won't say your guess is as good as ours, because we think our guess, informed by our experience, would be better. But that is no guarantee we'd be right. In fact, your guess might be prophetic because you're going to be the one that introduces a whole new genre to the game business. That amazing game coming out of nowhere could be yours.

Until very recently, video games have been in their adolescence. We've been through a childhood of mining other mediums. We're starting to break off to a golden age when games firmly establish themselves as their own vibrant medium. We've seen the start of this with many of the current hit franchises. Games are being seen as more than creatively ambitious and financially rewarding; now they are being recognized for their artistic merit.

As we write this, we are in the midst of several projects. With one project we are debating whether or not it is acceptable to withhold vital information on the main character from the audience. In other words, we're trying to figure out whether the player will feel cheated if he finds out that the character he's playing has a different agenda than was originally presented. Everybody has an opinion. We think it's worth taking a chance, and we are going to keep the twist. Taking chances is one of the main premises of this book.

We're in show business. The *show* guys might think it is really cool to take a chance, but the *business* guys, serving as counterweights, want a modicum of safety. Is there more risk in taking a chance or more risk in not taking a chance? That's one of the eternal dilemmas of the entertainment industry.

On another project, we're trying to figure out exactly how much we have to reveal about a mysterious, murky horror world. Is it more satisfying to reveal the entire mystery or to tantalize the player with clues, but never really tell all—or will they come away feeling cheated?

On still another project, we're trying to build a game around a movie script— to stretch the boundaries of the story at every turn. We want the movie story to be playing as an ambient narrative in the background of the game, but we don't want to contradict it or break it. In other words, the game is to be a companion to the movie, not duplicate the things that movies do better than games.

All these projects present really cool challenges. A successful solution will, in every case, rely on a team of very smart, very hard working people making a lot of right decisions and, more important, executing them.

During the process of writing this book, we feel that we've had you as our collaborator. So together, we've now reached gold. We hope, at the very least, that we've stimulated your creativity and given you the tools and maps you'll need for your own personal journey into the game-space. We hope to see you somewhere on that journey, as a designer, a writer, a creative executive, or even our competition. Who knows, maybe we'll even work together again.

Now, go and make some really cool games.

GAME GLOSSARY

Here is a list of definitions and game terms that you may find useful. Many are standard throughout the industry. Others are ones we've created over the years to help us shorthand issues and elements that we commonly encounter in game development.

007 Moments
An experience heightener. A special thing, which—when discovered—gives you a special attaboy, animation, and score point.

AAA Game (Triple a Title)
This is industry speak for a first-quality game. It could be translated like school grades: A in Art (graphics and story), A in Gameplay, A in Programming.

Ability Progression
A system that rewards players with new moves, new character attributes, and hit-ratio increases (higher jumps, more health, etc) after accomplishing certain things (defeating bosses, finishing levels, and minigame areas, etc.).

Acid Test
A methodology for validating ideas before implementation.

Adrenalizer Scene
A scene to get the action going if things seem to be slowing down.

Alignment Chart

A chart, which characterizes all characters as a combination of Good, Neutral, and Evil with Lawful, Neutral, and Chaotic. It comes from *D & D* and is a great way to build out and define a property.

Alpha, Beta, Gold

The three major milestones of game production. Alpha: You have your game completely put together, but assets, gameplay, and levels are still being tweaked and tuned. Beta: Your game is finished, and now subject to testing to find bugs, fine-tune gameplay, and deal with any last minute revisions. Gold (also Gold Master): The game is complete. Note that this is not always the case, and some games continue to be tweaked when they have gone gold.

Ammo Hunt

Shorthand for a specific type of gameplay involving scavenging for items or power-ups.

Amphetamize

The structural version of an adrenalizer scene. It is something that adds artificial urgency to the story. A Ticking Clock is an amphetamizer.

Animatic

A partially animated storyboard with voices, music, and/or sound effects. Gives a sense of the pacing of the final product.

Arcader

An arcadish minigame in the context of a larger nonarcade game.

Ass Cam

Camera that basically follows the player character from behind (usually below and behind). A standard gameplay camera for third-person action games like *Tomb Raider*.

Attaboys

Small celebrations in which the player is congratulated for accomplishing something (ant: spanking).

Auricular gameplay

Gameplay based on sound.

Axonometric

Total top-down view of a game. Flat world. Usually very abstract strategy games or military sims. *See* Isometric Camera.

Backhook
An unexpected payoff from something established earlier in the story.

Barneys
Incidental, and usually, expendable characters in a game. From the various security guard models used in *Half-Life*.

Beats
Story beats are the individual plot elements that go into making a larger story.

Bitching Bettys
Characters that pop up during gameplay to nudge and harass the player to perform specific actions. They also function as a warning device.

Blowpast
A feature in a game in which the player is allowed to blow past a level or challenge that he can't beat so that they don't get stuck at that point in the game.

Blue Shoes
If you are doing a project for a client, you must deliver a recognizable version of their idea, even if you think you have a better one. "Look, if the client wants blue shoes, don't try to keep shoving red shoes at them. They don't want your red shoes, they want blue shoes."

Blueprint Copying
Creative process that works by saying, "Let's copy this game, but we'll make it a western instead of a sci-fi adventure."

Bond Sense
Named after a feature in the Bond game that allows the player to go into a mode where he sees things that the gamer cannot see. These sometimes provide essential information or fun things to do. It deals with the issue, very elegantly, of the difference between the player and James Bond himself.

Botox Effect
The gulf that still exists between photo-realistic characters and the real actors.

Branch
A part of the story that splits off from the TRUNK (optimal path) of the story.

Branching
A name for interactive adventures in which the story splits into different outcomes or plot developments based on player interaction.

Breaking the Game
Finding some weakness in the code/A.I./design or whatever that allows a player to win the game in a way that wasn't intended. Sometimes, this turns into Emergent Behavior, as with LURKING in Asteroids.

Button Masher
A title where simply slamming the buttons, rather than learning combos, will get you through the game.

Call-Outs
Lines of dialogue that provide direction to the player.

Camedy
Simulated humor. The kind of thing you see in kid's comics where all of the characters laugh about something that isn't really trying to be funny, but trying to be symbolic of funny.

Camera Logic
The motivation behind the camera. Point of view of the killer. Voyeur. Teacher. The alignment of the person telling you the story.

CGI
Computer-Generated Images.

Character Adventure
A game in which the player controls a specific, iconic character throughout the game.

Cheats
Codes that allow the player to beat the game, or acquire collectables and power-ups, without earning them. Cheats are including for testing purposes during development, and left in the game to be discovered by the players.

CIG
Sounded good, as in, "sounded good in the room." This refers to the kind of idea that pitches great, but in fact ends up being either meaningless, or worse yet, an idea that cannot be implemented after everyone falls in love with it.

Cinematic
A narrative moment in the game. Usually involves some loss of control on the part of the player.

Cleansing
A cleansing is when you go through a script or a property with the purposes of wiping out every trace of creative involvement (usually to clear rights, etc). It

might involve changing all the names of the characters, locations, every word of description (though not the intent). It is changing something to get rid of Clingons or, alternatively, to take away creator's rights.

Clingons
Guys who cling on to a project that they have no legitimate right to cling on to.

Clown Car
An object that just keeps generating enemies for the hero to fight in a video game (or for that matter, a movie).

Collectable
Items and objects that the player picks up during gameplay to aid him on his journey, such as ammo, health packs, power-ups, etc.

Combos
Executing moves in succession to achieve more powerful attacks.

Completion Rate
The percentage of players who complete a game.

Conceit
An idea that requires a leap of faith on the part of the player. For instance, the conceit of a game might be that it is always raining.

Concept Document
This is a short document (approximately ten pages) that lays out the basic mechanics, mythology, look, feel, plot, characters, worlds, etc. of the game.

Conditional Objective
In order to do X, you must do Y first. In order to open the door, you must get a key card. See Lock/Key gameplay.

Consequences
The decisions a player makes earlier will come back to effect him later on. This goes with the fact that the world has a memory.

Co-Op
Multiplayer gameplay in which the players are on the same team against the computer. Also know as cooperative gameplay.

Critical Path
In a branching game, the main story/gameplay path to success. Also used in game development to describe the major path that must be taken to completion of the project.

Cut-Scene
Much like a cinematic, but more likely to be presented in real-time using the in-engine. Also known as an In-Game.

Death Equivalents
(*See also* Violence Equivalents): Especially in children's properties, these are thing we insert in order to avoid showing death. Example, *G.I. Joe*—we would shoot down planes, but then show the bad guys escaping in parachutes.

Deliverables
Actual work items that must be delivered when doing a project.

Denting the Batmobile
Messing with sacred stuff.

Design Document
The blueprint for the game. Subject to multiple revisions and iterations as development proceeds.

Destructible Environment
Geometry that can be destroyed within a level.

Developers
The company or team who actually produces a video game.

Diamond Branching
A short branch in gaming that splits off and very quickly returns to the throughline. Very limited branching.

Directed Experience
Player has control, but the overall game is structured to give him the maximum gameplay experience by having a defined, linear design.

DWUK
Design Wanker's Useless Concern (not unrelated to a L.I.N.F.). This is one of those things that usually involves a huge over-think.

Dynamic Music
Music that reacts to a situation or environment—not canned.

Elevator Pitch
The ultra-fast version of a pitch that you can tell to an executive or producer on an elevator. "X meets Y in the future, you interested?"

Emergent Gameplay

Things don't always work out the way designers expect them to work out. Sometimes players find a really fun way to exploit the game in ways that never could have been anticipated. Sometimes, they just figure out how to *Break The Game*. Sometimes a bug becomes a feature.

Engine

The code underlying virtually any game. There are a variety of subsets of engines, such as physics and graphics engines.

Event Trigger

An action, place or object that advances the game by triggering some new event to occur.

Exposition

Imparting information that establishes the story, world, and characters.

Extrinsic Value

Things that exist outside of the game proper that serve to heighten the experience websites, comics, marketing contests, etc.).

Eye Candy

Nice graphics and visuals.

Faux Pitch

An idea that sounds great in a pitch but is not producible as a game for any number of reasons.

Fear Object

In the fiction itself, it is the thing that the character is afraid of. In development of a project, it is the thing you're afraid of in the project. *See Protecting an Idea.*

Feature Creep

Adding additional gameplay components as the game is developed. Almost always used in a negative connotation, to denote that the team and design is losing focus.

Feedback Loop

You press a button. Something meaningful happens. You understand that happening. Repeat the process.

Fetch Quest

This is a quest wherein you are sent to get something. These are basic game design elements and get pretty tedious.

First-Person POV (1st-Person)

Where the game is seen from the point of view of the character—as if through their eyes—creating the illusion that the player and character are one.

Flow State

That state you get into when time passes and you don't notice it. Also called The Zone.

Flushed

Gone. Deleted from the design. Out of the game. "The prison level is flushed."

FMV

Full-Motion Video.

Foo

A bunch of technical stuff creative types don't need to know about.

Force

The magic and art of forcing the player in a specific direction, or to perform a specific action, while maintaining the illusion of choice.

Fractile Rewrite

A rewrite that systematically goes through the script, searching for a particular element—for instance, a character.

Freeze (code, art, design, feature)

No more changes. When a game has reached Code Freeze, nothing new can be added to, or taken away from, the game's engine. Also sometimes referred to as Lock, as in Feature Lock.

Fun factor

Just what it sounds like. "Yeah, that's a cool design idea, but is it ultimately fun for the player? What is the fun factor?" A surprisingly common question.

Game Logic

Game logic dictates that any function of the game must make sense.

Game Objective

The task at hand. What the player is trying to do.

Gamer Pride

The act of empowering your player through game design.

Giant Rat of Sumatra

A dangling, intriguing issue or story left over in a franchise. This is an homage to Sherlock Holmes.

Gibs (from Giblets)
Flying body chunks when a character is hit.

Glavotch
Overly complex contrivance.

Gornished
Out of fashion . . . Not quite "in the toilet" but certainly out of favor. Tired . . . "It was hot a while ago, but now it's pretty gornished."

Granular
Using the smallest kind of minutia in order to illustrate or make it easy to understand a bigger point.

Grognard
War-gamer.

Grok
To understand something so thoroughly that you don't even have to think about it.

Grounding
To ground a story is to make it relatable. Setting it in a familiar world, with familiar characters, or with a familiar genre.

Hack and Slash
Fighting through waves of enemies.

Hat on a Hat
Too many ideas jammed into one concept. One cowboy hat on a character makes him look like a cattle rancher. Put a baseball cap on top of the cowboy hat, and suddenly, he looks like an idiot.

Head Turn
Literally, a character's head turning in a scene to look at an object that might be significant. It is also another way of discussing how the player knows to look at something. (Any subtle nudge given to the player to notice an action.)

Hoppy-Jumpy (Platformer)
A game that requires the player to jump from platform to platform (Sly Cooper, Crash Bandicoot).

Hot Spot
A specific place on the screen that triggers a unique action when a player or cursor comes over it.

Idea Diffusion
Having the basic idea that weakens the more it is developed.

Idea Drift
Losing focus of the core elements of your design and/or story as more ideas continue to be added to the mix.

Illusion of Freedom
A good sandbox game tries to give you this impression. It is always an illusion. There are always constrictors and limits. You can't walk into all of the buildings, the world ends, eventually there are only so many challenges, there are only so many canned lines of dialogue—and so on.

Inevitable Game
The game that is really going to get made, once the initial excitement wears off and schedule and budget realities come into play.

Instant Fun
Pick up the controller and start playing.

Interface
Graphical game conventions that provide information to the player and help him interact with the game. Health bars, ammo meters, maps, etc.

Inventory
Objects that a character is carrying around.

Invisible Ramp (Level Ramping)
The game keeps becoming more challenging the further the player progresses. One of the fundamentals of design.

Isometric Camera
Top down at a slight angle so you have a sense of depth.

It's a Feature!
A happy accident in which something that starts as a bug or an error in the game ends up showing the way to a whole new kind of gameplay. Also used jokingly when a horribly obvious bug affects the game.

Iterative Process
Game design is, by its very nature, an iterative process. You do version after version after version. Usually, the changes between iterations are minor. Sometimes they are huge and disruptive.

K.I.N.F.
Kool Idea, No Fun. This is the kind of idea that is conceptually sound, but wouldn't lead to fun gameplay.

K.I.N.I.

Kool Idea, Not Implementable. Great idea, but it is not practical.

K.I.S.S.

Keep it Simple, Stupid. An old chestnut, but still worth remembering.

Keeping Alive

Reminding the player of a character who does not have essential business for segments of the game. This also goes for keeping various plot elements alive.

Killing Keyser

A note so devastating that an entire project collapses if the note isn't dealt with. If you kill Keyser Soze, then you don't have *The Usual Suspects*.

L.I.N.F.

Logical Idea, No Fun.

Laying Pipe

Setting up something that will pay off later on.

Learning Curve

Macro learning curve is learning skills and concepts that will take the player the game. Micro learning curve is learning how to beat individual things in the mission. This will also lead to greater speed and sense of mastery.

Levels

The environments of the game. Levels in a game work like chapters in a book. Most often, they are of increasing difficulty (though many designers like to alternate hard and easy levels to keep players interested). In plot-based games, each level should advance the story.

Look and Feel

Too often, this phrase is rammed together almost as if it was one concept. It is two concepts. Look is literally: the look of the game. Feel is how it feels to play it.

Luigi

A mock exercise to placate somebody.

Marquee

A phrase borrowed from the film industry. What it is you're selling—a famous license, a famous sequel, a famous designer? What is the marquee element of the game, if it has one?

Mechanic

The main way, or core play-pattern, in which the player will interact with the game.

Metastory

The metastory in an interactive project is the sum total of the known or implied stories of all of the characters in the story. It takes into account every part of every branch. All potential dialogue. All potential outcomes. All backstory. The world.

Middleware

Game engines that can be licensed to build titles.

Milestone

An objective that must be reached along the critical path before the project can move forward. For instance, you have to finish the outline of a project before you can move to script. Both the script and outline are milestones.

Mission-Based Gameplay

The player is given a series of missions to complete in order to beat a level.

Monotonatic

Same colors, same music, same gameplay mechanic. Blech.

Mouse Fishing

Refers to old-style CD-ROM games where you had to drag the cursor around until something interesting happens.

Moustache

A disguise on something new to separate it from its familiar source.

Now We'll Figure Out What the Real Game Is

This is an informal step in the process that occurs when people realize that there are limits to money, art, disc space, programming time, and that ultimately, life is too short. Rare indeed is the project that doesn't go through this phase. It is created by a fascinating number of phenomena, most of them involving excessive optimism, surprise input from publishers, inattention, and lack of desire to face the constantly shifting realities of the process (*see* Parallel Design Process).

NPC

Nonplayer Character. This is a term borrowed from role-playing. It is any character showing up on the screen that the player does not control.

Paradigm Buster

A game or film that is so radically different that it fundamentally changes the medium. It becomes a genre.

Parallel Design Process

Working on all three of the primary elements of a project simultaneously and immediately measuring the breakthroughs of one area upon another.

Pavlovian
It has been said that all game design is Pavlovian. Believe or disbelieve this at will.

Payoffs
Anything that rewards the player. Also, in a story sense, the narrative results of setups.

Pear-Shaped
A term used to describe the phenomenon when mission-based gameplay goes awry due to scripted or random events in which the player must improvise.

Pete Popcorn
The average guy in your audience. The point is to put a face, maybe even a broadly drawn one, on the audience.

Popcorning
One thing explodes, another thing explodes next to it, creating a chain reaction to destroy enemies.

Preliminary Design Document
This is a longer document (50–200 pages) that goes into much more detail on how the game works. Ideally, this also includes artwork.

Protecting an Idea
"What are you protecting?" Often arguments will take place because somebody is protecting something in a project, a scene, a character, or a gameplay device and feel that it is being threatened. Oftentimes, when somebody is behaving irrationally, they are "protecting" something.

Prototype
A working mock-up of the game designed to test the core gameplay concepts and whether or not the game can be produced in a timely, cost effective manner. Mostly prototypes have fallen out of favor with the advent of the Vertical Slice.

Publishers
The company that produces the game, markets it, sells it, and most often finances it, e.g., Electronic Arts, Activision. The publisher might also own the Developer.

Quickly Recognized Features (QRFs)
Players can pick up the game and start playing instantly because the controls are similar to other games of the genre (forward on the D-Pad moves the character forward, etc.).

Ragdoll
Realistic physics.

Red Shirt

A character that is doomed to die. From *Star Trek*.

Reference Titles

Products you should be aware of in order to understand a particular design, e.g., you should know about *Doom* in order to understand this game.

Reload Learning

This involves the learning you do as you try the same level multiple times. Basically, the more you do it, the faster and better you get at it. It is tied to the concept that each death means something.

Replayability (or lack thereof)

Any game with a linear story (containing an ending) is inherently limited in replayability. Once you have exhausted the story, the game is over. Replay can be extended with bonus rounds and serendipity objects, but once the story is told, it is over. Publishers used to be obsessed with replayability, but now, giving players a satisfying single-player experience is often enough.

Ripamatics

This is a term stolen from the advertising business where concepts for commercials are often put together using stock footage or elements borrowed from other movies, television shows, etc. In games, often edited sequences are compiled from other inspirational material, such as films, and used to give a sense of the general tone and intent of the game.

Rorschach

A document or demo designed to let the reader/viewer see what they want to see. Great for sales; not great for knowing what you've sold, later on.

RTM

Release to Manufacture. When you hear these words, you can finally breathe a sigh of relief. At this point, your Gold Disc is out of your hands and in the process of being pressed and printed. Of course, this also means that you get no more bites at the apple. When you reach RTM, you are done. Period. The end.

Sandbox

Area in a game where players feel free to roam around, do random missions, and are not pinned to the through-line of a story.

Schedule Monkey

That guy at every developer who tells that you can't do things because the schedule won't permit it.

Schlobongle
A complicated hassle.

Scriptment
A cross between a script and a treatment. Contains the entire story, snippets of dialogue, scenes, camera angles, etc.

Sense of Mastery
The feeling that a player has that he's in control of the game and the world.

Serendipity Factors
Unexpected elements in the game that serve as overall goals.

SFAR
Standard for a Reason. A game convention that is standard, because it makes a kind of intuitive sense. Moving the joystick to the right moves your character to the right.

SFX
Sound Effects.

Snags
Design elements you want to pull from other games and insert in yours.

Snipe Hunting
Endlessly wandering around in a game, looking for something that either isn't there or is badly hidden. This is often done to extend gameplay time or sell cheat books.

Spotlight on a Turd
Drawing unnecessary attention to a plot or game problem by putting too much emphasis on it.

Start to Crate Ratio
The time it takes from when you start the game until you run into the first gaming cliché.

Stealth Education
The concept that education can be "snuck" into products through immersive gameplay. The player will learn whether they know they're learning or not.

Storyboard
What the artist draws to visualize action before it is animated. Can also be used to give a sense of what gameplay will look like.

Tabula Rasa (blank slate)
The world or character starts out blank and the player creates the identity.

Technical Design Document
The complementary documentation to the Game Design Document that is focused on the programming and code issues in developing the title.

Tezstein's Law
When you get rid of an incompetent or intrusive manager he will inevitably be replaced by something worse.

Third-Handed
Used to describe gameplay that gets so complex that you'd need a third hand to operate the controls.

Third-Person Point of View
Where the main character in the game is seen on screen.

This Is Not My First Picnic
You've done this before and you understand the issues and risks involved.

Thumb Candy
Fun gameplay.

Ticking Clock
Anything that increases suspense by giving the player a limited amount of time.

Title
A game.

TMI
Too Much Information. What does the player really need to know to understand gameplay conventions and story, etc.? Do we need a huge backstory—do we need a labored logic for the game convention?

Toyatic
Will this franchise make good toys? Is it *toyatic?*

Trench Coat
Device for covering something very ugly.

Trivbits
Things to insert into a game that may be irrelevant to the game, but build the franchise that the game is based on.

Trunk

In limited a branching game, the trunk is the through-line of the story—the optimal path—to which the branches reconnect.

Tune and Tweak

To optimize the gameplay and details of a level.

Turnip Truck Gambit

People offer you the "sucker deal," thinking you don't know what you're doing. Often it is insulting.

Turtling the Ninja

This is taking a concept that might be offensive to some and softening or spinning it to make it acceptable. It comes from *Teenage Mutant Ninja Turtles*, a 1980s toy line that cleverly sold a cute turtle to Mommy and a ninja swordsman to the little boy.

USPs

Unique Selling Points—special elements and features of the game that will make people want to buy it.

Value System

What is valued in the "world" of a game? What is the "morality" of the world? There is the fictional value (such as saving the world) and there is the gameplay value, and that is a power-up, a health pack.

Vector Check

To check your project and say, "Is this going where we intended it to go?" or has it incrementally strayed into being something else.

Vertical Slice

A specific type of game demo in which a very small portion of the envisioned game is developed to "final" quality, including design, game mechanics, art, and engineering. Think of it as taking a slice out of a completed game. Very common these days, as too many publishers have been burned by demos that never really advance beyond the temp stage in quality or gameplay.

Violence Equivalents

Especially with children's properties, ways of having guns without having guns (goo shooters). Ways of softening violence (silly sound effects).

Vision

The intangible, hopefully shared, view of a project that drives it forward.

W-5-H
Who, What, When, Where, Why, and How of the game's story structure.

Walkthrough
A written description of the gameplay experience for a given level (or game).

Waypoints
Key locations with a level.

Weed Eating
The process of eliminating unnecessary elements from the design and story.

Zerging
Unskilled gameplay that is more dependent on numbers than tactics (from a specific alien type used in *Starcraft*).

Appendix A

Backwater
Game Design Document

BACKWATER
The Ultimate
Survival Horror Experience

Game Proposal by Ground Zero Productions
Version 2.1
Proprietary and Confidential

ONE-SHEET—SUMMARY

TITLE
Backwater

GENRE
Survival-Horror/Action-Adventure Hybrid

VERSION
2.1—Preliminary Proposal

CATEGORY
Backwater is an exciting, heart-stopping action adventure that brings a number of unique gameplay elements to its terror-inducing thrills. The game combines exploration, combat and puzzles with an innovative character interaction system that allows the Player to hide, fool and trap the main antagonist, Mr. Jangle.

PLATFORMS
PS2 and Xbox

THE BIG IDEA
Through the course of one horrible night, the Player's Character (PC), Eden, must outwit and outfight her tormentor, a classic horror villain named Mr. Jangle, through the backwater swamps and bayous of the deep south. However, unlike most games in the genre, in *Backwater*, the PC is the prey, not the hunter. Throughout the gameplay experience, players will be constantly confronting their feelings of vulnerability and fear as they develop strategies to fight, trap and contain Mr. Jangle. As they advance through the completely nonlinear gameplay, they reveal more of the backstory that will ultimately help them defeat Mr. Jangle.

PLAY MECHANIC
Players will control Eden as she moves through the various locations that comprise the worlds of *Backwater*. Eden can walk, run, crawl, climb, hide, fight, shoot, use items, sneak, manipulate props, solve puzzles, interact with other characters, jump, and control her breathing. Exploration and combat are key components of gameplay. Most interaction happens in highly cinematic third-person perspective.

However, Eden will also have a look function, which will allow the player to see the world through her point of view, or first person.

LICENSE

Backwater is envisioned as a franchise with immense ancillary market potential. The main villain, Mr. Jangle, has an elaborate fiction and backstory that puts him squarely in the realm of other classic horror creations, such as Freddy Kruger, Hannibal Lecter, and Michael Myers.

TARGET AUDIENCE

Targeted for 16- to 35-year-old gamers, both male and female. *Backwater* has a strong female heroine and eerily beautiful worlds that will appeal to fans of strong gameplay and visual stunning experiences. To reach the broadest possible audience, the game will have intuitive controls and a quick learning curve.

CONCEPT

Backwater is a game in which you are the prey of a modern-day boogieman. The entire game happens over the course of one night in and around a Louisiana swamp.

If you are to succeed, you must survive until morning. To do so, you will have to hide, run, distract, and repeatedly kill your antagonist, Mr. Jangle, as he relentlessly pursues you.

Backwater turns the standard 3D game on its head. Unlike traditional 3D action-adventures, you must both evade and attack your pursuer. Your options are to both fight and flee. Rather than firepower alone, your wits and courage are also your tools of survival.

Backwater will be designed as a real-time horror game, one in which creating a tension-filled, heart-pounding experience is the ultimate goal. Playing the game should not only be fun . . . it should be terrifying.

The story of the game unfolds as you move your way through the world on that fateful evening. The narrative will be filled with crosses and double crosses, and by the time the story ends, the real identity of our killer, Mr. Jangle, the unfortunate tow-truck driver, will create the final jolt of terror.

Designed to be an interactive *Deliverance* and *Southern Comfort* meets *Halloween* and the *Scream, Backwater* is an intense, heart-racing action-adventure. Danger and death lurk around every tree, horror hides in the shadows . . . even the crickets sound menacing.

You are an outsider in this world, with a simple objective: Stay alive and get to the highway by morning. To do that you will have to face your tormentor, Mr. Jangle, and find a way to destroy him.

GAME SUMMARY

In the tradition of story-driven experiences like *Fear Effect* or *Half-Life*, *Backwater* is about creating emotional responses that move beyond the satisfaction of pressing buttons.

Because we are putting you into the familiar world of 3D, but standing the expectations of this genre on its head, we are creating a new gameplay dynamic. The intent is to make *Backwater* not only the most frightening game ever created, but to make it the most terrifying experience one can imagine.

Currently, we are planning to license an engine to build *Backwater*. Traditional level building techniques will be employed to create the worlds. Aggressive AI structures will be implemented to bring our main antagonist, Mr. Jangle, to life. This is especially true since many of the sequences in the game will involve extended sequences in which Mr. Jangle will be moving and searching for you, and you will need to study his actions if you are to escape.

As the game progresses, the story of *Backwater* unfolds. For instance, you might make it to a side road when you see a state trooper's vehicle. You scream for help, but when you arrive, the trooper is nowhere to be found. You climb into the vehicle and try to get the shotgun locked inside when you see Mr. Jangle holding the key and the trooper's severed hand . . .

In addition to exploration of the world, you will be able to gather objects that will help you in avoiding/and or distracting Mr. Jangle. Objects you can gather might include: Flashlights, flares, rope, welding torch, etc. These and other items may also become Weapons of Opportunity.

Because the objective of the game is survival, rather than ammo counters and health meters found in traditional 3D games, there will be a Fatigue Meter.

Running causes you to become fatigued, eventually slowing you down and causing the sound of your breathing to become louder. This increases the chance of being detected by the killer as he searches for you, so part of playing the game is balancing your energy as you avoid Mr. Jangle. And facing Mr. Jangle is always a dangerous proposition in *Backwater*.

You will also be able to utilize an Adrenaline Rush. A Rush will increase speed, coordination and stamina to perform actions during gameplay. Rush moments can come in one of two ways. You may either Scream (which will, of course, let Mr. Jangle get a bead on you) or perform a specific milestone within the game to obtain the Rush moment. Over time, the Rush will dissipate, and your abilities will return to normal. The Scream "power-up" can also be utilized while facing Mr. Jangle.

During gameplay, you will come to realize that although you can kill Mr. Jangle, you cannot stop him until the very end of the game. In fact, the objective of the game is to kill Mr. Jangle thirteen times. You see, much like a cat, he has many lives.

The mythology of why Mr. Jangle has thirteen lives can be found within the ritual of the Black Milking, which is explained in the **Backstory** section of this document. However, this conceit allows you a number of unique opportunities to kill Mr. Jangle, including impaling him, crushing him under a freight car, tossing him into a metal shredder, shoving him into an alligator pit and igniting him with high-octane whiskey from the moonshine still.

However, like the Terminator, Mr. Jangle is an unstoppable machine until the very end. And every time Mr. Jangle is dispatched, he returns with even more power (though he will look the worse for wear). In fact, Mr. Jangle, in essence, is an ever-evolving level boss that becomes more and more disturbing in both appearance and action as the game progresses. This means that although you will interact with Mr. Jangle often, his fantastical nature will create a variety of game-play opportunities and "new" enemies to face.

And in addition to Mr. Jangle, you will be faced with all manner of enemies and creatures related to the powers of the Black Milking that he can manipulate.

Only after you have caused Mr. Jangle to use up his thirteen lives can he truly be destroyed. To aid you in dealing with Mr. Jangle, you will be able to gather weapons of opportunity, such as a rack, an ax handle, a shotgun, a welding torch, etc.

Mr. Jangle's Achilles' heel is the thirteen snakes that created him. There will be one snake located in each of the Thirteen Locations of the game that must be captured into Miss Lady Em's suitcase (which you will find early in the game).

Once the snake is back within the case, the power of that lifetime's evil is vulnerable to attack. This creates the hunting and gathering component of *Backwater*. Many of the snakes will be in difficult locations to obtain, and require creative solutions and/or puzzle solving to acquire. (Once again, the mythology and explanations of *Backwater*'s story are discussed later in this document.)

With these ground rules firmly established, you will be as concerned with your own survival as with trying to destroy Mr. Jangle. The design of the game is based around your role as prey and all level design and story points will reinforce your vulnerability.

The best defense throughout the game is to run, distract, trap, and/or hide from Mr. Jangle as he continues to chase you until the snakes of the Black Milking are collected.

There will be unique opportunities for concealment during the game, including climbing trees, or perhaps hiding underwater with a breathing straw fashioned from the plants growing along the water.

However, that is not to say that you are without an offensive capability to attack Mr. Jangle. Once a snake has been trapped in the suitcase, you can then go on the attack and try to take away one of Mr. Jangle's lives.

In fact, in a number of instances, doing battle with Mr. Jangle and other enemies within the *Backwater* universe is the only path to survival. The key point is that your character, Eden, will never come across unlimited ammo, über-weapons, or other gameplay conceits that create the sense of invincibility. Throughout the game, you will always feel vulnerable to both Mr. Jangle and his minions.

TARGET PLAYER

Our Target Player is a fan of the survival-horror genre, and also action-adventure games in general. *Backwater* will appeal to horror fans, both the hard-core gamer and the casual player.

While *Backwater* is not about overt violence and massive bloodshed, its tone and content will make it an MA title.

The game is about an ever-increasing tension brought on by your need to confront your fears. To survive in, and ultimately win *Backwater*, you will engage in a number of terrifying gameplay elements, including having to defeat Mr. Jangle multiple times. While the game has crossover appeal, it falls strictly into the same category as Resident Evil, Silent Hill, System Shock, etc.

Our goal is to create the most horrifying, terror-inducing interactive experience ever. To accomplish this, *Backwater* will be designed within the MA guidelines structure.

INTRODUCTION

The following is a potential opening cinematic that establishes the mood and overall sensibility of *Backwater*.

```
OVER BLACK we HEAR a young WOMAN'S voice that betrays an
urgency that will soon become panic . . .

                    WOMAN
           That last stop was at least fifty miles
           back.

An apologetic MAN'S voice responds.

                    MAN
           I'm sorry, okay? You're right, Eden, I
           should've checked . . .
```

We FADE IN on . . .

EXT. GAS STATION—NIGHT

The CAMERA MOVES in on a deserted and long-abandoned Gas
Station deep within the heart of the Bayou. Greenery crowds
what remains of the equipment under the awning. A broken sign
on rusting hinges reads "KINDLY SERVICE AND GAS".

Struggling with one of the '40s-style pumps is the man whose
voice we've heard. His name is TED, early twenties and in good
shape, obviously the adventurous-type. He pulls the fuel nozzle
away from his late model SPORTS CAR.

> TED
> Nothin' . . .

TED gets into the car where the woman, EDEN, waits anxiously in
the passenger seat. Early twenties, Eden has more curves than
Ted's German wheels, and one suspects from her pout on her
beautiful face, a better motor as well.

Ted fires the engine and looks at the FUEL GAUGE. It is pinging
EMPTY. He puts the car into gear and it pulls out of the
station, showering a trail dust and debris.

The CAMERA tracks through the empty station, until it stops in
front of the darkened service bay beside the pumps. Inside, we
can see an old, beaten and battered TOW TRUCK. A beat, then
suddenly . . .

The LIGHTS of the Tow Truck turn ON, blasting the screen with
illumination. A split second later, the engine of the truck
ROARS to life with a menacing rumble.

Kindly Service is back in business . . .

DISSOLVE TO:

INT. TED'S CAR—LATER

Ted is negotiating with his car and losing.

> TED
> Come on, come on . . .

He looks at Eden as he pulls over. The engine of Ted's car
complains loudly as the fuel tank can no longer quench its
thirst. Ted drives across a small rickety BRIDGE and onto a
dirt culvert beside the road as the car sputters to a stop.

                              EDEN
                   So now what, Ted?

                              TED
                   Guess we walk . . . Forgive me?

                              EDEN
                   You _are_ kidding, right?

Ted closes the difference between them, moving his face next to
Eden's.

                              TED
                   Please, Eden. I'll make it up to you . . .
                   right here if you'd like . . .

                              EDEN
                   Now you _are_ kidding.

                              TED
                   Why not? It'll give us something to talk
                   about while we hike. Besides, who's out
                   here but us and the
                   gators . . .

                              EDEN
                   Shut up.

Eden pulls Ted to her, and they begin to kiss when the entire
rear window of the car is BLASTED with light. Ted and Eden
struggle to look out into the light.

EDEN'S POV

We see the outline of the Tow Truck from Kindly Service BACKLIT
against the night sky of the Bayou.

                              EDEN
                   Looks like a tow truck.

                              TED
                   I'll be damned. I was kinda hoping that
                   this crisis would've lasted a little
                   longer. I could ask him to come back in
                   fifteen if you want . . .

Eden smiles and laughs disarmingly.

                              EDEN
                   What I want is gas and directions.

<pre>
                        TED
              Right. Lock it behind me.
</pre>

Eden gives Ted a peck on the cheek as he exits the car. He
shuts the driver's side door and Eden reaches across, locking
it.

Eden loses sight of Ted as he steps into the light radiating
from the Tow Truck. She is alone for a painfully long moment,
then SPLAT . . .

Ted, bloodied and screaming, crashes into the side window of
the car. Eden SCREAMS. Tow HOOKS attached to metal CHAINS are
painfully imbedded into Ted's SHOULDERS.

<pre>
                        TED
              Help me, EDEN . . . Help ME!
</pre>

The sound of a WINCH drowns out Ted's pleas for help and Eden's
terrified cries. Ted claws at the car window as he is suddenly
jerked backwards by the Chains toward the tow truck.

Eden is in shock, breathing heavily. As she sits alone and
terrified in the car, we hear Ted's anguished scream fade, then
abruptly stop. Eden doesn't move. And we realize that she
won't. The next move Eden makes is ours to control.

It's time to play . . .

GAMEPLAY DESCRIPTION

What follows is a description of the opening few minutes of the *Backwater*
Gameplay Experience that would come after the introduction found at the beginning of this document.

Player-Controlled Actions and Effects are CAPITALIZED. Your PC
is Eden.

Following the opening Cinematic, Eden USES the car door and
exits the vehicle. She finds herself outside among the dangers
of the Bayou. In the distance, Eden LOOKS toward the tow truck.
Its engine is running and its lights are on. Eden CROUCHES,
then CRAWLS away from the car towards the brush beside the
road. Her FATIGUE METER is still at the minimum, so her
breathing is quiet as she HIDES under a fallen tree and LOOKS
for a path toward the bridge behind the tow truck.

To her right, Eden HEARS the metallic jangling of keys. She
LOOKS back toward the sound as the side window of Ted's car
CRASHES OUT. Eden SEES the shadowy FIGURE of MR. JANGLE blur
past in the Background. The SOUND of the keys grows louder as
Mr. Jangle comes nearer.

Eden slips from her hiding spot and RUNS for the tow truck. As
she moves, her Fatigue Meter begins to RISE. Her breathing
INCREASES in volume, and her coordination is affected. Eden
stumbles as she LOOKS behind her while RUNNING toward the
truck.

Reaching the cab of the truck, Eden USES the door. A large
BLACK, WATER MOCCASIN strikes out at her, then quickly slithers
down onto the floor of the truck as she WATCHES. Eden HEARS the
sound of the keys getting louder still. Her FATIGUE METER
begins to return to normal as she reaches the back of the truck
and finds TED flailed upon the towing arm. Eden SCREAMS,
increasing her ADRENALINE METER and rewarding her with a RUSH.
She USES a BOX of FLARES in the bed of the truck, and adds the
FLARE to her INVENTORY. Then Eden DASHES for the bridge, her
speed increased by the RUSH. She looks back and sees MR. JANGLE
closing on her as she reaches the bridge.

As the RUSH expires, Eden stumbles, falling BACKWARDS onto the
bridge as Mr. Jangle appears beside her.

Eden USES the FLARE from her inventory, and attacks with the
FLARE as a weapon. It ignites, shooting flame into Mr. Jangle's
face. He cries out as he is driven back. Then, seizing the
moment, Eden LEAPS onto a branch beside the bridge. She CLIMBS
down the branch toward the water below, but her FATIGUE METER
is maximized, so she can't SWIM into the water. Instead, the
FLARE that Eden holds illuminates a drainage pipe under the
bridge. Eden hesitates for a moment until her FATIGUE and
ADRENALINE METERS stabilize, then she CLIMBS into the pipe and
begins to CRAWL, hoping the flare burns long enough for her to
find the other side. Her FATIGUE METER begins to rise as she
struggles to find her way through the pipe.

From the shadows, Mr. Jangle watches the red glow of the flare
radiate from the drainage pipe and begins to move.

Eden can HEAR the sounds of the keys once again.

MR. JANGLE

Mr. Jangle, the killer, is a classic horror movie villain. Mr. Jangle gets his name from
the hundreds of keys he wears around his waist. We will find out that these are the

keys of his victims, his trophies, and he plans to add yours to the collection of Janitors keychains he wears on his belt. As Mr. Jangle moves closer to you, you can hear the rattling of the keys. That is how you know that he is getting nearer.

Mr. Jangle can be killed, but only temporarily. And each time he returns from the dead, he is progressively more powerful and supernatural than before. Mr. Jangle is relentless in his pursuit, and won't stop until he finds you. But Mr. Jangle can be distracted, giving you time to escape. You will also be forced at times to hide from him.

For instance, you may have to seek cover in a tool locker located within the engine room of the Sunken Riverboat as he searches for you.

In addition to Mr. Jangle, you will have to face other dangers, including Alligators, Water Moccasins, Bogs, Quicksand, collapsing Mine Shafts, etc.

As the story and game move forward, the supernatural aspects of Mr. Jangle will begin to be revealed. Before the game is over, you will find ourselves facing Mr. Jangle's unique powers and abilities as reality bends to the magic of the Black Milking. However, you may find a way to use the power yourself . . .

NONLINEAR GAME STRUCTURE AND STYLE

The world of *Backwater* is composed of real-time 3D Interior and Exterior Environments.

The feel of the locations is very Gothic. Everything is overgrown with weeds and vegetation. The world is damp. The colors are cool with dark tonality. Fog lies close to the ground.

Stylistically, the characters and worlds, although 3D, will have the illustrative look of a graphic novel. The intent is to put you into a stylized hyper-reality, creating a unique and compelling world to explore.

Since all of the action of the game takes place within a moonlit Louisiana Bayou, you will not only have to explore the swamp, but also a number of unique locations within it. All of the locations are disturbing and scary, adding to the ever-increasing sense of dread. Each location includes plenty of places where Mr. Jangle might suddenly appear. They all project a sense of dread and foreboding. Heavy shadows, creaking floorboards, windswept trees, etc.

The game is built around thirteen chapters with unique end-level narratives that can be played in a nonlinear fashion. Each of these narratives represents one part of the larger backstory fiction that will finally be revealed and will give you the ultimate solution on how to defeat Mr. Jangle once and for all. Other game narratives that relate to what is happening that evening in the swap are location (level) specific, and will be revealed when preset triggers are hit.

All of the narratives in *Backwater* will be RTV (in game) Cinematics.

At the end of each level, the player will unlock a backstory narrative as part of winning (completing) the level.

To accomplish this, the player must destroy Mr. Jangle and gather the snake rattle hidden with the location. This is our established gameplay mechanic for the entire game. The main object is to find the snake and destroy Mr. Jangle. Subobjects will include fighting other NPCs, solving puzzles, finding items, exploring environments, etc.

Visual representation of the uncovered backstory narratives in the game shell will be a Circle, so that the beginning and the end of the story will not be obvious until it is almost completed.

Snake rattles will serve as placeholders for the missing story lines. The rattles of the snakes will shake when highlighting a finished backstory element. Art direction will make this look like the final sacrificial voodoo circle that releases Mr. Jangle's power.

When you have all of the elements of the backstory completed, they will unlock the final location of Mr. Jangle's wrecking yard (Kindly Service).

The beginning and end of the game happen in linear fashion at their respective locations (the abandoned road and the wrecking yard) and are not part of the thirteen chapters, but bookends on the overall fiction and gameplay.

The rest of the game and story are nonlinear, and it is completely up to you to decide on how you wish to tackle the game. A foreshadow element will preview each separate location (level), before you enter the level, because once a location is entered, a "door" is locked behind the characters, trapping them in that chapter of the experience until they have reached the end of the level, found the snake rattle, dealt with the unique enemies and puzzle challenges of the location, and defeated the level-boss version of Mr. Jangle.

Listed below are the level/locations in the game. Each of these locations will be populated with a number of NPCs; some human, some creature, and later in the game, some supernatural.

* **Swamp/Bayou Location.** The classic Bayou. Waist-high water filled with trees. A thick canopy of vegetation overhead. Sounds of creatures in the darkness. Stillwater on a moonlit night. Fireflies and insects. Alligators, snakes . . . the works.

* **Abandoned Mansion.** Overgrown with swamp foliage. A classical southern mansion, huge in scale. Inside, sheet-covered furniture, cobwebs, etc. You can move through the location, and search all of the various room of the place. Plenty of places for you to hide. Unfortunately, plenty of places for Mr. Jangle to hide as well.

❋ **Destroyed Bridge.** Part of the old interstate, but left to rot in the damp swamp for thirty years. Could be a bridge of a canal, with a mechanical room full of gears, etc.

❋ **Cemetery.** The classic southern cemetery, with crypts above ground because the water table is so high that burying the dead is not practical. Much of the Black Milking secrets can be found within the gates of this eerily silent place.

❋ **Sunken Riverboat.** Destroyed casino, wheel house, engine room, paddle wheel, etc.

❋ **Moonshine Still.** Drums for the ingredients, machinery. Maybe a couple of guys working at the still. A fast '49 Mercury with its key in the ignition. But will they help you, or are they out for something?

❋ **Deserted Oil Platform.** Drilling equipment, Rough-necks huts, office trailer etc. Oil drums everywhere.

❋ **Alligator Farm.** Complete with worn-out, tired attractions and very hungry Alligators.

❋ **Mardi Gras Float Storage-yard.** An overgrown lot of abandoned floats from the Mardi Gras festivals. Surreal and terrifying in equal measure.

❋ **Railcars.** Rusted track with a few passenger and freight train cars that can be explored.

❋ **Voodoo Shack.** The location in which the Black Milking took place. Disturbing, dark. This location will contain a number of items that you will need to unleash the Black Milking's power. This is also where the final, thirteenth snake must be captured.

❋ **Old-Timer's Cabin.** Right out of *Deliverance*. Could have a Swamp Boat nearby that would have enough fuel to take us across part of the Bayou.

❋ **Kindly Service and Gas Station/Junkyard.** Your final location, and where you will find the ultimate truth about Mr. Jangle. You will also discover Mr. Jangle's other victims, or what remains of them. Filled with rusting hulks of cars. Weeds and car parts everywhere. A Vehicle grave-yard that is home to rats, maggots and half-dead victims welded into steel boxes. In the back, a shack with car winch, underground mechanics pit, etc. Off to one side, a huge car-crusher and shredder (where Mr. Jangle meets his final demise).

GAMEPLAY HIGHLIGHTS

There are two main components to playing *Backwater*. They are exploration (including object gathering/usage, trap setting and NPC interaction) and combat. All of the elements of *Backwater* will be tied together with seamless RTV and Pre-rendered Cinematics.

EXPLORATION/INVENTORY ITEMS

Exploration of the world will involve searching through the various environments in the experience, meeting up with other characters that may be out to harm or help you, and looking for areas to hide from or trap Mr. Jangle.

When objects are found, they can be added to your inventory. Objects will include items like lanterns, racks, moonshine etc. Occasionally, you will also be able to get your hands on some weaponry, but the inventory system of *Backwater* is based on realism.

The more items you are carrying, the slower and less agile you are, which will of course have a direct effect on your encounters with Mr. Jangle. Also, the inventory will not be Felix the Cat's bag of tricks. There is a finite number of items that can be carried at any one time. Part of the game strategy will involve which items to carry. For instance, you won't be able to carry a shotgun, a rake, and a pick-ax all at the same time. However, there will be places in the worlds where items can be hidden and later retrieved.

The most important objects that you must find during gameplay are the thirteen snakes that created Mr. Jangle. Through the course of *Backwater*, you will come to know their significance, and realize that the Water Moccasins are the Achilles' heel of Mr. Jangle. The snakes will have to be gathered, along with the other items needed for a ritual sacrifice to free the evil they possess. Some of the snakes will be difficult to find, others will be easy to find but difficult to gather.

For instance, when you reach the Alligator Farm, you can see one of the snakes on a small island. Unfortunately, that island is in the middle of an Alligator Pit. Also, some of the snakes will put up a fight and become boss-characters that must be subdued.

As the thirteen snakes are collected and you tick off Mr. Jangle lives by confronting and repeatedly killing him, the experience will become more supernatural because the powers of the Black Milk are beginning to come under your control.

Using the environments and objects found within them to create traps to slow down Mr. Jangle will also be a key gameplay component. You will have the opportunity to set traps that will hurt or distract Mr. Jangle, giving you time to make your escape.

For instance, you will be able to booby-trap the still so that when Mr. Jangle opens one of the moonshine barrels, the still will explode. To accomplish this, you will have to find the necessary elements that make the bomb, and then find a way to lure Mr. Jangle to search for you in the still.

COMBAT

In addition to surviving Mr. Jangle's numerous attacks, you will also find yourself facing off against a number of diverse enemies, both real and supernatural, in *Backwater*.

As an example, as you approach the Moonshine Still in the above example, the Good Ol' Boys brewing the white lightning may think that you are the local police, and open fire on you. You will have to dodge their fire until you've convinced them that you are not the cops. However, they have no intention of being friendly. In fact, you are an outsider in their backyard, and although you think that the Moonshiners will help you once they hear your story, instead they attack you.

You must now combat the Moonshiners, knowing that all the while Mr. Jangle is on your trail.

When the magic of the Black Milking come into full force later in the experience, you will find yourself facing the undead victims of Mr. Jangle, reanimated by his powers. This means you will be fighting horrific creatures brought back into existence by the Voodoo that created Mr. Jangle. And the only way to defeat them will be to use the Black Milking talents that you acquire, such as Paralysis (freezing internal organs and brain functions), Immolation (causing enemies to ignite into flames), Projection (instantly moving from one area to another), and Splintering (shattering limbs with directed thoughts).

To ultimately defeat Mr. Jangle, you may have to use his own power against him, and infect yourself with the Black Milking. This will give you not only additional strengths and abilities, but also allow you to resurrect yourself by gaining a life. This twist will be the ultimate leap of faith within the game, since the evil and consequences of the Black Milking must be accepted to reap its power.

KEY GAMEPLAY FEATURES

Because *Backwater* is about moving beyond traditional expressions of 3D gaming, we will incorporate a number of features that are designed to heighten the gameplay experience. These include both unique elements and also re-interpretations of standard gameplay devices:

SCREAM/ADRENALINE RUSH

A big part of any horror experience is the scream of terror that your character cries out when faced with a frightening situation. In *Backwater*, your scream can both help and hurt your character. Unlike traditional survival-horror games, your character Eden will react to the fear she experiences, rather than moving through the world without emotion.

In *Backwater*, things will make both you and your character scream. When Eden screams, she receives an Adrenaline Rush Power-Up. These are triggered, pre-scripted events controlled by the design of the game. These events can also be conditionals, and determined by your proximity to Mr. Jangle, your current status, etc. While you cannot control the scream, you can exploit the power that it provides.

The scream induces an adrenaline rush giving you additional power for a brief period of time, but causing your energy to drain faster.

The game will have a adrenaline and status "bar" to monitor during the game. Adrenaline (character energy) reduces over time as distance from Mr. Jangle increases and activity slows down. Status (character health) regenerates over time.

Adrenaline directly affects your Status.

The scream power up will actually boost adrenaline beyond what is possible by simply acting within the environment. For instance, Eden can never get her adrenaline past 80 percent by simply running through the swamp. However, the scream can jolt the adrenaline up to 100 percent. The Status of your character affects your ability to perform actions such as climbing, jumping, weapon targeting, hiding, etc.

The more "rushed" (adrenaline high/status low) Eden is, the more noise she will make (heavy breathing), which means that Mr. Jangle will be able to more easily track her. You will also be less agile, which will affect all of your skills.

When you are at Maximum adrenaline, you can take more damage and perform at enhanced levels. However, the game remains basically one or two hit death, so increased adrenaline only gets you so far. When status reaches zero, your character dies.

Note: If we have a health kit in the game, it will only exist in a logical location and will be story related. (This rule applies to ammunition and any other usable items that the player can interact with during gameplay.)

CINEMATIC VS. FIRST-PERSON CAMERA

Our intention with *Backwater* is to create a highly playable, addictive gaming experience that is also both beautiful and disturbing. A first-person horror game is really not feasible to create the experience we are after, so a cinematic, third-person camera will be our default view.

However, you will be able to go into first-person (Point of View) mode if desired, when an indicator lets you know that it's active. As mentioned, this option is accessible through a toggle command.

Smart Camera

The smart camera (real-time director) will create a unique, cinematic feel to the game. The camera might actually help you by providing clues and foreshadowing danger that Eden might face. Camera views will include all of the elements relevant to your character within specific situations, i.e., enemies, traps, puzzles, etc.

We will create an aggressive design flowchart consisting of conditionals that will affect the camera AI.

This will include issues such as relative distance to Mr. Jangle and other NPCs, world geometry, plot points, level triggers, time, character adrenaline, previous cameras, continuity, etc.

From these conditionals, the camera will create a cinematically viable choice that also is optimized for the gameplay that is happening. For instance, we may weight certain conditionals for combat so that most of the time the smart camera might choose a higher angle overhead shot when this occurs. We will also create "magnetic" locations within the levels that will attract the cameras to specific, prescripted areas for maximum impact.

However, as stated, it is the camera AI that will ultimately create the angle.

First-Person Look Function with Tracking (Padlock)

First-person view is only available at specific locations and at certain triggers within the game.

In *Backwater*, you will normally explore the world with cinematic third-person perspectives of Eden, your PC. However, an indicator will at times activate, letting you know that a first-person view is available. In this mode, you can go into Eden's Point of View (POV) to look for items, manipulate objects, solve puzzles and target enemies.

This mode also allows you to constantly track Mr. Jangle (or any other selected target) while moving as long as that object remains within the field of view. This will be especially useful in watching Mr. Jangle approach while you search for cover.

This feature allows you to keep Mr. Jangle in constant view. This is only available as first-person view. You can trigger this action with a function button when first-person view is available as an option.

We will place this feature on a toggle so that it doesn't clutter the controller.

OTHER KEY FEATURES

✻ **H.U.D./On-Screen Interface.** All H.U.D. functions, including inventory, adrenaline and status "bars" will only be visible when the player activates a hot-button. This will keep the clutter off the screen during most of the game, but allow you to always have it available when you need it.

✻ **Useable Items.** Any item that you can interact with has value, and therefore you know that this item is something that you need to use, take or destroy if you are to succeed.

  Puzzles are built around this idea, encouraging interaction with the environment. We will attempt to keep the worlds tactile, and to feature elements that are obvious to use. The goal is to avoid wall-surfing or mouse-fishing while playing the game. Instead, logical reasoning and common sense will address the problems the game presents and help you find the items that can be used.

✻ **Hide Mode.** In Hide Mode, you can slow your breathing, creating as little noise as possible while presenting the smallest visual profile. You will be forced to hide often if you are to survive. However, if Mr. Jangle discovers you, hiding is the hardest action to start running from.

✻ **Player-Directed RTV.** Throughout *Backwater*, you will be able to control how you choose to experience the game by having the ability to change camera angles during specific sequences and view the action in ways that are unique to your style of play. Extreme camera angles preset by the director with real-time editing will be the default during RTV. However, you may choose to see the sequence through the POV of any of the NPC or enemy characters as well, including Mr. Jangle. In addition to adding visual complexity and interest, this feature also will allows you in certain sequences to keep track of Mr. Jangle by seeing what he sees, enhancing gameplay.

CONTROLS

Listed below is a possible controller configuration for *Backwater*. All forward movement is on the shoulder buttons, freeing the D-PAD for movements in any direction.

Up	Action Up (Stand Up, Climb Up, Reach, Hang) Look Up
Left	Action Left (Roll, Crawl, Duck) Look Left
Right	Action Right (Roll, Crawl, Duck) Look Right
Down	Action Down (Climb Down, Crawl) Look Down

Triangle	Target Nearest Enemy or Object
Circle	Mode Toggle (Walk, Run, Sneak, Crawl, Hide)
X	Fire Selected Weapon or Use Selected Object
Square	Jump
Select	Inventory
Start	Pause
L1	HUD/Display Toggle
L2	POV (First-Person) Toggle
R1	Move Forward
R2	Move Backward
Left Analog	D-Pad
Right Analog	Move Forward/Backward

TECHNOLOGY

We are currently exploring Licensed Engine Technology as our first choice (Unreal, Quake, or Lithtech).

Main issues that the engine must support are the aggressive AI for Mr. Jangle, including complex animation trees.

Since Mr. Jangle is constantly on the prowl, and may appear at any time, we need to be able to elegantly incorporate his presence within *Backwater*. His AI must be able to identify triggers such as an open door, and know to explore the room that connects to it. Mr. Jangle should also try and trick the player if they are hiding by stepping out of a room, taking a beat, then suddenly reappearing once the player thinks that the coast is clear. As mentioned, a main element of the gameplay experience is feeling vulnerable in Mr. Jangle's presence. Much of the Technology R and D will go into delivering this component of the game.

For instance, you may be hiding under the bed while Mr. Jangle explores a room. He may pause for a couple of minutes, then search again before he goes. You will have to keep your cool during this entire episode. This is part of the game mechanic that builds tension, because the design will force you into these life or death situations.

And once Mr. Jangle discovers you, he will be relentless in his pursuit.

BACKSTORY

The story of *Backwater* is a fusion of mythologies that exists around Bayou cultures, including, but certainly not limited to, Voodoo Worship and Fundamentalism.

25 YEARS AGO

EXT. BAYOU—RAINY NIGHT

Over BLACK, we hear RAIN and then the slow but steady crescendo of a throaty V8 engine . . . a big block American with its carburetor wide open.

We FADE IN on a desolate and muddy road cutting through the middle of a swamp so overgrown with vegetation that the sky has little hope of intruding on the scene with anything other than the continuing downpour. In the BG, a single-lane BRIDGE, wooden and weathered, crosses over some of the deeper water of the swamp.

On the side of the road sits a dark maroon PACKARD with a blown rear tire. The car at first looks abandoned. But as the sound of the distant engine grows louder and louder we realize that there is someone waiting by the Packard. A figure is silhouetted against the approaching headlights. A stranded motorist. It is a slender WOMAN clutching a large SUITCASE. She stands in the center of the road, shielding her eyes from the light as help arrives.

The sound of the engine abruptly stops . . .

From a REVERSE LOW ANGLE, we see the side door of a TOW TRUCK. Torn fifties-fenders, dented body, rusting paint, the patina that only comes from work and abuse. In the BG, we see the woman. She is black, middle-aged, wearing clothing that implies that she is unconcerned with the water pouring down on her. She squints through the light toward the truck, pulling the suitcase closer to her as if it can offer some security, some protection while she scans for her savior.

The door of the Tow Truck simply reads "TOWING." It opens and a pair of well-worn DICKIES shop BOOTS steps down from the cab of the truck into one of the large puddles hiding most of the pavement. The camera moves UP to reveal the back of the MECHANIC, a large man wearing grease-stained OVERALLS. We do not see his face. The Mechanic wears a large leather belt, with

an industrial-sized janitor's KEYCHAIN attached. From it hang
what appear to be hundreds of keys. They glimmer like jewels as
he moves toward the woman, taking measured and deliberate
steps.

We don't see what happens next . . .

INT. CAR—CONTINUOUS

Three TEENS roar through the night in huge, black, sixties
CONTINENTAL with suicide doors. THUMPING MUSIC and whoops of
joy drown out the sound of the land-yacht's motor.

Behind the wheel is KAI. Asian cool. Nineteen. All attitude and
slick haircut. Sitting next to him is his girlfriend PETRA. She
is a swirl of dyed hair and flesh, just about eighteen.
Curvaceous. Deep eyes. Petra's transition from cute to
beautiful is not quite complete, yet her crooked smile easily
straightens all the boys who know her.

Sitting in the back of the car is MARCUS, eighteen. Everyone
calls him Cus. Clearly a follower. He is dumb-jock blond and
muscular.

The teens are talking about swamp. Petra wants Kai to slow down
a little, but he replies that that's why there out on these
roads. No other cars, no speed limits, no rules. Cus readily
agrees, goading Kai into going faster.

Kai lets out a whoop, then gives it the gun as the car leaps
forward at what is obviously an increasingly unsafe speed.
Reluctantly, Petra plays along, smiling at Kai as Cus fights to
hold on to the front seat and stay in the conversation. The
laughter, music and engine get louder as the car races over the
single-lane bridge.

It happens so fast that Kai is not on the brakes until it's
over.

Petra SCREAMS.

Through the windshield, we SEE the mechanic working on the flat
tire. The black woman holding the suitcase stands alongside
him. They both look up just as the hood of the Continental hits
them squarely. Metal tears against metal as the sides of the
cars scour past each other.

Petra, Kai, and Cus are tossed around the inside of the car as
the out of control Continental careens over the side of the
road and violently impacts the moss-covered trees beside the
roadway . . .

All is quiet. Kai and Cus come around, checking on Petra and swearing beneath their breath. After they regain their composure, they tell Petra to wait in the car, then bail out to have a look at the damage. Petra watches as Kai and Cus step through the rain toward the twisted wreckage, illuminated by the Tow Truck's headlights.

Upon seeing the destruction they've caused, the teens panic. Kai and Cus put the body of Miss Lady Em back into her car, then push it into the swamp. Petra can only watch in disbelief as Kai and Cus then drag the lifeless body of the Mechanic back to the Tow Truck and shove him inside. As the are pushing toward the water, Petra sees the suitcase. She grabs it and gives it to Kai. He opens the door of the Tow Truck and tosses the suitcase inside the cab, hitting the Mechanic and causing him to move ever so slightly.

Kai realizes that the man is alive, but its too late . . . the Tow Truck is already sinking below the swamp water. The mechanic comes to and looks back through the rear window at the teens on the road, not quite comprehending what is happening as he sinks below the surface.

As the mechanic struggles to free himself, he inadvertently kicks open the suitcase. Thirteen Water Moccasins are released into the cab of the truck from the broken suitcase.

The snakes attack . . .

In time we will learn that the Woman on the Road was in fact a Voodoo Priestess on a mission. Her name is MISS LADY EM. Inside of her suitcase were THIRTEEN SNAKES, Water Moccasins that were used in a ceremony for the dying known as the Black Milking (extracting snake venom is known as milking).

Miss Lady Em visited the soon to be departed and performed a ritual in which a snake bites the subject. She and her followers believed that the snake's venom would drive all of their sins from the bloodstream before they die.

Unfortunately for Mr. Jangle and you, these snakes were used on the most vicious and vile individuals, murderers whose families agreed to the Black Milking as a last chance at salvation for their fallen relatives.

When bitten, the sins of the subject are released and the evil is transferred to the snake. To get rid of it once and for all, the snakes must be buried on sacred ground within the swamp. And the snakes must be buried in a group of thirteen, without food or water. Eventually, the snakes feed on each other, and in the process, evil devours evil until only one Water Moccasin remains. Miss Lady Em then retrieves the final snake and, having now identified the most dangerous evil, sacrifices it in a ritual that proves the triumph of man over his sins. She was on her way to perform this ritual when she met the bumper of Kai's Continental.

This is the mythology that forms the foundation of BACKWATER, and drives the gameplay and story forward. When the lowly tow-truck driver from Kindly Service and Gas kicked open the suitcase full of snakes, they had something more to feed on than themselves, and they wasted no time in getting started. Every strike was another lifetime's worth of sins and evil from the murderers transferred to the mechanic.

This is how Mr. Jangle was born.

And because the Black Milking was not completed, each of the murderers that was to have been saved by the ritual have instead become spiritually undead. They are trapped within Mr. Jangle, driving his power and his appetite for mayhem.

We will also learn of the legend of Mr. Jangle and how the three teens each met a horrible demise within a couple of years of this horrible event. Finally, before the game is over, we will realize that Eden has arrived at the Bayou by more than just a random chance. She will be revealed as Marcus's and Petra's daughter, whose search for the truth turns into a chaotic struggle for survival against the horror her parents helped create.

ADDITIONAL MARKETS

As content creators, we are uniquely positioned to exploit *Backwater* in a number of other markets and media. Since our talents include success as game designers, producers and writers, as well as successful film-makers with established relationships in traditional media and proven track records in delivering hi-profile, hi-impact, hi-production value entertainment, our intention is to develop *Backwater* as a franchise . . . a license that can seamlessly move into other media, including an original sound track CD, a Graphic Novel Serialization, and Feature-Film/TV possibilities.

Backwater is envisioned as a three-act story, with the first act (including character back-stories, mythology and establishing the worlds) playing out on the Internet during production of the game. This allows a community of Players interested in *Backwater* to be built in conjunction with the game.

The released game will pick up at the end of the online story experience. Those who have not followed along online will have no trouble following the story, but those Players who've experienced the online component of *Backwater* will have a greater understanding of the situation confronting them.

PRELIMINARY PRODUCTION SCHEDULE—EIGHTEEN MONTHS

What follows is a rough preliminary schedule. A detailed MS Project schedule will be completed during the initial design stage.

QUARTER 1

Programming
> Engine Acquisition
> Tool Path Planning
> AI Research and Development
> Engine Modification Planning

Production
> Design Document
> Narrative Scripting
> Level Layout Planning

Art
> Character Concepts
> World Concepts
> Art Direction with Color and Style Layouts Bible

QUARTER 2

Programming
> Tool Path Programming
> AI Design Document
> Engine Mod Document

Production
> Design Document Completion
> Puzzle Design
> Narrative Scripting Completed
> Level Layout with Tools for First Level
> Sound Design and Voice Casting

Art
> Character Modeling
> Texture Map Imagery
> Narrative Storyboards

QUARTER 3

Programming
> Level and Puzzle Programming
> AI Programming

Interface and Inventory Programming
Multiplayer Engine Modification Documents
Production
   Multiplayer Design Document
   World Building
   NPC and Enemy Placement
   Testing of Levels with First-Pass Art Assets
   Voice Talent Recording
   Sound Efx and Music Composition
   Web Site Up and Online Serialization of Story Begins
Art
   Interface Concepts
   Inventory Screens
   Game Shells
   Object and World Modeling
   Texture Mapping
   Character Modeling

QUARTER 4

Programming
   Level and Puzzle Programming
   AI Programming
   Interface and Inventory Completed
   Sound Programming and Tools
   Multiplayer Programming
Production
   Single Player Levels Complete
   Multiplayer Levels Functional with First-Pass Art
   NPC and Enemy Placement Complete
   Testing of All Levels
   Original Sound Track Production
   Online Serialization Continues
   Sound Editing of Vocal Performances
   RTV Sequences Directed
Art
   Interface Completed
   Inventory Screens Completed
   Character Models and Maps Completed

World Art 50 Percent Complete
Sprites and Visual Efx
RTV Sequence Production Begins

QUARTER 5—ALPHA
Programming
    Puzzle and Level Programming Complete
        AI Programming Competed
        Multiplayer Programming
        Bug Fixing
        RTV and Gameplay Integration
Production
    All Levels Complete for Single Player
    All Levels Complete for Multiplayer
    Testing of Puzzles, Levels and NPC/Enemy Placement
    Revisions as Needed
    Sound Complete
    Online Serialization Continues
    Sound Track Completed
Art
    All Art Complete
    Art Revisions as Needed

QUARTER 6—BETA
Programming
    Bug Fixes and Revisions as Needed to Gold
Production
    Playtesting and Revisions
    Release of Multiplayer Level to Beta Testers
    Online Serialization Dovetails into Release
Art
    Art for Online Promotions
    Revisions as Needed

CONCLUSION
At its core, *Backwater* is about confronting fear.

Designed to be one of the most horrifying games ever created, *Backwater* will deliver the jolts and scares, but also the satisfaction that only comes from having looked death in the face and lived to tell about it.

With compelling characters, rich worlds, varied gameplay, a sympathetic yet complex hero and an archetypal antagonist, *Backwater* will exceed the expectations of what's possible in a gaming experience.

Backwater is innovative game design, stories and characters with impact, forward-thinking technology and high-production-value imagery fused into a seamless entertainment experience.

Firmly establishing a commitment to the gamer, while creating a new survival-horror franchise and character, *Backwater* is addictive, challenging gameplay, intelligently presented.

CONCEPT IMAGES

Early concepts of Mr. Jangle are included below.

1.

2.

Appendix B

Sample Sequences

NARRATIVE CUT-SCENES: SETUPS

This is a sample Setup cut scene from our script for the video game *Constantine*. It is the opening narrative of the game:

```
FADE IN:

CLOSE ON an amber liquid. Whiskey. No ice. Short glass. It
moves ever so slightly, then is lifted up . . . out of FRAME.
Beneath it, a couple of face-down Tarot Cards are being used as
a coaster.

A moment, then the glass returns, much lighter. On its edge, a
trickle of BLOOD.

                    JOHN (V.O.)
          I was hoping for a quiet night.

The blood runs down the glass until it fuses with the liquor.

EXT. RAMSHACKLE HOLLYWOOD APARTMENT BUILDING—NIGHT

The places reeks of desperation. Older. Probably built by a
studio mogul back in the '30s as a henhouse for his starlets.
Then, it was something to behold. A nice place to live. But not
anymore. And especially not tonight.
```

Now, it is a bad place to die.

From one of the floors above, a LOUD CRASHING SOUND. CAMERA
shoots up from the street, past an old PHONE BOOTH, through the
"X" of a couple CROSSED PALM TREES . . . the tall, Los Angeles
ones, with balls of fronds on the top . . .

. . . and into . . .

INT. THOMAS ELRIU'S APARTMENT

THOMAS ELRIU is being violently attacked by some unseen
opponent. THWAAAAKKKK!

He crashes into the furniture of his small apartment. Tries to
fight back, swinging wildly. Clearly not a match for his
assailant. Then, off his feet and tossed sideways through the
air.

CRASH

Thomas is hurled through a wall. Plaster and wood splinters hit
the CAMERA as limbs break. And something else . . . a flash of
an image . . . a broken wing, perhaps.

Then it is gone.

Thomas struggles. Crawls across the floor. Begins to chant.
Latin. Under his breath . . .

                    THOMAS
              (struggling)
          Ego operor non . . . vereor nex.
          Ego . . . sum procul unus per . . . lux
          lucis.

Thomas hears a low hissing sound, part groan. It grows louder.
His killer is getting closer.

Thomas looks at the approaching SHADOW. A DEMONIC HAND catches
the light. Extends its index finger.

The finger waves in the air. Back and forth. A "don't do that"
gesture. Instead, Thomas chants louder. The finger moves toward
a leathery face we can almost see.

The low groan becomes a "Shhhhh . . ." Quiet, yet forceful.

Thomas lowers his head. Waits for the inevitable. It comes
quickly, in a blur.

                                             CUT TO:

INT. PAPA MIDNITE'S BAR—LATER

CLOSE ON HANDS AND A WHISKEY GLASS

Smoke trails upwards. A COUGH. A cigarette comes to a face, is
lit. Inhale. Deep . . . down to the lungs. You can almost feel
it, taste it. The smoke mingles with whiskey in suggestive
shapes. Like one of those old Subliminal Seduction Ads.

Then another cough, silenced as JOHN CONSTANTINE takes a swig
from his drink. He notices the blood swirling in the alcohol,
refusing to mix with it.

Oil and water.

He stares at the glass. Wipes his mouth.

Suddenly, Constantine looks upward, a split second
before . . .

A PHONE RINGS

Like an alarm clock you're trying to ignore. The DEMONIC BARMAN
answers. He sounds like he got a hot poker in the larynx
somewhere down in Hell.

> DEMONIC BARMAN
> Yeah? Papa Midnite's.
> (then, loud)
> Constantine. For you. Ever think of goin'
> wireless?

The barman hands Constantine the phone. John COUGHS.

> JOHN
> What is it?

> HENNESSEY (V.O.)
> I'm callin' you right off this time, John
> . . .

EXT. RAMSHACKLE HOLLYWOOD APARTMENT BUILDING - SAME TIME

Hennessy at the phone booth. Same one we have seen before.
BLACK AND WHITES in the BG. Maybe a CORONER TRUCK. Lots of
flashing red and blue LIGHTS.

> HENNESSEY
> . . . so don't go complaining when I tell
> you I don't know anything . . . but a
> name. Elriu.

INTERCUT PAPA MIDNITE'S BAR—CONSTANTINE

John hears the name. Reacts. Puts some CASH on the bar.
Finishes his drink. Empty glass back down on the Tarot Cards.

Constantine gets up. Heads for the door.

> JOHN (V.O.)
> Yeah . . . I was hoping for a quiet night.

The Barman buses the glass. Notices the two Tarot Cards
underneath.

> DEMONIC BARMAN
> (seeing cards, calls to John)
> Hey . . .

No response. The Barman flips the cards over. An ANGEL and a
DEMON.

> JOHN (V.O.)
> But it wasn't in the cards.

The Barman reaches for the cash. As he does, John snaps his
fingers. The money bursts into FLAMES.

> DEMONIC BARMAN
> Damn you, Constantine.

The Barman hits the bills with a half-empty glass of beer.

> JOHN
> I've been damned by worse.
> (beat)
> Much worse.

A half-smile across Constantine's face. Then he is out the
door.

> END CINEMATIC:

SAMPLE SETUP CUT SCENE

This one from our script for *The Chronicles of Riddick: Escape* from Butcher Bay:

INT. INTERSTELLAR TRANSPORT—(SPACE)

Johns stands over Riddick, weapon drawn.

>   JOHNS
>   Rise and shine, Riddick. It's time for you
>   to earn me some money.

Johns triggers a series of release mechanisms. The restraints
holding Riddick in place snap away, and Riddick slowly stands.
He looks at the weapon Johns is holding.

>   RIDDICK
>   Be careful with that, Johns. You could
>   hurt somebody.

RIDDICK AND JOHNS

exchange a look, then . . .

>   CUT TO:

EXT. BUTCHER BAY LANDING DOCK—CONTINUOUS

Riddick walks ahead of Johns as they move away from the
Transport Ship and toward the hell-hole that is Butcher Bay.

>   RIDDICK
>   (sarcastically, referring to surroundings)
>   Butcher Bay. You know, you always take me
>   to the nicest places, Johns.

>   JOHNS
>   I hear the food stinks as well.
>   (beat)
>   Can't say I'm gonna miss you, Riddick.

>   RIDDICK
>   Then don't.
>   (spotting Hoxie in the distance)
>   . . . oh, he doesn't look happy to see
>   you.

ANGLE ON HOXIE

Approaching from further down the platform is HOXIE, the Warden
of Butcher Bay. His Second-in-Command, ABBOTT, as well as a
detachment of armed GUARDS follows closely.

                    JOHNS
        Hoxie is a businessman. Now, play nice and
        we can get this over with quickly.

                    RIDDICK
        This is already over, Johns.

Hoxie and his men reach them. The Guards quickly surround Johns
and Riddick.

                    HOXIE
        Secure your weapon, Johns.

                    JOHNS
        Good to see you, Warden.

JOHNS HOLSTERS HIS GUN AS HOXIE APPROACHES RIDDICK.

                    HOXIE
        So . . . the famous Mr. Riddick.

                    RIDDICK
        Hoxie.

                    HOXIE
        Finally come to stay, eh? Well, as of this
        moment, Butcher Bay owns your ass . . .
            (then, in Riddick's face)
        I own your ass.

Riddick watches Hoxie as Johns tries to cut in.

                    JOHNS
        He's all yours once I sign him over,
        Hoxie.

                    HOXIE
            (closer to Riddick, ignoring Johns)
        You're not going to be a problem, are you,
        Riddick? 'Cause my boys and I like . . .
        solving . . . problems.

                    RIDDICK
            (flatly)
        Johns said you were ugly up close. For the
        first time, I gotta agree with him.

Hoxie and Riddick stare at each other. Then . . .

                    HOXIE
        Hmmm . . . Nice try.

>   RIDDICK
>   I do what I can.

>   HOXIE
>   (circling Riddick)
>   Not at Butcher Bay but a few minutes and
>   already trying to get under my skin, eh,
>   Riddick?

>   RIDDICK
>   Be easier if you'd give me something
>   sharp.

Johns moves toward Hoxie, breaking the moment.

>   JOHNS
>   Bounty plus fifty on Riddick, right Hoxie?

Hoxie turns his attention to Johns as Riddick tilts his head
and gives him a "told you so" look.

>   HOXIE
>   (cutting him off)
>   I think Riddick about covers what you owe
>   me, Johns.

>   JOHNS
>   There's plenty of other slams I can take
>   Riddick if you can't afford him.

Johns and Hoxie try to stare each other down. Then . . .

>   HOXIE
>   Alright . . . alright. Perhaps we can come
>   to a number. But don't push it, Johns.
>   "Extra" or no, Riddick stays at Butcher
>   Bay. Period. Full stop.

Hoxie signals his guards, who move in and start to lead Riddick
away.

>   HOXIE (CONT'D)
>   (to Abbott)
>   Let's get him processed.

>   ABBOTT
>   Yessir.

Riddick moves ahead of the guards.

>   RIDDICK
>   (smiling, to Johns)

        Better luck next time.

Johns and Hoxie watch Riddick as he's led away.

                                         GO TO GAMEPLAY

SETUP CUT-SCENE FROM *TEEN TITANS*

INT. POWER PLANT—LATER

Robin and Cyborg step back as Plasmus and Cinderblock close in.
Starfire is watching . . .

OVERLOAD

. . . as he draws power from the electrical GENERATORS of the
Power Plant. Sparks and whipping ARCS of electricity surround
him.

                    CYBORG
                (to Robin)
            Each jolt of electricity is making
            Overload stronger.

                    BEAST BOY
            Talk about your power-ups . . .

                    ROBIN
            He'll soon be a mass of pure energy. If
            that happens, they'll link up to form . .
            .

                    BEAST BOY
                (to Robin)
            Don't say it, dude.

Robin stops, but Cyborg finishes the thought.

                    CYBORG
            Ternion.

They all look toward Cyborg.

                    CYBORG
                (off their looks)
            What? You didn't tell me not to say it.

                    RAVEN
            Plasmus and Cinderblock are bad enough as
            solo acts.

> STARFIRE
> Then I believe we must keep this band of
> villains from getting together.

> BEAST BOY
> Yeah, really together.

> ROBIN
> Take 'em down, Titans. Go!

GO TO GAMEPLAY:

NARRATIVE CUT SCENES: PAYOFFS

PAYOFF sequence. This one is near the end of *The Chronicles of Riddick: Escape from Butcher Bay.*

INT. HOXIE'S OFFICE—CONTINUOUS

The destruction is complete. Riddick moves through the remnants of the office toward Hoxie's capsule, which sits high up against the wall.

Riddick stops by one of the guards, bends down and reaches for his arm.

He pulls the arm up and aims its mounted weapon toward the capsule and . . .

FIRES

The capsule splits open and Hoxie tumbles and crashes to the floor.

Hoxie slowly gets to his feet as Riddick approaches.

> HOXIE
> Now, Riddick, there must be someth . . .

Off Riddick's look, Hoxie immediately shuts up.

> RIDDICK
> I want the codes to your ship.

Hoxie hesitates. Riddick lowers his weapon.

> HOXIE
> Shit, Riddick. You wouldn't . . .

                          RIDDICK
                    (cutting him off)
               Wouldn't what? What wouldn't I do, Hoxie?

                          HOXIE
               Oh . . . Of course . . . the codes are in
               my desk.

Johns is coming around. Riddick calls out to him without taking
his focus off Hoxie.

                          RIDDICK
               You walk, Johns?

                          JOHNS
                    (recovering)
               Yeah, I think so.

                          RIDDICK
               Run?

                          JOHNS
               Maybe . . .

Riddick gives him a quick look.

                          JOHNS (CONT'D)
               But I won't try to find out.

                          RIDDICK
               Good.
                    (turning back to Hoxie)
               How's your eyesight?

Hoxie looks at Riddick, confused.

                                                    FADE OUT

PAYOFF SEQUENCE FROM *CONSTANTINE*

Notice the number of Alternate Lines (Alts.) in this script. At the time we were finishing our draft, the final projected rating for the game was still under discussion

with the developer and publisher, so we included alternate lines for both a harder and softer rating. Also notice that sometimes a Payoff sequence—in this case, the end of the boss battle with Balthazar—can, and often does, include Setup information for the next objective. You should always look for ways to maximize the amount of mileage you can get out of your cinematics.

Timing—2 minutes

EXT. BALTHAZAR'S BUILDING ROOTOP

Constantine has Balthazar right where he wants him. He closes, raising his Holy Shot gun to his hip. He turns it until the cross is revealed.

> JOHN
> There are things I need to know. You're going to tell me.

> BALTHAZAR
> Fuck you, Constantine.
>   (alt.)
> Screw yourself, Constantine.
>   (alt.)
> Burn in Hell, Constantine.

> JOHN
>   (smiling)
> I'm taking requests. How 'bout . . . "Our father, who art in . . ."

> BALTHAZAR
>   (in pain)
> NO! Stop! Please . . .

> JOHN
> Don't beg, Balthazar. Not yet.

> BALTHAZAR
> What happened . . . to . . . turn the . . . other cheek?

> JOHN
> Got the wrong J.C.
>   (alt.)
> Got the wrong guy.
>   (beat, lowering the Holy Shotgun)
> Now, why the hard-on about the upstairs, huh?
>   (alt.)
> Now, why's the upstairs got you so worried?

Constantine begins to raise the Holy Shotgun.

>   BALTHAZAR
>   (spitting it out)
>   The food sucks. Milk and honey . . . give
>   me a fucking break . . .
>   (alt.)
>   The food sucks. Milk and honey . . .
>   they've got to be kidding . . .

Balthazar is in Unspeakable Pain as Constantine raises the
Shotgun Crucifix . . .

>   JOHN
>   Wrong. Try again.
>   (back to the Prayer)
>   Thy Kingdom Come . . . thy will be done,
>   on earth . . .

>   BALTHAZAR
>   All right. Stop . . . just stop . . .
>   (beat)
>   Perfection . . . it's torture . . . to . .
>   . the damned.

Constantine lowers the Holy Shotgun.

>   BALTHAZAR (CONT'D)
>   (catching his breath)
>   The Spearhead . . . it's the weapon that
>   killed Christ. On the Cross. God's
>   Sacrifice. It has His blood.
>   (alt.)
>   The Spearhead . . . it's what the Roman's
>   used on Christ as he hung on the cross.
>   God's sacrifice. It has His blood.

>   JOHN
>   And Angela?

>   BALTHAZAR
>   Mammon will use her . . . as a bridge . .
>   . to cross over.

>   JOHN
>   That wasn't so tough.

>   BALTHAZAR
>   Just for a moment . . . imagine it,
>   Constantine. Imagine the glory of this
>   city, of this world, when Mammon takes
>   over.

Balthazar manages a smile.

CONSTANTINE'S POV—MAMMON'S LA (FANTASY SEQUENCE)

Looking out, we see the city-scape change. Earth to a vision of Hell. An illustration of things to come should Mammon succeed.

JOHN LOWERS THE SHOTGUN

His eyes move back to Balthazar.

>   JOHN
>   Where do I find her?
>
>   BALTHAZAR
>   Ravenscar Mental Hospital. But you're too
>   late.
>   (laughs)
>   Mammon's almost here. I've been stalling
>   you, Constantine. You should never trust a
>   demon . . .

KABLAM!

Constantine pumps a round into Balthazar. He looks up in disbelief.

Constantine lowers the holy shotgun

at Balthazar's head. Point blank. The barrel smokes.

>   JOHN
>   . . . or a man with a loaded cross.
>   (he pulls the trigger)
>   Burn in heaven, asshole.
>   (alt.)
>   Burn in heaven.

>   GO TO GAMEPLAY:

PAYOFF SEQUENCE FROM *TEEN TITANS*:

INT. THE TENT

As Mumbo Jumbo collapses, we see the TENT collapsing with him.

>   RAVEN
>   Your circus is going dark, Mumbo.

                    CYBORG
          . . . turns to Mumbo Jumbo.

                    CYBORG
          You've got some 'splaining to do, Carny.

                    MUMBO JUMBO
          I'll be honest . . .

                    ROBIN
          That'll be the day.

Raven moves to Mumbo.

                    RAVEN
          All of this is beyond your ability. How'd
          you do it?

                    MUMBO JUMBO
          I have no idea. It was . . . magic.

Robin is concerned.

                    ROBIN
          First someone was messing with time . . .
          now someone is manipulating space.

                    BEAST BOY
          Dude, this is totally outta control . . .

                    ROBIN
               (thinking, to himself)
          Control.

                                   DISSOLVE TO:
                                   IN-GAME DIALOGUE

IN-GAME DIALOGUE

The following is a sample sequence from *Constantine*. In-game dialogue is used to reinforce the objectives of the mission as well as provide subtle hints and direction to the player without the need for a complete cut-scene. In this case, all of the dialogue belongs to the Player Character, John Constantine. Also note that rather than screenplay format, these lines are written within a table. This is very common for in-game dialogue.

Dialogue—John Constantine	Gameplay Need
Something really enjoyed itself up here.	Foreshadow boss battle to come
The party had come to me.	The enemy attacks
The Naissance de Demoniacs. A real "page-burner."	John needs this book to advance
Ah, the final shotgun piece, I'll be taking that.	John can now assemble the shotgun
Guess they know I'm coming.	Foreshadow enemy attack
No way through.	John needs to find another way through the level
My bad.	The item didn't work
I had to keep moving.	Reinforce timer
I didn't need the attention. But, strangely, I didn't mind it all that much either.	John's comments on fighting the last wave of demons
Locked. Figures.	The door is locked
I needed to get inside.	Alternate for the locked door
In hell, it's always a warm welcome. Very, very warm.	General comment. Use when needed
How do I get over that?	Hint to get over obstacle
I knew I had to get on with it.	Reinforce timer
Sucks to be you.	Payoff line for defeat of mini-boss demon
I did the least I could. Sometime in my future, I knew I'd be there on that stake, or worse.	Mercy kill victim
A primordial flamethrower . . . Dragon's Breath.	John finds a new weapon
I had to get the hell outta hell. But I knew the book was close.	Hint: the book is close
The dead were stacked like cordwood. More fuel for the fires of hell.	John comment on hell